THE PRESENCE OF FORD MADOX FORD

Ford Madox Ford, 1930s. (Courtesy Princeton University Library)

THE PRESENCE OF
FORD MADOX FORD

A Memorial Volume of Essays, Poems, and Memoirs

edited, with an introduction, by
S O N D R A J. S T A N G

UNIVERSITY OF PENNSYLVANIA PRESS
Philadelphia 1981

This work was published with the support of the Haney Foundation.
Copyright © 1981 by the University of Pennsylvania Press
Drawing of Ford Madox Ford by Juan Gris Copyright © by ADAGP, Paris 1981
Printed in the United States of America

Library of Congress Cataloging in Publication Data

Main entry under title:

The Presence of Ford Madox Ford.

  "Chronological list of Ford's books": p. 240
  "Books in print": p. 243
  1.   Ford, Ford Madox, 1873–1939—Criticism and inter-
pretation—Addresses, essays, lectures. 2.   Ford, Ford
Madox, 1873–1939, in fiction, drama, poetry, etc.
I.   Stang, Sondra J.

PR6011.053Z82   823'.912   80–52811
ISBN 0–8122–7794–5

Contents

Illustrations

Acknowledgments

I wish to thank William Gass for his enthusiasm and help in planning this volume, for enlarging my idea of what its direction and scope ought to be, and for being the first to offer an essay. I am indebted to Holly Hall, excellent and rare librarian and chief of the Rare Book Room at Olin Library, Washington University, St. Louis, for giving herself so generously to the pursuit of information and materials I constantly needed. I am grateful to Jarvis Thurston for urging me on when I first mentioned the idea of a memorial volume for Ford, and I thank him and Mona Van Duyn for reading manuscripts and giving me their sensible advice. I also would like to thank George Core for his attentiveness to the progress of the book and for many excellent suggestions, beginning with the suggestion that I ask Allen Tate for an essay. I thank my husband, Richard Stang, for asking useful questions, reading manuscripts, and giving me wise counsel; and my son Sam for copying most of the photographs lent to me for inclusion in this book.

Janice Biala has generously given permission to use all the unpublished material by Ford that appears in this volume. I am indebted to her for that permission as well as for granting the interview, answering still further questions, and lending photographs; and I thank her and Daniel Brustlein for their hospitality in the course of an interview that ran to several days.

I am grateful to Julia M. Loewe for kindly lending family photographs and supplying information for this book; and to Edward Naumburg, Jr., for giving me the privilege of finding my way through his collection, for having particular documents copied, for lending photographs, and for making suggestions.

For information, suggestions, and help of a general or specific nature, I am greatly obliged to the following persons: Roger Hecht, Glenway Wescott, Monroe Wheeler, Frank MacShane, Robie Macauley, Andrew Lytle, Telford Taylor, J.H. Hexter, Gordon Craig, Howard Nemerov, Bernd Witte, Peter Marsden, Tony Gould, Robert Buffington, Ashley Brown, Candace MacMahon, Helen Vendler, James Laughlin, Sally Bixby Defty, Willard R. Trask, Todd Bender, James Phelan, Susan Fox, Douglas Cooper, Lawrence D. Steefel, Jr., Mrs. William Van O'Connor, Stanley Elkin, Peter Taylor, Mary Heath, Pamela Roper, William Karanikolas, Miriam Selvansky, Alma Denny Kaplan, Laura Popenoe, Devora Schwebel, Mary Gallatin, Joan Givner, Richard Ludwig, Alasdair Clayre, Clyde Logan and the B.B.C., Margaret J. Cox, Robert Wilson, Barbara Howes, Sidra Stith, Steven Zwicker and Carter Revard.

Various libraries at various times supplied me with information and material. I wish particularly to thank William Matheson and Leonard Beck of the Rare Book and Special Collections Division of the Library of Congress; Ida Holland, Harold Jordan, and Timothy Murray of the Rare Book Room, Washington University; Kay Shehan, Victoria Witte, Terrence Keegan, Kenneth Nabors, and the staff of the Reference Department, as well as the Inter-Library Loan Department of the Washington University Library; the staff of the Reference Department, Saint Louis University Library; Janette B. Rozene, Reference Librarian, the Museum of Modern Art, New York City; Robert L. Beare, McKeldin Library, University of Maryland; Patrick M. Quinn, University Archivist, Northwestern University Library; Marilyn Gould, Special Collections, University of California, Davis; Jean F. Preston and Charles Green, Princeton University Library; Robert J. Bertholf, Curator of the Poetry–Rare Books Collection, the State University of New York at Buffalo; and the library of the Institut für Anglistik, RWTH, Aachen, Germany.

I acknowledge my very good fortune in having had Robert Erwin, former director of the University of Pennsylvania Press, and Gail C. Levin as the editors of this book; and Deborah Stewart, Jane Barry, and Lee Ann Draud as my copyeditors.

For permission granted to publish pertinent material, I am indebted to Graham Greene and The Bodley Head Press; David Dow Harvey; Helen Tate; the *New York Review of Books;* the *Minnesota Review;* the *Sewanee Review;* the *Southern Review;* Carcanet Press; Barbara Howes; Julia Madox Loewe; James Laughlin, New Directions Publishing Corporation; the Princeton University Library; the Cornell University Library; Richard Elman; KPFK in Los Angeles; WBAI in New York City; Pacifica Tapes; Tony Gould; Jenny Bradley (Mrs. William Aspenwall Bradley); Frank Bidart; and Georges Gonzalez-Gris.

WILLIAM TREVOR
Foreword

Thirty-two years have passed but I still take pride in the fact that I discovered Ford Madox Ford for myself. I bought the Tietjens novels and *The Good Soldier* when they came out as Penguins in 1948: one and sixpence each, and I notice from the dates I jotted down on the flyleaves that I couldn't afford to run to all five in the same month. Many years later I heard myself saying in a London pub that *The Good Soldier* must surely be one of the best novels written in this century. To prove my point I lent my copy and never got it back. But the Tietjens story is still alive on my bookshelves, tattered now and exuding that distinctive papery smell that cheap editions acquire with time.

I reread *The Good Soldier* in order to write this brief foreword: it still seems to me to be a masterpiece. I did not reread the Tietjens quartet, because I have carried its world about with me for so long that I prefer it to exist as it does in my imagination, without interference. My memory of Tietjens himself, of Sylvia, Valentine Wannop, Mrs. Duchemin, Macmaster, and all the others, may be faulty; I may have come to exaggerate certain of their characteristics, incidents may have been lost in the fog of the intervening years, the order of events dislocated. But I remember the novels and their people as one remembers life, and I think that is as it should be. Tietjens is still the Tory gentleman, dressed carelessly yet with a note of style, resembling a sack of potatoes when he sits down in an armchair. Whether she said it or not, I recall Sylvia most vividly as the source of the remark that the really divvy moment of an illicit love affair is when you watch the man you're spending the weekend with buying the tickets at the railway station. Some do not in the Tietjens world; some endlessly do. Some marry in order to have conversations over breakfast; some don't converse at all.

My debt to Ford Madox Ford is that of any reader to the writer of good books, but for me there is just a little more to it, for those books introduced me to an England I did not even know existed. I was nineteen when I first read them, a student at Trinity College, Dublin, who had never been outside Ireland and could only guess what England, so long a trouble to us, was like. As a child in such provincial towns as Skibbereen and Tipperary and Enniscorthy, I had formed an impression of a very splendid place indeed: leafy and beautiful, with no burnt-out houses or smashed castles, no brambles growing through rusty baronial gates, as we had in Ireland. "England," I have written elsewhere, "spelt elegance, and style and graciousness." I read my way through a mass of English public-school stories, through Bulldog Drummond and all of Edgar Wallace, Dickens, Jane Austen, the Brontës, A. J. Cronin, Francis Brett Young, Somerset Maugham, Aldous Huxley, Evelyn Waugh, and almost everyone else. But it wasn't until I came across Ford that England and the English took real shape, and having come to know both rather well in the meanwhile I am repeatedly aware of how accurate, and how perceptive, he was in painting his picture. And not only in depicting life in the country he so valued and loved did Ford display these qualities: they are even more to the fore in his continuous investigation of the ever-interesting kaleidoscope of the human predicament everywhere.

Ford shatters the surface of things and even out of the fragments creates an extra pattern of truth. The honor and decency of which he wrote so movingly—and the England which had cosseted them for so long—no longer exist. But his voice remains, echoing always more powerfully as the bleaker years pile up.

Ford at the typewriter (Courtesy Edward Naumburg, Jr.)

"His influence was immense, even upon writers who did not know him, even upon other writers today, who have not read him."

—ALLEN TATE

". . . to understand a composer's musical language you have to know most of his output. If you come upon enigmas in a certain piece, they may be unraveled by analogy to a composer's other works. Even if you compare piano sonatas to string quartets or symphonies, you can understand and dispel many puzzles."

—CLAUDIO ARRAU

Of Ford's "other" novels: "No one has read them."

—V.S.PRITCHETT

The General was expatiating on the solidity of a squat castle, like a pile of draughts, away to the left, in the sun, on the flatness. He was saying that we didn't build like that nowadays.

Tietjens said:

"You're perfectly wrong, General. All the castles that Henry VIII built in 1543 along this coast are mere monuments of jerry-building. . . . 'In 1543 *jactat castra Delis, Sandgatto, Reia, Hastingas Henricus Rex'* . . . That means he chucked them down. . . ."

The General laughed:

"You are an incorrigible fellow. . . . If ever there's any known, certain fact . . ."

"But go and *look* at the beastly things," Tietjens said.

—FORD MADOX FORD

Introduction

Ford Madox Ford is a special case. There is probably no other major figure in twentieth-century letters whose achievement is so generally unacknowledged as his.

In his lifetime he won no prizes, except for one from *Poetry* magazine for his poem *A House;* and there were no posthumous awards—only a niche of sorts as an almost-underground figure with enough of a reputation to keep the prices of his out-of-print books modestly rising. Hugh Walpole observed in 1929, ten years before Ford's death: "there is no greater literary neglect of our time in England than the novels and poems of Ford." "Why," he went on to ask, "doesn't someone write a proper critical article on Ford? Here is a subject crying out to be used."

A number of critical articles have been written since that suggestion was made—and whole books—but the subject is still, fifty years later, "crying out to be used." Perhaps it is only fair to add that the subject is a very large one, so large and complex that it is beyond the scope of any single critical article, no matter how proper.

This volume of essays, poems, and memoirs was conceived as a memorial to Ford for the fortieth anniversary of his death, no special notice having been taken of the hundredth anniversary of his birth in 1973. The critics and poets assembled for this occasion wish to pay tribute to Ford's presence in literature—by looking for themselves at Ford's achievement and inquiring into its significance and value for us today.

The sixties produced over a dozen books on Ford, but given our rapidly evolving attitudes in the last decade, it is time now to reread him, not through the eyes of another period, with its assumptions and limitations, but through our own eyes, seeing for ourselves, as Christopher Tietjens advised General Campion to do. For this reason, it seemed best, as a plan of action for a memorial volume, to gather together critics and writers who had written with great distinction about the twentieth-century novel (half of them novelists themselves), but who, for the most part, had not yet written about Ford. The purpose then was to generate fresh criticism, bringing into the discussion new critical personalities who might ask new questions, discard some old ones, report on their experience of reading Ford, and tell us of any discoveries they might have made in their reading.

The book is divided into two parts—critical essays and poems in the first half; memoirs, an interview and an essay in the second. One of the rules for the book was that it contain only new writing, done in response to the invitation to honor Ford, or writing that had never been previously published. Among the essays, there are three exceptions to the rule: (1) Graham Greene offered his two essays from The Bodley Head edition of Ford, never published as a pair in the United States. (2) Allen Tate died within half a year after accepting the invitation to write a memorial essay for this book; with Mrs. Tate's permission and the help of George Core, editor of the *Sewanee Review,* Tate is represented here by a series of short pieces written on several occasions and made into a statement as sequential as possible by assembling and cutting and pasting what seemed most appropriate. (3) The only other essay included but not written especially for this volume is a section from the unpublished introductory essay by David Dow Harvey to his splendid and indispensable *Ford Madox Ford: A Bibliography of Works and Criticism.*

Part Two contains a group of new or unpublished memoirs by men and women who knew Ford at different times in his life—three generations of contemporaries who tell us what they observed and remember. To preserve points of view that might otherwise be lost and to enlarge the body of primary material we have, every attempt was made to reach the dwindling number of people who can write about Ford today from their own knowledge of him as a man. All but a few of the memoirs were written specifically for this volume. The pieces by Ford's daughter Julia Madox Loewe, by Janice Biala, and by Robert Lowell come from a little-known tape made in 1961 and have never before been published. Mary McIntosh's piece was written in 1965 but not published. In addition to the 1961 taped memoir, Janice Biala consented to be interviewed, thus breaking a silence of almost two decades and adding significantly to the biographical material we already have.

This volume also presents previously unpublished writing by Ford. A fairy tale called "The Other," from the Cornell University Department of Rare Books, is appended to Alison Lurie's essay on Ford's fairy tales for children. A sonnet in the late nineteenth-century manner that Ford wrote during one of his "bouts-rimés" evenings in Paris was saved by Willard R. Trask and appears at the end of Mary McIntosh's memoir. Edward Naumburg, Jr., in opening his collection to the readers of this book, has published for the first time a number of letters to and from Ford, as well as an early version of a chapter from *Some Do Not . . . ,*[1] the opening novel of *Parade's End,* found in a dummy of the *Transatlantic Review* that Ford, as editor, had

---

[1]*Editor's note:* This chapter was heretofore believed to be the alternate ending of *Some Do Not. . . .* It appears to be a draft of the first chapter of Part Two.

circulated in order to advertise the forthcoming magazine. Among the other rare items presented in Edward Naumburg's essay is a newly surfaced contribution by Ford to a symposium on women's suffrage published in 1912. It is known that Ford wrote a pamphlet for Mrs. Pankhurst in 1913, *This Monstrous Regiment of Women,* but the earlier piece seems to have eluded the Ford bibliographies.

Omitted from this volume, regrettably, are two projected pieces—an essay on Ford's poetry, which could not be written in time for publication, and an essay on *The Good Soldier,* which the late Professor Sheldon Sacks of the University of Chicago had planned to write.

This book set out to represent in as balanced a way as possible both the familiar and the less familiar books of Ford. Denis Donoghue writes about *The Good Soldier;* Roger Sale, about *The Good Soldier* and *Parade's End;* Howard Nemerov and Andrew Lytle, about *Parade's End.* William Gass writes about *The Fifth Queen;* C. H. Sisson, about *The Critical Attitude;* William H. Pritchard, about *The March of Literature;* Alison Lurie, about *The Brown Owl, The Feather, The Queen Who Flew,* and *Christina's Fairy Book;* and L. L. Farrar, Jr., about *When Blood Is Their Argument* and *Between St. Dennis and St. George.*

It seemed important in planning the book to suggest something of the range and variety of Ford's work—fairy tale, criticism, the historical novel, historical and cultural essay, and the literary magazine. The two short but brilliant runs of the *English Review* and the *Transatlantic Review* are the subject of Edward Krickel's essay.

And the critics themselves are sufficiently different from one another in taste and sensibility and experience to impart a sense of balance to the collection. Their essays are strong and original readings—neither hagiography nor polemic, but independent and vigorous criticism that reaches past the wearying and restrictive issues in which so much criticism of Ford has been so long detained.

Why Ford has been considered a peripheral rather than a central figure in the canon of twentieth-century writers is a perplexing question, one that probably has more to do with accident and the way in which reputations are made than with the substance or nature of the work itself. They are really two separate matters, and if ever criticism had a job to do it is to see them as separate. Whether Conrad learned more from Ford than Ford learned from Conrad; whether or not a man should conduct his private life monogamously and stick to one woman of his own age; whether or not Ford can be "exonerated" from the charge of lying about real events and real people (including himself) in his written reminiscences and his conversation—these questions have aroused high passion and partisan feeling and the sense that it is necessary to cast a vote. But they are all false issues for criticism to concern itself with, when they are seen by themselves apart from matters of sensibility and temperament—and when more meaningful questions about Ford's powers as a novelist have not yet been sufficiently considered.

Ford's reputation as a man was formed in another age. Early in the century the suggestion of impropriety attached itself to him, first in a divorce case and a brief imprisonment that were widely publicized by the press and then in his union and subsequent break with the novelist Violet Hunt, widely publicized by her. Edwardian England made its Edwardian judgments about his character, a good many of his friends and acquaintances, among them Joseph Conrad and Henry James, dropped away from him, and even now the suspicion that there was something dubious about Ford, something not quite respectable, lingers on—an idea that is, as Janice Biala points out in her interview, quaintly incongruous with our present view of the relations between men and women.

Ford was a raconteur. A good many of the stories he told seemed very wild to his contemporaries, who were not amused ("As always, Ford told lies which made those who knew the truth gasp and stretch their eyes"—David Garnett). Ford never retold a story in quite the same way, and he reinvented real people living and dead. "Most writers dealing with real people find their invention confined," Graham Greene observes, "but that was not so with Ford." The issue has assumed an inordinate importance; and though it may some day be laid to rest, it will have been largely responsible for a widespread feeling among reviewers and critics that if Ford could not be trusted as a character witness, how could he be trusted as a novelist? What is surprising is how little scrutinized the matter has been, how little critical imagination has gone into the effort of understanding what Ford might have been up to in those stories of his.

There was, to be sure, a certain amount of pure high jinx, and he knew how to tell a story: "The humorous story," Mark Twain advises, "is told gravely; the teller does his best to conceal the fact that he even dimly suspects that there is anything funny about it." Ford liked to tell stories that stretched probability, to see how far he could go. He expected resistance, skepticism, interpretation; what he got was belief or disbelief, indignation, and even a sense of outrage.

"You can write about anything if you know how," he told a young writer in the late thirties.[2] This statement, at once liberating and cautionary, he made not long after he had written his last novels—daring, original, still unread. The important thing for him was knowing how—and as he grew older he wished that novels could be written like fugues, where knowing how is everything and the subject or subjects merely an occasion for the working out of the form, through which the expressive power of the writer transmits itself. What all this suggests is not that Ford was careless of content,

[2]Quoted by Wanda Tower Pickard in a letter to the editor, 3 April 1980.

or careless of truth: his novels attest, it has been observed, to how powerful a truth-teller he was, a teller of the truths that matter most. Denis Donoghue makes the essential distinction in his essay: "Truthfulness, rather than truth, since truth refers to the facts of the case and truthfulness to the spirit in which they are to be declared."

It seems reasonable to suppose that Ford, after a certain amount of looking around, doubted the possibility of finding an objective fact. How can we know the world as it really is? Ford did not fool himself into thinking that he could; all he could do was record what he saw and heard from moment to moment, given the changes in himself as an observer and the changes in the light, and his possession of the novelist's equipment to do all this more accurately than most men can. He called himself an impressionist because he felt it was the most honest thing he could be. What philosophers call the epistemological problem was a pervasive one for Ford, and perhaps one of the remarkable things about him was the seriousness and consistency with which he applied his understanding of truth—that a multiplicity of truths is possible but no single version, at least that men were capable of—both to his own life and to the novels he wrote, in which the form was so much determined by questions of point of view.

Although his books could not have been written by such a person, he was regarded as a buffoon, a megalomaniac, a posturer, a deliberate liar, an unreliable narrator—in short, a sort of Rameau's nephew. But these improvisations imply an author behind them, and few critics have bothered to look for him. "What I am trying to say," Allen Tate said very well, "is that Ford's best biographer will understand at the outset that Ford himself must be approached as a character in a novel, and that novel a novel by Ford." The outrageous stories were largely inventions by a man who deliberately invented himself and who was writing all the time, even—and especially— during those hours when he left his writing table and was making wonderful conversation, as Robert Lowell tells us, conversation that was indistinguishable in quality from his written words.

Other writers may have departed from literal truth as much as Ford, but they were more circumspect and less prodigal. Ironically, Ford was probably as private a person as Conrad or Faulkner, but he was also more gregarious, and his stories, his themes and variations, enjoyed very wide currency, as he dragged his career through three countries (Ezra Pound's description). Ironically too, the stories he told *viva voce* left the literary world unwilling to take him seriously, and the novels he wrote were, for the most part, left unread, little read, or misread. But as Robie Macauley has pointed out,[3] Ford harmed no one—unlike Ernest Hemingway, who reinvented Ford out of malice and destructiveness. Ford cared about the shape, the telling, the effect of the

[3]*Encounter* 23, no. 3 (September 1964): 56–58.

story, and if he aggrandized himself, it was at no one else's expense. He did so in a spirit of irony so oblique and elusive that it all but concealed the ultimate self-deprecation and self-knowledge behind the apparent vanity. Even a partial awareness of his indirections and the extraordinary subtlety of his sense of play would change the way in which he is read. Out of himself he created a personality that was as distinctive a contribution to literature as his best work—and was indeed inseparable from it. Its particular tonality, related to yet distinct from that of Montaigne or Stendhal, has been described by Edward Krickel in his essay on Ford as an editor.

> Pound, who knew Ford well, said he was "almost an halluciné." But most of Ford's anecdotes about himself were deftly sliced and pricked by his peculiar "Fordian irony," for which I have no technical name, but in which are an awareness and a self-mockery, and also in which what is said is meant not quite as stated—though it might be true; yet at the same time it is riddled with the awareness that his claim is too high. He would prefer that we make it for him, so he could deny it, including the component of truth in it, which is assuredly there. . . . The bearing of all this is the multiple awareness Ford held in regard to his work, his exploits, and his tales about them.

But the astonishing thing that we are beginning to learn, as we learn more about Ford, is that some of the "Huefferisms" (Olive Garnett's term for his stories) were in fact true, in the most ordinary sense. As Thomas C. Moser has discovered, "Time and again Olive's diary serves to confirm Ford's much later autobiographical statements."

> The diary naturally deals at great length with the two chief crises of Ford's early years, his forbidden marriage and his nervous breakdown. In *Return to Yesterday,* Ford told in detail only about the breakdown. His account has probably struck many readers as wildly improbable; and yet, though written twenty-seven years after the event, it is amazingly accurate, even to the fabulous tale of Elsie's accursed opal that Ford after much trouble managed to give away.[4]

And Louise Bogan, in a 1961 radio tape, commented: "As I knew him better . . . it was possible that a good many of these tales could be true." If even some of them were true, and they seem to have been, Ford must have been fascinated by the uncertain relation between plausibility and truth, and he was always testing it—not just for comic effects. He believed that there is a certain wildness inherent in events themselves. His money really had been snatched by the mistral while he was standing on the bridge at Avignon; and the subtitle he gave to one of his books—"A Just Possible Story"—referred

---

[4]Thomas C. Moser, "From Olive Garnett's Diary: Impressions of Ford Madox Ford and His Friends, 1890–1906," *Texas Studies in Literature and Language* 16 (Fall 1974): 3.

to a sense he had about his own life. For him the fantastic was probable: on what other premise could a character like Sylvia Tietjens have been created? Even Pound, who thought of himself as Ford's champion, left the impression of his inability to tell truth from fiction. But a good deal remains to be learned, and the whole issue is far more complicated than Pound saw it to be. Looked at with any care, these complications ought to call into question the judgments about Ford that have preceded, rather than followed, full knowledge.

Critic after critic in this collection of essays is drawn into the matter of Ford's idea of the truth, and the essays in this book concern themselves with it in one way or another. For the serious critic the problem leads directly into the heart of Ford's work; it is one of his great themes. But to follow the reviews of Ford's books as they were published, one after another—over eighty books in about forty-five years of writing—is to be struck forcibly by a history of condescension, a long illustration of the power of received ideas on the part of critics whose minds were made up beforehand to belittle or dismiss what they were about to consider or what they could not easily understand, to take Ford's "inaccuracies" as an excuse to look no further. If criticism were not still infected by this attitude, there would be no need to raise the point.

The title of *Some Do Not . . .* is a quotation from Ford's own poem "Mr. Bosphorus and the Muses" (1923).

> The gods to each ascribe a differing lot:
> Some rest on snowy bosoms! Some do not!

The lines are misquoted by Macmaster at the opening of the novel because he thinks only of his career:

> The gods to each ascribe a differing lot:
> Some enter at the portal. Some do not!

Some writers receive, in their own lifetime, the attention that is commensurate with their powers; some do not. Ford understood this and would have called it the rubs of the game. But he did not despise a popular success; it would have signified to him that he had succeeded in "the highest form of communication between person and person"—his definition of an art.

> It is nothing more and nothing less. The more attractive the personality making the communication, the wider in extent, the deeper in penetration and the more lasting, will be the appeal.[5]

He so believed in the future and the importance of "the humaner letters"

[5]*The March of Literature,* Introduction.

in bringing about an integrated culture that he wrote his last book, *The March of Literature* (1938), to induce "a larger and larger number of my fellows to taste the pleasure that comes from always more and more reading."

Some writers—Blake, Jane Austen, Stendhal, Melville—gain in significance in the course of time. At some moment in history they come to assume an importance in our consciousness that rescues them from total or relative obscurity because of what they have to tell us. It is not really a question of rehabilitating Ford or trying to bring about a "revival"; it is a question of investigating a mainly unknown literary territory and seeing for ourselves what is there, what we can find that we can use.

How are we to regard the vast bulk of his work today? Are *The Good Soldier* and *Parade's End* aberrations in an otherwise bewildering output? The critics writing for this collection would probably not agree on any answers here, nor do they always agree about other questions, and perhaps that is as it should be. Every reader ideally should read for himself and exercise what Ford called the critical attitude. Writing in 1963, Allen Tate remarked: "The staggering disproportion between the number of books about Ford and the number of his own books . . . in print will be an anomaly of Anglo-American literary history. It will be easier to read about Ford than to read him." The books, the greater part of them, are still out of print and in their total number available in only a few rare-book rooms; until they are republished, no real reevaluation can take place.

"Homo scriptor," Richard Howard calls Ford in his poem of homage—

> to whom
> literature and fiction
> were different, irreconcilable dooms,
> literature being a luxury and
> fiction a necessity.

Subtract the thirty-two novels from the over eighty books, and what is left is a large mass of books that (apart from the volumes of poetry) can be designated, more or less, if one wishes to be orderly, as art criticism, literary criticism, autobiography, biography, history, sociology, travel; but in fact the crossing over of reminiscence, anecdote, speculation, commentary, and digression in these books would make it arbitrary to speak of genre. It would be more accurate to speak of a certain transparency of genre, a fluidity that suggests a vast and continuous notebook, each section concealing a structure akin to the characteristic structure of the novels, where fluidity is a determining value. C. H. Sisson, in his essay on Ford the critic, speaks of "an atmosphere, an uncertainty in the air, which is really the critical benefit received." No final truths, no incontestable logic, method, or theory—but plenty of contradiction, "the endless qualification of one view by another." In short, what Ford has to give to the reader is a sense of enlargement and life and pleasure in reading; he offers "the civilized wisdom of his hesitations" and "the lighting up of the *reader's* picture." In his unwieldiness and refusal of categories, a spirit large and generous and full of surprises: William H. Pritchard's appreciation of Ford's daring and freedom as a critic—his "audacities and heresies"—suggests, as C. H. Sisson's essay does, how much there is for us if we refuse the stock response of outrage at Ford's inconsistencies, hyperbole, misrepresentations, and lack of system. Wisely, neither essay concerns itself with *progression d'effet* and time shift and the rest of the terminology Ford and Conrad liked to use between themselves in their conversations about the writing of novels. Rather, both essays bring up questions about the nature of responsibility in the literary critic, and beyond that, the question again—this time triggered by so apparently anomalous a critic as Ford—of the purpose, or the purposes of criticism. The Pritchard essay looks at Ford in a context of other critics—Samuel Coleridge, Pound, T. S. Eliot, D. H. Lawrence, Wyndham Lewis. Ford did not, as Mr. Sisson points out, wish to be taken literally, but he did wish to be taken seriously, and he deserved to be. His seriousness as a critic, emerging from "the recesses behind his casual and often throw-away tone" is a subject that future critics might further consider.

How much of Ford can be read today—and taken seriously? More, it would seem, than conventional wisdom has allowed.

Alison Lurie opens the fairy tales Ford wrote as a young father and finds *The Queen Who Flew* (written when he was twenty-one). It is "a first-rate story, lively, imaginative, and well written. . . . It compares favorably with contemporary fairy tales by writers like Andrew Lang and Oscar Wilde, and should be far better known today than it is."

William Gass reads *The Fifth Queen* trilogy (1906–8) and concludes: "It is a virtuoso performance—the first of Ford's great shows—and closes out the historical novel like an emptied account." Mr. Gass goes on:

> The neglect of this novel, the critical obtuseness which the Tudor trilogy has had to endure, the indifference of readers to an accomplished art, and a major talent, the failure of scholarship even to disclose the real clay feet of the real Ford, even the esteem in which *The Good Soldier* is held, as if that book were being used to hide the others, but, above all, the unwillingness of writers to respond to a master, constitute a continuing scandal which hushing up will only prolong; yet one does wonder what is to be done. Certainly no adequate history of the recent English novel can be composed that does not recognize the door through which that novel passed to become modern.

A little-known pair of books Ford wrote as part of the official British propaganda campaign against Germany in 1915 is the subject of an essay by the historian L. L. Farrar. "Generally unknown to historians," the two books, *When Blood Is Their Argument* and *Between St. Dennis and St. George,* are seen as a significant source of information "about the wartime attitudes of the English ruling class" and should be known as well to literary critics interested in the literature written in response to World War I. The books are, in addition, discussions of the ideological background that *Parade's End* grew out of, and to some degree, away from. Written the same year as Veblen's book on Germany, they were not intended to be more than what Wyndham Lewis characteristically called Ford's "blast" against Germany. They turned out, because Ford was incapable of sustaining such an unmixed genre, to be a good deal more. Mr. Farrar examines these books as propaganda, as history, and as novels *manqués.*

Clearly there is matter in Ford's oeuvre to sustain more than a single collection of critical essays. If this volume could have given representation to Ford's *The "Half Moon"* or *The Call* or *The Simple Life Limited* (written under the pseudonym Daniel Chaucer!) or *Ladies Whose Bright Eyes* or *The Young Lovell* or *Zeppelin Nights* or *The Marsden Case* or *A Little Less Than Gods* or *No Enemy* or the four last novels *(When the Wicked Man, The Rash Act, Henry for Hugh,* and *Vive le Roy)*—it is possible that yet more discoveries would have been made, perhaps comparable in excitement to those contained in this memorial volume. The question remains open for future criticism.

The books we already know—*The Good Soldier* and *Parade's End*—we know better by virtue of the essays written about them here.

Roger Sale looks at both works in the same essay and makes as strong a case as has been made for *Parade's End:* it is "one of the few irreplaceable novels of the century"; and, unlike *The Good Soldier,* as he reads it, *Parade's End* is "a work of strength, health, and joy."

> Its length is a pedagogical inconvenience; a course with *Ulysses* and the major Lawrence in it may seem weighted down enough already without it. But, for me at least, it is those books that it should be placed alongside, better than Conrad or Woolf or Forster or Huxley or Waugh, and it should never be allowed to disappear again.

Set against this claim, long overdue, is a view of *The Good Soldier* that connects it with the Flaubertian tradition and its limitations:

> For Ford as well as for James, concealment and revelation are exercises in seeing how it can best be done, and for both what is revealed is a sexual horror that will, in turn, conceal a deeper sexual horror the reader is left to imagine more than see. The besetting weakness of the Flaubertian tradition is that artfulness is often mistaken as an end in itself, and concealment and revelation, when not informed by some-

thing really worth seeking, can seem either empty gesture or strip-tease.

Denis Donoghue reads *The Good Soldier* not primarily as a novel owing to a given tradition its way of being *written* but as a story, a tale, with an "insistently oral" element. And he sets aside one of the much-vexed questions in the accumulated criticism of the book.

> The question of reliable and unreliable narrators has often been raised in reference to him, but it is not the real question. . . . The real question is: what remains, now that nearly all the ostensible significance of the facts has been drained from them by Dowell's scepticism? And the answer is: Dowell himself remains. . . . The more he disputes the significance of the facts he recites, the more indisputable he becomes.

"We listen to his voice": Denis Donoghue works out the implications of Dowell's language, a poetic diction akin to that of Stephen Daedalus or Prufrock and, like theirs, "an exercise of the only power [Dowell] commands, the power to draw every event into himself and convert it into privacy and inwardness."

The social changes behind the aesthetic impulses that translate an alienated universe into a private language are of course the great subject of *Parade's End.* The statements of four writers in this collection—Andrew Lytle, Roger Sale, Howard Nemerov, and William Trevor—provide a powerful reconsideration of that work.

Andrew Lytle interprets the tetralogy as a rendering of "the given moment of history as people make it and in peace time the cultural conditions through which and by which all human beings are effectively moved." His essay elucidates the moral issues involved in the great social changes of the twentieth century, changes which Ford understood and projected as very few writers have been able to. Mr. Lytle clarifies, point after point, the many submerged particulars of the action as well as the larger meaning of the outward signs of change. He takes up the question of whether *The Last Post* is integral or not to the design of the Tietjens story: "Without it the ending would have emphasized the union of the two lovers beyond the meaning of the whole."[6] Always the meaning of the whole: the essay will be essential to a new generation of readers; it takes them from the clearly understood detail—matters that even older readers no longer seem to know about—to "the full-rounded meaning of what happens to the hero and the heroine in their persons and as they reflect the matters common to what was Christian Europe."

One of Ford's characteristic subjects, the experience of losing and

---

[6]Compare Graham Greene's argument, in his second introductory essay, against the inclusion of *Last Post;* see also Roger Sale's comments.

finding, grew out of his profound understanding of what was being lost, in terms of human and civilizing values, as the nineteenth century yielded to the twentieth. Ford understood that great historical shift and its implications for the future as only a very great writer born in one century and confronting the other could. The nineteenth-century world behind the emerging one— seen as both history and literary history—is the subject of Howard Nemerov's poem:

> Beginning your four gospels about a world
> Threatened by nothing more than suffragettes,
> As outward and as *there* as it had been
> For Jane and George but showing its omens forth. . . .

When Ford was elegiac it was not for the loss of the past or the fact of change; what he regretted was the discontinuities, the element of rupture inherent in the kinds of change taking place in his lifetime. What he feared is what we have, a culture of disjunctions, with very little to bind us, "each to each." Ford belonged with the Renaissance humanists to whom the past was something present and living that could be drawn upon. Montaigne read Plutarch as if he were a contemporary; Ford read Juvenal and Petronius as if they were no more distant in time than Stendhal or Flaubert.

But he thought of himself, insofar as he was a novelist, as the historian of his own times. As a historian of the culture he knew—during the same years Freudianism came to dominate our psychology—Ford gave us some of the most powerful delineations we have of repressed feeling, and the questions he raised about the cost of civilization to the individual personality were questions raised by Freud after *The Good Soldier* was written and made more familiar to us from our reading of *Civilization and Its Discontents.*

Ford's view of European culture in the earlier part of our century is very close to Freud's, and both were formed independently although from a shared intellectual background; but these matters have not had much attention, and Ford, when he is noticed by literary historians, is remembered for advancing, in Conrad's company, particular practices in the construction of the novel, in the building up of its surface.

"If we owe a great deal to James or Ford," Allen Tate wrote, "we may appear to owe them less if we acknowledge debts to writers to whom we owe very little." If we owe a great deal to Ford, we may appear to owe him less if we acknowledge smaller debts for matters removed from the most central concerns of literature. It should be remembered that Ford thought of technique—"that harsh dissyllable"—as "the most odious word in the English language."[7] What he meant was that technique could not be regarded as an end in itself; a writer has to search for a method in which to work that would

---

[7]Ford Madox Ford, "Techniques," *Southern Review* 1 (July 1935): 20–35.

allow him to work in it "as easily as he can live in an old and utterly comfortable coat . . . or dressing gown."

> So long as you remain a live writer, you will forever be questioning and re-questioning and testing and re-testing the devices that you will have evolved. . . . You must have your eyes forever on your Reader. That alone constitutes. . . . Technique!

An educated European knows who William Faulkner is, or James Joyce, but Ford Madox Ford, one must explain, was Joseph Conrad's collaborator. "I am a little tired of being tacked onto C's coattails,"[8] Ford wrote in 1928, with all of *Parade's End* behind him, the most important English novel to come out of World War I. Over a decade before that, he had written *The Good Soldier,* the novel that Rebecca West has recognized as having "set the pattern for perhaps half the novels which have been written since."

Ford liked to say that the word *author* derived from the Latin *auctor,* someone who adds to what we already have. How much Ford added to our knowledge of life William Trevor suggests in his Foreword:

> It wasn't until I came across Ford that England and the English took real shape, and having come to know both rather well in the meanwhile I am repeatedly aware of how accurate, and how perceptive, he was in painting his picture. . . . Ford shatters the surface of things and even out of the fragments creates an extra pattern of truth.

William Gass calls attention to the splendor of Ford's writing, the living English he wrote even in his recreation of sixteenth-century English—prose that is "the recovery of poetry itself." Beyond even this

> In an arrogant display of literary genius, Ford Madox Ford brought the nineteenth-century novel, in each of its principal areas of excellence, to its final and most complete expression.

What he gave, besides, to English literature—if it were necessary to give more—was, C. H. Sisson has said, the contribution "of a man who has something to inject from outside the insular stream"—an awareness of the mainstream of European culture that Hugh Kenner has fully appreciated: "It was Ford, and Ford almost alone, who in the first decade of this century absorbed and retransmitted the discoveries of Stendhal and Flaubert on an English wavelength."[9] Allen Tate, in his essay on Faulkner, suggests a direct line from the European novel to Faulkner and sees him in the tradition of Stendhal and Flaubert as "one of the last great craftsmen of the art of fiction

---

[8]Arthur Mizener, *The Saddest Story: A Biography of Ford Madox Ford* (New York: World Publishing Co., 1971), p. 385.

[9]*Gnomon* (New York: McDowell, Obolensky, 1958), p. 145.

which Ford Madox Ford called the impressionist novel"—a hovering point that a future critic may develop.

Even in his poetry—which was to have been the subject of an essay for this volume—Ford was an influence, unacknowledged except by Pound, who was an intermediary in the line of influence that radiated out. The poet Basil Bunting, who worked as Ford's secretary in the early twenties and as a subeditor of the *Transatlantic Review,* talks about Ford's influence as a poet.

> He wrote poems which take some time to make their point, and make it by rhythms which repeat with variations from line to line, which have a relation to prose rhythms and which have a vocabulary which is not merely a prose vocabulary but a colloquial vocabulary; and that had an enormous influence. He was the first to do it on a large scale and was imitated by one poet after another. Perhaps the only one who directly learned from him was Ezra Pound. But through his use of it, it came to be in the air, and without knowing where it originated hundreds of poets in England and America began to write in ways which would hardly have been possible unless Ford had shown them how.[10]

This sort of assessment confirms what Lowell reports in his Introduction to Ford's *Buckshee:*

> I heard someone ask [Ford] about Pound's influence on Yeats's later style. "Oh," Ford said, "I used to tell Ezra that he mustn't write illiterate poetic jargon. Then he'd go to Yeats and say the same thing." This was tossed off with such flippant finality that I was sure it was nonsense. Years later, however, Pound told me the same story.

Ford had an extremely delicate ear for the rhythms of speech, and what Robert Lowell noticed in his memoir about the closeness of Ford's conversation to his writing draws attention to the spoken and the heard element of his work—consider Denis Donoghue's point that the narrator of *The Good Soldier* is to be listened to, heard with the ear. Lowell heard in Ford's writing "that quality of someone speaking." Conversely, "he was the most astonishing speaker you'd ever heard." We have fascinating evidence of Ford's subtlety and accuracy of perception as a listener (not just to human speech, but to all sound) in two of four letters from Edward Naumburg's collection written by Ford to Conrad from the trenches in 1915. These letters are full of precise observations about what Ford was hearing, observations he wished to put in Conrad's safekeeping in case he was killed in the war. Only a musician could have attended so particularly to matters of pitch, dynamics,

---

[10]From an unpublished transcript of a B.B.C. program by Tony Gould on Ford Madox Ford, "The Only Uncle of the Gifted Young," February 1974.

timbre, color, duration, and resonance.[11] The only thing like these "renderings" I have come upon is a description by Fritz Kreisler, who was listening carefully and taking notes in another trench, on the Eastern front, in the very same year.

> My ear, accustomed to differentiate sounds of all kinds, had some time ago, while we still advanced, noted a remarkable discrepancy in the peculiar whine produced by the different shells in their rapid flight through the air as they passed over our heads, some sounding shrill, with a rising tendency, and the others rather dull, with a falling cadence. . . . I could actually determine by the sound the exact place where a shell coming from the opposing batteries was reaching its acme.[12]

The statements in the second half of this book by those who knew Ford have a common theme—that he was magnanimous to a fault, and Frank Mac-Shane's essay draws out some of the implications of his generosity to other writers. When Lionel Trilling wrote "On Not Talking" in *A Gathering of Fugitives,* he was reflecting on the habits of American artists and intellectuals of not talking to each other. Ford had found the habit an English vice as well, and believing—like all the great writers of the nineteenth century—that art is a binding force among men and women, he also believed it could be a binding force among artists. So he carried this belief to the United States and organized the Friends of William Carlos Williams to create a framework for some sort of community for the writers he knew here, and he organized Dinners—for Williams, for E. E. Cummings, for Theodore Dreiser, for John Crowe Ransom, for Edward Dahlberg; and he organized a tribute to Pound: *The Cantos of Ezra Pound: Some Testimonials by Ernest Hemingway, Ford Madox Ford, T. S. Eliot, Hugh Walpole, Archibald MacLeish, James Joyce and Others.*[13]

We are reminded of a line from Conrad's *Amy Foster:* "There is no kindness of heart without a certain amount of imagination." Not only did Ford have more than a certain amount of imagination, but he believed that "imaginative culture" was necessary for civilization because it would make the world a less inhuman and less unfamiliar place. He believed that it could be made that, though the odds seemed to be against it. Even his detractors would not deny the force of his belief in the value of art, his sense of a calling to be a writer. "Somebody is telling me," Basil Bunting remarks, "that Ford had strong passions, violent hatreds and loves and so on. I saw no sign of it whatever. . . . His only real passion, the only thing that he was so devoted

---

[11]Ford's unknown musical compositions, "written between c. 1894 and c. 1905"—one hundred twenty pages of music—have recently come to light (summer, 1980) in the sale of papers and manuscripts by John Lamb, son of Ford's daughter Katharine.

[12]Fritz Kreisler, *Four Weeks in the Trenches: The War Story of a Violinist* (New York: Houghton Mifflin Company, 1915).

[13](New York: Farrar and Rinehart, 1933).

to that it would take him from his meat or anything else was the English language." "A true literary man," Sherwood Anderson called him in the New Directions memorial gathering of 1942, "the very type of the artist man." "He understood the obligation taken on. . . . He was a professional writer who didn't soil his tools. He was . . . a real workman, a man who understood what it is that gives a man's own life some significance." Graham Greene sees Ford in the same way: "No one in our country except James has been more attentive to the craft of letters. . . . He was a carpenter; you feel in his work the love of the tools and the love of the material."

Edward Crankshaw gives us a picture of Ford as he remembers him:

> This heavy, rather lumpy figure in shapeless, battered tweeds, panting, often gasping like a fish, would sit upright, legs apart, on a hard chair in a bare attic room like a king on his throne—and talk like an angel about everything under the sun—without the faintest suggestion that he had no idea where next week's rent was coming from—showering on his listeners pure gold. His possessions when he died were minimal. One of his favourite remarks was that he enjoyed luxury but despised comfort; but the discomfort of some of his perches was excessive—and unrelieved by the least touch of luxury.

Pound said that Ford "actually lived the heroic artistic life that Yeats talked about." We are left with the paradox that the idea of heroism Ford knew to be a lost cause in the real world (the world his novels project) sustained him in his own life so that he could be a writer and keep on going as a writer. He invented himself, as we now know; and he became a hero as Carlyle meant it—a great personality expressing itself through a way of life his genius has determined for him, leaving a heroic stamp on his achievement. A fabulous monster, one of the scamps of literature, a scamp of a literary critic, a natural and incorrigible Bohemian, a Baron Munchausen, Falstaff, Lord Plushbottom, Don Juan, Don Quixote, Sancho Panza perhaps—all these names for him if we wish, and they have been used both in and outside this volume; but also a great European man of letters, a hero of letters, and a hero, even on second thought, in Carlyle's sense.

RICHARD HOWARD
Homage

Mid-August, the mid-twenties,
writing from Guermantes—I saw the French postmark;
you could have made it up, of course, another
    of your fat, nourishing fibs,
but there they were, Proust's own "orange" syllables
incontrovertible on the envelope
    (some truth is close to being
only a consistent lie, as we shall learn
when the last of your memorialists dies off)—
    you more or less volunteered
for the obsessional task which lures me still:
"it would amuse me to translate *Swann.*" Ever
    the good soldier ("I somehow
pine to publish a volume of poems before
the war ends or I am killed"), you knew
    the way the saddest story
ought to go, leading us (not only Marcel)
slowly back down from the heights, following some
    path of blithe declivity—
the reason for a mistress. Proust escaped you:
now you would have to produce, as all of us
    long to do, a great dreary
masterpiece everyone must claim to have read;
it was either happiness or art. By then
    you had invented yourself
under (or over) the emblematic name,

bringing out your fiftieth book and the first
        novel by "Ford Madox Ford";
losing a father, gaining a fatherland
in that neat reversal, repudiating
        his tainted Teutonism
(though Provence was "in the family" for good)
for a new-made man, *homo scriptor,* to whom
        literature and fiction
were different, irreconcilable dooms,
literature being a luxury and
        fiction a necessity.
"I have for facts a most profound contempt," though
after dozens of books and two daughters, sighing
        "I do wish I had a son,"
enmeshed from divorce to divorce by a strong
if sleepy sexuality which somehow
        worked against the grain of love
(what was saucy in the gander, I daresay,
was not saucy in the goose). Meanwhile you ditched
        your legacy, the dry glare
of pre-Raphaelite masters *and* the wet mist
of Impressionism, steeping yourself instead—
        "to discover where we stand"—
in that inclusive negative, the Modern:
"but for Conrad, who told me 'put more shadow
        in it, there *is* more shadow,'
I should be merely a continuation
of Dante Gabriel Rossetti." Which is
        what it has been my study
to continue, if headway can be something
besides continual parricide, eager
        to commit poetic acts
between consenting adults and managing
to ravel a sow's purse out of that silk ear . . .
        You smile at my ambition,
you forbid nothing, suggesting only—do
I hear you?—that poems, even your poems,
        be labelled, like medicines:
Shake Well Before Using. How you got away
from them—from "Aunt Christina" and the others
        was your great exploit, how you
survived originality, whereas I . . .
I go round on the back of that other life

my reading relinquishes
like the little Egyptian heron that lives
on the backs of cows. The shoe fits perfectly.
    There is no getting beyond
without first getting as far, you remind me,
part "denture," part "danger," the self-proclaimed
    model for James's Merton
as he (HJ, not Densher) was yours in all
but success: "I am a half-way house between
    the unpublishable young
and real money, a sort of green baize swing door
to kick on entering and leaving, both ways."
    Well, who has got beyond *you,*
who wants to? I cannot bear to imagine
your last years—did it *have* to be Michigan,
    when all America seemed
like a bluepoint oyster, very large, very
insipid? You wanted countries built out of
    obstacles and boundaries,
like Guermantes, say—the fields that resemble
a dinner-table one has just left, gardens
    gently warding off darkness
with red flowers . . . I leave you there, confronting
"with a certain erudition most of the things
    which make for the happiness
of mankind," the shadows deepening, the light
orange as Proust said it sounded: *Guermantes . . .*
    Just light enough to read by,
reading what? Joyce, or Yeats, who died your last year?
No, some new writer not even printed yet,
    formal as the familiar
rapturous sentences in the first lessons
of a French primer: *il aime, il écrit, il meurt.*

PART ONE
The Critical Attitude

GRAHAM GREENE
Two Introductory Essays

Introduction to Volume I of *The Bodley Head Ford Madox Ford*

I

Ford Madox Hueffer, the name under which he was first known, was born in 1873 and died, in France, in 1939. His first book was published in 1892, his last in 1939, and between those dates some seventy-five books appeared, novels, poems, reminiscences, essays, biographies, histories, books of travel, topography, criticism, sociology. I have chosen for the present selection his finest novel—and perhaps one of the finest novels of our century—*The Good Soldier,* passages from his volumes of reminiscence (the headings and divisions are my own*), a few poems, and his historical trilogy *The Fifth Queen* which has never before been published in one volume. There is a conspicuous absentee which is sometimes known as the Tietjens Saga, after the name of its principal character—the series of war-novels, *Some Do Not, No More Parades, A Man Could Stand Up* and *Last Post,* but those books have already been published in one volume in the United States, and, remarkable though they are, they do not stand up to the erosion of time so satisfactorily as *The Good Soldier.*

Ford was not a man who loved fools or bad writing, and his enemies have been almost as persistent as his friends have been loyal. He was a great editor: in *The English Review* before 1914 he published Conrad, Hudson, Hardy; in the years between the wars in Paris he edited *the transatlantic review* in which he published Gertrude Stein, the early Hemingway, E. E. Cummings. The better the editor, the more numerous his enemies. He was a man too of a passionate nature; his marriage, a Catholic one, was unsuccessful, but divorce was impossible; his long love-affair with the novelist Violet Hunt, of which the reflection is to be found in his poem *On Heaven,* came to a confused

Introductions by Graham Greene to Volumes I and III of *The Bodley Head Ford Madox Ford* reprinted with permission of The Bodley Head.
*The dots which break out like a rash in his later work, for example in *The Pines, Putney,* are Ford's own and do not indicate omissions by the editor.

and miserable end. On one occasion he tried to leave his country for good and to become a German citizen (that strange episode is recounted in *The Desirable Alien,* a collaboration with Violet Hunt published ominously in 1913). When war broke out, in spite of his age he joined the army and saw service on the Western Front. Finally he came through the troubled years with his appetite for life undiminished, and was happy in his final relationship. My only memory of him dates from about 1938, a stout sanguine man walking over the fields with the air of a country gentleman—which always, with one side of his nature, he had wanted to be, though the nearest he came to realizing his ambition was on the small property he owned in Provence.

II

Ford had once described himself, before the great disaster of 1914; 'I may humbly write myself down a man in his early forties a little mad about good letters.' By the very nature of his birth and early years he was condemned to the life of an artist. Son of Hueffer, the distinguished musical critic of *The Times* and grandson of Ford Madox Brown, the famous Victorian painter, brought up in the strange mansion in Fitzroy Square immortalized by Thackeray in *The Newcomes,* with small Rossetti cousins tumbling downstairs at his feet and Swinburne, as like as not, lying drunk in the bath on the top floor, he had little choice: one might have prophesied almost anything for him from a staggered laudanum death to membership of the Royal Academy.

One would have been wrong about the details, but not about the fact that, in the age of Kipling, Haggard, and Wells, an age of increasing carelessness among good writers, he was an artist. No one in our century except James has been more attentive to the craft of letters. He was not only a designer; he was a carpenter: you feel in his work the love of the tools and the love of the material. He may sometimes have been over-elaborate, an accusation which after he had spent more than forty years in writing fiction can be brought against his last novels. But who else, except James, has shown such a capacity for growth, even misguided growth, over so long a span of years? Ford's first novel was published in 1892 and his last in 1937. Even so, when he died, he had not reached the limit of his technical experiments.

How seldom a novelist chooses the material nearest to his hand; it is almost as if he were driven to earn experience the hard way. Ford, whom we might have expected to become a novelist of artistic bohemia, a kind of English Murger, did indeed employ the material of Fitzroy Square incomparably well in his volumes of reminiscence—and some people might regard those as his finest novels, for he brought to his dramatizations of people he had known—James, Conrad, Crane, Hudson, Hardy—the same astonishing knack he showed with his historical figures. Most writers dealing with real people find their invention confined, but that was not so with Ford. 'When it has seemed expedient to me I have altered episodes that I have witnessed, but I have been careful never to distort the character of the episode. *The accuracies I deal in are the accuracies of my impressions.* If you want factual accuracies you must go to . . . but no, no, don't go to anyone, stay with me.' (The italics are mine: it is a phrase worth bearing in mind in reading all his works.)

In fact as a novelist Ford began to move further and further from bohemia for his material. His first period as an historical novelist, which he began by collaborating with Conrad in that underrated novel *Romance,* virtually closed with his Tudor trilogy. There were to be two or three more historical novels, until in *Ladies Whose Bright Eyes* . . . he came half out into the contemporary world and began to find his true subject. It could even be argued that in *The Fifth Queen* he was nearest as a novelist to Fitzroy Square. There is the sense of saturation: something is always happening on the stairs, in the passages the servants come and go on half explained errands, and the great King may at any moment erupt upon the scene, half kindly, half malevolent, rather as we feel the presence of Madox Brown in the gas-lit interstices of No. 37.

Most historical novelists use real characters only for purposes of local colour—Lord Nelson passes up a Portsmouth street or Doctor Johnson enters ponderously to close a chapter, but in *The Fifth Queen* we have virtually no fictional characters—the King, Thomas Cromwell, Katharine Howard, they are the principals; we are nearer to the historical plays of Shakespeare than to the fictions of such historical writers as Miss Irwin or Miss Heyer.

'The accuracies I deal in are the accuracies of my impressions.' In *The Fifth Queen* Ford tries out the impressionist method which he was later to employ with triumphant ease in the great confused armistice-day scene of *A Man Could Stand Up.* The whole story of the struggle between Katharine and Cromwell for the King seems told in shadows—shadows which flicker with the flames of a log-fire, diminish suddenly as a torch recedes, stand calm awhile in the candlelight of a chapel: a cresset flares and all the shadows leap together. Has a novel ever before been lit as carefully as a stage production? Nicolas Udal's lies, which play so important a part in the first volume, take their substance from the lighting: they are monstrously elongated or suddenly shrivel: one can believe anything by torchlight. (The power of a lie— that too was a subject he was to pursue through all his later books: the lies of Sylvia Tietjens which ruined her husband's army-career and the monstrous lie of 'poor Florence' in *The Good Soldier* which brought death to three people and madness to a fourth.)

If *The Fifth Queen* is a magnificent bravura piece—and you could say that it was a better painting than ever came out of Fitzroy Square with all the mingled talents there of Madox Brown and Morris, Rossetti and Burne-Jones —in *The Good Soldier* Ford triumphantly found his true subject and oddly enough, for a child of the Pre-Raphaelites, his subject was the English 'gentleman,' the 'black and merciless things' which lie behind that façade.

Edward Ashburnham was the cleanest looking sort of chap;—an excellent magistrate, a first rate soldier, one of the best landlords, so they said, in Hampshire, England. To the poor and to hopeless drunkards, as I myself have witnessed, he was like a painstaking guardian. And he never told a story that couldn't have gone into the columns of the *Field* more than once or twice in all the nine years of my knowing him. He didn't even like hearing them; he would fidget and get up and go out to buy a cigar or something of that sort. You would have said that he was just exactly the sort of chap that you could have trusted your wife with. And I trusted mine and it was madness.

The Good Soldier, which Ford had wished to call *The Saddest Story,* concerns the ravages wrought by a passionate man who had all the virtues but continence. The narrator is the betrayed husband, and it is through his eyes alone that we watch the complications and involvements left by Ashburnham's blind urge towards satisfaction. Technically the story is undoubtedly Ford's masterpiece: the book is simultaneously a study of the way memory works. The time-shifts are valuable not merely for purposes of suspense— they lend veracity to the appalling events. This is just how memory does work, and we become involved with the narrator's memory as though it were our own. Ford's apprenticeship with Conrad had borne its fruit, but he improved on the Master.

I have, I am aware, told this story in a very rambling way so that it may be difficult for anyone to find their path through what may be a sort of maze. I cannot help it. I have stuck to my idea of being in a country cottage with a silent listener, hearing between the gusts of the wind and amidst the noises of the distant sea, the story as it comes. And when one discusses an affair—a long, sad affair—one goes back, one goes forward. One remembers points that one has forgotten and one explains them all the more minutely since one recognizes that one has forgotten to mention them in their proper places and that one may have given, by omitting them, a false impression. I console myself with thinking that this is a real story and that, after all, real stories are probably told best in the way a person telling a story would tell them. They will then seem most real.

A short enough book it is to contain two suicides, two ruined lives, a death, and a girl driven insane: it may seem odd to find the keynote of the book is restraint, a restraint which is given it by the gentle character of the narrator ('I am only an ageing American with very little knowledge of life') who never loses his love and compassion for the characters concerned. 'Here were two noble people—for I am convinced that both Edward and Leonora had noble natures—here, then, were two noble natures, drifting down life, like fireships afloat on a lagoon and causing miseries, heartaches, agony of the mind and death. And they themselves steadily deteriorated. And why? For what purpose? To point what lesson? It is all a darkness.' He condemns no one; in extremity he doesn't even condemn human nature, and I find one of the most moving under-statements in literature his summing up of Leonora's attitude to her husband's temporary infatuation for the immature young woman, Maisie Maidan: 'I think she would really have welcomed it if he could have come across the love of his life. It would have given her a rest.'

I don't know how many times in nearly forty years I have come back to this novel of Ford's, every time to discover a new aspect to admire, but I think the impression which will be left most strongly on the reader is the sense of Ford's involvement. A novelist is not a vegetable absorbing nourishment mechanically from soil and air: material is not easily or painlessly gained, and one cannot help wondering what agonies of frustration and error lay behind *The Saddest Story.*

Introduction to Volume III of *The Bodley Head Ford Madox Ford*

It seems likely that, when time has ceased its dreary work of erosion, Ford Madox Ford will be remembered as the author of three great novels, a little scarred, stained here and there and chipped perhaps, but how massive and resistant compared with most of the work of his successors. *The Fifth Queen* trilogy and *The Good Soldier* have already been published in the first volumes of The Bodley Head Ford, and there remains *Parade's End,* the title Ford himself gave to what is often known, after the name of the principal character, as the Tietjens tetralogy—the terrifying story of a good man tortured, pursued, driven into revolt, and ruined as far as the world is concerned by the clever devices of a jealous and lying wife.

Ford always wanted to see his novel printed as one book, but he wanted to see it as a trilogy, consisting only of *Some Do Not . . ., No More Parades* and *A Man Could Stand Up—*the final book, *Last Post,* was an afterthought which he had not intended to write and which later he regretted having written. In a letter dealing with the possibility of an omnibus edition, which is quoted by Mr John A. Meixner in his critical study, *Ford Madox Ford's Novels,* Ford wrote: 'I strongly wish to omit *Last Post* from the edition. I do not like the book and have never liked it and always intended to end up with *A Man Could Stand Up.'* It can be said therefore that in this edition, for the first time, we have Ford's own version of *Parade's End.*

I think it could be argued that *Last Post* was more than a mistake—it was a disaster, a disaster which has delayed a full critical appreciation of *Parade's End.* The sentimentality which sometimes lurks in the shadow of Christopher Tietjens, the last Tory (Ford sometimes seems to be writing about 'the last English gentleman'), emerged there unashamed. Everything was cleared up —all the valuable ambiguities concerning the parenthood of Christopher's son (the suggestion chosen by his wife Sylvia to torture him), his father's possible suicide, his father's possible relationship to Valentine, Christopher's

8

mistress—all, all are brought into the idyllic sunshine of Christopher's successful escape into the life of a Kentish small-holder. Even Sylvia—surely the most possessed evil character in the modern novel—groped in *Last Post* towards goodness, granted Christopher his divorce, took back—however grudgingly—her lies. It is as though Lady Macbeth dropped her dagger beside the sleeping Duncan.

This is a better book, a thousand times, which ends in the confusion of Armistice Night 1918—the two lovers united, it is true, but with no absolute certainties about the past so deformed by Sylvia's lies (if they are lies) or about the future with that witch-wife still awaiting them there. Those of us who, even though we were children, remember Armistice Day (so different from that sober, reflective V.E. day of 1945) remember it as a day out of time —an explosion without a future. It was the Armistice only which counted, it was the Armistice too for the poor tortured lovers: perhaps there would never be a peace. . . .

> They were prancing. The whole world round them was yelling and prancing round. They were the centre of unending roaring circles. The man with the eyeglass had stuck a half-crown in his other eye. He was well-meaning. A brother. She had a brother with the V.C. All in the family.
> Tietjens was stretching out his two hands from the waist. It was incomprehensible. His right hand was behind her back, his left in her right hand. She was frightened. She was amazed. Did you ever! He was swaying slowly. The elephant! They were dancing! Aranjuez was hanging on to the tall woman like a kid on a telegraph pole. The officer who had said he had picked up a little bit of fluff . . . well, he had! He had run out and fetched it. It wore white cotton gloves and a flowered hat. It said: "Ow! Now!" . . . There was a fellow with a most beautiful voice. He led: better than a gramophone. Better . . .
> *Les petites marionettes, font! font! font . . .*
> On an elephant. A dear, meal-sack elephant. She was setting out on
> . . .

This is the end of *A Man Could Stand Up,* and this—not the carefully arranged happy *finale* of *Last Post*—was the true conclusion of a story of unhappy marriage, of Sylvia's tortuous intrigues which had begun, before the so-called Great War had closed in, in a little resort among the pine-woods of Lobscheid. 'They were sitting playing bridge in the large, shadowy dining-hall of the hotel: Mrs Satterthwaite, Father Consett, Mr Bayliss. A young blond sub-lieutenant of great obsequiousness who was there for a last chance for his right lung and his career, and the bearded Kur-doctor cut in.' Sylvia had not yet entered 'like a picture of Our Lady by Fra Angelico,' but I have always been reminded of another wicked setting, in a poem written at much about the same time:

9

In depraved May, dogwood and chestnut,
    flowering judas,
To be eaten, to be divided, to be drunk
Among whispers; by Mr Silvero
With caressing hands, at Limoges
Who walked all night in the next room;

By Hakagawa, bowing among the Titians;
By Madame de Tornquist, in the dark room
Shifting the candles; Fräulein von Kulp
Who turned in the hall, one hand on the door.

This is not a war-book in the ordinary sense of the term; it was produced by the experiences of 1914–18, but while a novel like *All Quiet on the Western Front* confined its horror to the physical, to the terrors of the trenches, so that it is even possible to think of such physical terrors as an escape for some characters from the burden of thought and mental pain, Ford turned the screw. Here there was no escape from the private life. Sylvia pursued her husband even to the headquarters of his regiment. Unlikely? Read in *The Memoirs of Lord Chandos* how, just out of the heavily shelled Ginchy valley, he and his friend were greeted by the disquieting telegrams from home. I remember a week-end reunion in the dug-outs of Dien-Bien-Phu, as the troops waited day by day for the assault. The private life cannot be escaped and death does not come when it is most required.

ALLEN TATE
Ford Madox Ford

I

Ford was one of the great men of the twenties. He had had a great literary career before the twenties but he came into his own at that time. He had been born in London in 1873 with a formidable and rather suffocating background to deal with. He was the son of old Dr. Hueffer, an Alsatian who had come to London as the music critic on the *Times* and had married the daughter of the pre-Raphaelite painter Ford Madox Brown. Algernon Charles Swinburne was Ford's godfather, his uncle was William Michael Rossetti, and a more impossible background a poet-novelist could scarcely have. Ford told me that up until the time he was twelve years old he had to wear one purple stocking to show that he was a pre-Raphaelite. But there were certain advantages in this background, and Ford acquired an immense literary culture—through the pores of his skin, so to speak. When I knew him he was a man in his fifties. He was the last great European man of letters. They don't produce them anymore—anywhere. He knew everything, Latin and Greek literature, French literature, Italian and German. He was tri-lingual—English, German, and French, and read Italian. When his perhaps greatest novel, *The Good Soldier,* was brought up for translation into French in the late 1920s, the publisher asked Ford to suggest a suitable translator. Ford said, yes, I'll find one. Six weeks or two months later, Ford produced the manuscript. He had rewritten the novel in French himself without referring to the English text. If you compare the two versions, the English and the French, they are sentence-by-sentence identical.

Ford was not only a great writer. He was a great teacher. He believed in literature, in its dignity and value to civilization; he spent hours encourag-

Editor's note: The following pages from various scattered published pieces by Allen Tate are brought together here to take the place of the essay he wanted to write for this volume but could not in the months before his death. "I should like very much to write a memorial essay on Ford. . . . Ford is a great writer and I am glad other people besides myself think so" (letter to the editor, 18 July 1978).

The first section is from "Random Thoughts on the 1920's," *Minnesota Review* (Fall 1960): 52–53.

ing young writers and helping them—not merely encouraging them but going over their manuscripts, and getting them published. I could name dozens of writers from Ernest Hemingway to Katherine Anne Porter whom he helped. He helped me a great deal and I'm still grateful to him. He was also, of course, a great editor. In 1908 he founded the *English Review*—he used to say, rather plaintively, to publish a poem of Thomas Hardy's that nobody else would publish. People like Wyndham Lewis and D. H. Lawrence were first brought to the public through Ford, and he was one of the first editors of Ezra Pound. He was at the center of international literary life for some thirty years.

II

From 1927 to the year before his death in 1939 I knew Ford very well, as well as a man so much younger could have known him. I knew him first in New York, where he had for a few months rooms in a brownstone house in Perry Street in which I had a free apartment in exchange for being the janitor. In the winter of 1929, while he was in the United States again, he lent us his flat in Paris at 32 rue de Vaugirard. In the thirties he visited me several times in Tennessee, first at Memphis, and then at my farm near Clarksville where in the summer of 1937 he wrote much of *The March of Literature.* In that summer he brought with him his wife Janice Biala, the painter, and her sister-in-law, Mrs. Jack Tworkov, his secretary; Robert Lowell lived in a tent on the lawn, where he intoned the Miltonic blank verse that he wrote every morning. My wife Caroline Gordon, with one idiotic servant, ran the precariously balanced *ménage.* Ford could eat French food only, but Ida, with the occasional assistance of her mother Electra, the washerwoman, could not even cook Tennessee, much less French. Ford was unhappy in the 95° F. but every morning he paced the columned gallery—which had nothing but the earth to support it—and dictated to Mrs. Tworkov several pages of *The March of Literature.* There was a persistent tide that seldom ebbed of visitors from Nashville, from Louisville, from New York, from Europe. It was a situation perversely planned by fate to expose human weakness. There were no scenes. Were we not, like the Ashburnhams and the Dowells, "quite good people"? Yet much became known to us about one another that we could have written, as "trapped spectators," of what might have happened but didn't.

After Ford's death I began to feel that I had perhaps written a novel that I had put away and all but forgotten: had written it as the trapped spectator John Dowell in *The Good Soldier,* who "knew Edward very well" but then at last knew nothing at all about him. To this day I know nothing of Ford, except

From "FMF," *New York Review of Books* 1, no. 2, special issue (Spring/Summer 1963). Reprinted with permission from the *New York Review of Books.* Copyright © 1963 NYrev, Inc.

his great kindness to me as a young man. Ford's biographers at their peril will set up as omniscient narrators: they will have to assume the role of Dowell, the hesitant prober of motive with the intimate but obfuscated view, and through *progressions d'effet* come out in the end with the image but not the essence of the man. For he was a character in one of his own later novels. Will not his "method" be the best one possible for his biographers? His conversation either illustrated or was the source of his theory of fictional dialogue. Dialogue must never convey information; it may be about nothing at all so long as it is in character. ("Just might do it," says Ashburnham on a polo field. "Shuttlecocks!" says Nancy Rufford repeatedly.) Ford's casual observations could be detached from their occasions without loss of meaning, for he always spoke in character.

I remember a fine evening in Paris in the autumn of 1928 when I was walking with him by the Petit Luxembourg, and he suddenly spoke, as if to himself (as Ashburnham seems always to speak): "One might be a peer of the realm or a member of the Académie Française. There is nothing else." It had no "context." Was it really as fatuous as it sounded? I think not. John Dowell would have let the remark drop casually, but with shocking force, and then through some thirty pages of "time-shifts" show how it came out of the total "affair" which was Ford's life. We shall never know much more *of* Ford—however much his biographers may find out *about* him—than the brief self-revelation which reveals little. Ford, like Ashburnham and Tietjens, will be made "known" to us through the Jamesian-Fordian technique of "gradual revelation" and *progression d'effet,* by which we will witness the "affair," the significant action of a given moment of history, and then the pathos which will fall just a little short of tragedy, as *The Good Soldier* falls short of tragic action. And why should this be so? It is Ford's great theme that tragic action must be incomplete in a world that does not allow the hero to take the full Oedipean responsibility for the evil that he did not intend but that he has nevertheless done.

What I am trying to say is that Ford's best biographer will understand at the outset that Ford himself must be approached as a character in a novel, and that novel a novel by Ford. The complaint, often heard today, that James, Conrad, and Ford were each in his own degree obsessed by "form" or "method" is of course nonsense; but if it were true, would it be less damaging to the vitality of the novel in our day than the obsession with the expressionistic egotism and disorder of American novelists since the war? Ford was not, in the pejorative sense, a formalist. Ford's technique *is* Ford, and he could have had no other. So the biographer must collect and compare the views —as Dowell collects and compares—of Jessie Conrad and Violet Hunt, and attend closely to the correction of these views by Mr. Douglas Goldring, whose two books, *South Lodge* and *Trained for Genius,* though necessarily incomplete in documentation, will have to be accepted as the Ford primers by their more scholarly successors. Mr. Goldring knew Ford "well," but being the younger man could not have been in the action of the novel which was Ford's life. He will probably remain the best contemporaneous witness.

There are now in print three large critical studies of Ford which are the ostensible subject of this article. Mr. Cassell, Mr. Meixner, and Mr. Wiley —each has his particular insight; we shall remain permanently in their debt. I must have read *The Good Soldier* some thirty-five times; I imitated it, in the way Johnson imitated Juvenal in *London,* in a novel I wrote about twenty-five years ago. My novel might have been better had I understood the construction of *The Good Soldier* as shrewdly as Mr. Cassell does: that, I think, is Mr. Cassell's virtue—his grasp of the symmetries and correspondences of form. Mr. Meixner is, I believe, more than his rival colleagues, sensitive to the nuances of Ford's style: its great flexibility, its tightrope virtuosity which combines colloquial rhythms and idioms with high eloquence. For this reason he understands better than anybody I have read the role of Dowell in *The Good Soldier;* it is his awareness of what style does in this great novel that enables him to put Mr. Mark Schorer's Introduction to the Vintage edition out of court. Mr. Schorer suggests that the novel is a comedy of humor, the humor being phlegm, because Dowell is passive and obtuse. I am surprised that a critic of Mr. Schorer's experience could take a personal narrator at his word; I surmise that he would believe everything that the governess says about what she thinks is happening in *The Turn of the Screw.* Through subtle shifts of tone Dowell brings to bear upon the "affair" two points of view, his own and that of Ford, who is standing over his shoulder: the tragic action is delineated by Ford (through Dowell's eyes); the irony of this action is established by Dowell's faltering perception of it; and Dowell is the world. It is as if *Oedipus Rex* were a novel told in the first person by Creon. The action would be the same, but our access to the action would be delayed by Creon's limited perception. Mr. Wiley's book is less concerned than the two others with style and form, but his book is nevertheless a valuable addition to our understanding of Ford. His object is to show Ford's development from the early novels, up to *The Good Soldier* and through *Parade's End* to the decline in a late work like *When the Wicked Man:* this development is simply an increasing sense of the "affair" most deeply significant of the shift from decadent aristocracy to middle-class liberalism, along with a sharper sense of the fictional techniques best adapted to render the affair in its complete objectivity. All three of our critics agree that *The Good Soldier* offers us the most nearly perfect fusion of subject and method.

Besides these three books, there is also the formidable bibliography of Ford's writings and of writings about Ford, by Mr. David Dow Harvey. Mr. Harvey lists 1,053 titles beginning with a review of *The Brown Owl* in the London *Times* in 1891 and ending with Richard Foster's essay on *Zeppelin Nights* in the *Minnesota Review* of Summer 1962. Since the Second World War the number of articles about Ford has increased yearly at a rate that suggests geometrical progression; and it must also be said that there has been an increase not only in quantity but in the informed intelligence paid him. Recent studies and reviews of Ford, with the exception of the prefaces and articles by Graham Greene and Caroline Gordon, are by younger writers who could not have known Ford *en pantoufles* and who are not blinded by the fog or war that settled upon his reputation after the affair with Violet Hunt and the attacks upon him for his version of the collaboration with Conrad. If the essays published so far by Richard W. Lid and Richard M. Ludwig are parts of books yet to appear, as I hear they are, there will shortly be five books about Ford since 1961. There is still in manuscript a biography by Frank MacShane; and another biography, which I understand will have the full support of Miss Janice Biala, who owns the letters and other private papers, will appear in the next few years from the hand of Mr. Arthur Mizener. If this book comes out, say, by 1966, and Mr. MacShane's not much later than that, there will have been by 1966 seven full-length biographies and critical studies of Ford within five years. The staggering disproportion between the number of books about Ford and the number of his own books that may then be in print will be an anomaly of Anglo-American literary history. It will be easier to read about Ford than to read him.

Is it possible that all these studies will inspire publishers to lose money by getting back into print the minor works, and to sacrifice themselves in an heroic effort to hush up the scandal of this anomaly? Ford knew a great deal about scandal, but this sort never came within his purview. I think that the irony might have pleased him, but he would say, were he alive, as he often said about matters that he didn't want to discuss, "I am too old and too distinguished to think about it."

The future of his reputation is further complicated by the critical distinction of the three books so far published. This may trap us in the illusion that there is a Ford revival. There may be one soon, if Mr. Greene's plan to republish Ford, a few books a year, meets with any success at all. But for the moment only a few scholars and critics will be introduced to Ford, and his old admirers edified, by the three books here under review. It is not likely that the general reader (if he exists) will get further than hearing about them.

III

How shall we learn what to say about particular effects of the story, without which the great overall structure and movement of the human experience which is the entire novel cannot be made credible to us? The professional critics pause only at intervals to descend to these minor effects which

From "Techniques of Fiction," *Sewanee Review* 52 (Spring 1944): 214-15.

are of course the problems without which the other, more portentous problems which engage criticism could not exist. The fine artists of fiction, I repeat, because they produce these effects must understand them. And having produced them, they are silent about the ways they took to produce them, or paradoxical and mysterious like Flaubert, who told Maupassant to go to the station and look at the cab-drivers until he understood the typical cab-driver, and then to find the language to distinguish one cab-driver from all others in the world. It is the sort of *obiter dicta* which can found schools and movements, and the schools and movements often come to some good, even though the slogan, like this one, means little.

I suppose only the better novelists, like Defoe, Madame de La Fayette, Turgenev, Dickens, Flaubert, many others as great as these, some greater, like Tolstoy and Dostoevsky, knew the special secrets which I am trying, outside criticism, so to speak, to bring before you. There is almost a masonic tradition in the rise of any major art, from its undifferentiated social beginnings to the conscious aptitude which is the sign of a developed art form. Doubtless I ought to repeat once more that for some reason the moment the secrets of this aptitude come within the provenance of formal criticism, they vanish. They survive in the works themselves, and in the living confraternity of men of letters, who pass on by personal instruction to their successors the "tricks of the trade." The only man I have known in some twenty years of literary experience who was at once a great novelist and a great teacher, in this special sense, was the late Ford Madox Ford. His influence was immense, even upon writers who did not know him, even upon other writers, today, who have not read him. For it was through him more than any other man writing in English in our time that the great traditions of the novel came down to us. Joyce, a greater writer than Ford, represents by comparison a more restricted practice of the same literary tradition, a tradition that goes back to Stendhal in France, and to Jane Austen in England, coming down to us through Flaubert, James, Conrad, Joyce, Virginia Woolf, and Ernest Hemingway.

IV

Perhaps Ford knew in the winter of 1939 that he was going to die soon, for he went to France in the spring to spend the summer, as he had not done for several years; he had been going over in the autumn and coming back to America in the spring. It was well that he died in France, a country that he not only loved but that he represented far more than he ever did England, his native country. It is not too much to say that he was a French man of letters who wrote his principal works first in English, then rewrote them in French.

From "To Ford Madox Ford," *Chimera* (Spring 1942); also published as "Homage to Ford Madox Ford: A Symposium," *New Directions*, no. 7 (1942).

He was a man of letters too on the French model of the mid-nineteenth century: a man of "culture" who had survived into an age that no longer assumed the autonomy of the arts but had gone off into varieties of neo-primitivism or into "politics." As the heir of Flaubert and the avowed disciple of Henry James, Ford believed passionately in the novel as a form of art, a distinct genre to be explored and developed in terms of form, not of social ideas or of mere subject matter.

This point of view went into an eclipse at the end of the last decade, giving way to the cruder social-political novel, or even cruder than that, to the personal or expressionist novel of the sort written by the late Thomas Wolfe. And Ford's reputation, after a brief rise in the middle twenties, declined.

But it seems to me that if the novel is to survive the heresies of mere ideology and reporting, it will have to return to the great tradition of Flaubert and James—and of Ford Madox Ford, in whose three or four great books that tradition is most immediately available to us. If the future does not go back to this masterful tradition, it will have to learn its lesson all over again at great cost of energy and of time. The other, temporarily dominant school purports to teach us about life, and that is perhaps what the public reads for. But it is fatal for a literary artist to get life out of novels; what he must look for is the lesson of form.

Ford touched more phases of contemporary literature than any other man of our time in the Anglo-American world. It was inevitable that he should make innumerable enemies. He will make no more enemies, and the great distinction of his service to literature can now be assessed.

I cannot end this tribute to Ford without some comment upon his qualities as man and friend. In the fifteen years of our friendship I saw in him —as he doubtless saw in me—great faults of character, which seemed to me to proceed from a special romantic sensibility. One fault he did not have: I shall call it the artist's cowardice. He had, as a man of letters, an immense courage; through poverty, through prosperity, through the complications of his personal life, he *wrote;* and in writing he never ceased to explore his medium for new effects or to learn wherever he could. One day he brought me a sentence, and like a young beginner he asked me, a beginner: "Do you think it will do?" He could ask this because the dignity and the unremitting demands of his art came first.

DAVID DOW HARVEY
Ford and the Critics

In 1930 when Granville Hicks devoted an essay to Ford, "Ford Madox Ford: a Neglected Contemporary," he found it necessary to explain in what sense Ford had been "neglected": this was not another case of a forlorn and undiscovered "genius starving in a garret" but the "story of a man who has been in the thick of every literary fray and yet is ignored by the literary historians, a man whose individual books have, as they appeared, been greeted as unusual achievements but whose work as a whole has made little impression on the contemporary mind."[1] That Ford should be "ignored by the literary historians" is not to be greatly regretted when one thinks of the sketchy inadequacy and conventionality of most literary histories. This oversight in the survey books is only an outward indication of a neglect that should be the real cause for regret: the general ignorance, in academic circles and among intelligent lay and literary people, of Ford's achievement. Ford's varied labors should come automatically under study by anyone seriously interested in the development of modern English literature. Although *The Good Soldier* is often used now to introduce students to the formal complexities of the modern novel, the danger is that Ford will continue to be dismissed as a literary "sport" who told some wonderful lies, who was the subject of some juicy literary and domestic scandals, and who accidentally threw off a small masterpiece in something called *The Good Soldier.*

Ford's alliance with Ezra Pound also deserves second thoughts. Pound's 1914 essay, "Mr. Hueffer and the Prose Tradition in Verse," was not only the first magnanimous tribute to Ford but also the first piece of serious criticism to be devoted to Ford.

In a country in love with amateurs . . . it is well that one man should have a vision of perfection and that he should be sick to the

From the unpublished introduction (1961) to *Ford Madox Ford: A Bibliography of Works and Criticism* (Princeton: Princeton University Press, 1962).
[1]*Bookman* 72 (1930): 364–70.

death and disconsolate because he can not attain it. . . . It is he who has insisted, in the face of a still-Victorian press, upon the importance of good writing as opposed to the opalescent word, the rhetorical tradition.[2]

In Ford he thought he found an ally against "the old crusted lice and advocates of corpse language," and he could write of Ford's literary significance, as in his obituary essay, in words that chisel truth in stone. His writings on Ford show both the intense perception and the distortion one may expect from a great poet who is also a critic. Pound paid tribute to Ford's "humanitas" in his eighty-second Canto, but it is this quality one misses in Pound's writings about Ford, an understanding that literature is as much a business of "human vicissitudes" as revolutions of the word.

> Madox Ford's aim toward the just word was right in his personal circle of reference. He was dealing mainly with visual and oral perceptions, whereinto come only colours, concrete forms, tones of voice, modes of gesture.
> OUT of these you build sane ideogram.[3]

Pound seems to neglect here and elsewhere the fact that Ford also was "dealing mainly" with transforming words into human flesh. Ford's admiration for Flaubert's *mots justes* was interwoven with his appreciation for Flaubert's morality. Again and again Ford argued that if France had read and fully understood *Education sentimentale,* future wars would have been avoidable; more than once Ford used Flaubert's Emma to exemplify a successful heroine, fully created because she was deeply loved by her creator, not in spite of that fact.

It may seem strange to an age whose interest in Ford, such as it is, is centered upon his novels to discover that only his poetry was for many years deemed worthy of serious critical assessment. Pound's 1914 essay and his reviews of *High Germany* and *Collected Poems* may have encouraged this emphasis. Another early American essay of distinction reflects some of Pound's enthusiasm: "In *High Germany* . . . we get the real Hueffer, the innovator."[4] Harold Monro's evaluation of Ford's poetry in *Some Contemporary Poets* is not extensive but contains some cogent remarks. "He hates Victorianism as a reformed drunkard may hate whiskey. He has brain, style and vision. . . . He is too serious to take himself seriously."[5]Both Bronner and Monro show

[2]*Poetry,* 4 (1914): 111–20.
[3]*Polite Essays* (1914; Norfolk, Conn., New Directions, 1937), p. 53.
[4]Milton Bronner, "Ford Madox Hueffer: Impressionist," *Bookman* 44 (1916): 170–75.
[5](London: Leonard Parsons, 1920), pp. 82–87. See Monro's magazine, *Chapbook;* in the June 1920 issue appeared a checklist of Ford's books of poetry and a brief commentary ("It is one of the most remarkable features in the annals of modern poetry that Mr. Hueffer is unknown, unread and almost untalked about").

some knowledge of Ford's poetry in all its stages and are able to comment appropriately on his development from *The Questions at the Well* to *Collected Poems.* (No such enthusiasm for or knowledge of Ford's career as a novelist appears in criticism before the 1930s, and then hardly conspicuously. Ford had to die before his novels received the serious critical attention due them.) This critical neglect of his poetry today is not simply the result of changing tastes but owes something to limited distribution. His *New Poems* and 1936 *Collected Poems* were published in America, and even the British Museum lacks copies of these books; few American libraries have copies of the 1913 English printing of the *Collected Poems.*

Douglas Goldring, in *Trained for Genius,* bewailed the inadequacy of Ford's obituary notices but overlooked the essays of Graham Greene, Ezra Pound, and Joseph Brewer, which could scarcely have been improved upon. Perhaps the best monuments, though, were wrought by the poets, William Carlos Williams, Robert Lowell, and E. E. Cummings. It is perhaps fitting that Ford should be thus memorialized, and by three Americans who knew him personally. All three, oddly enough, echo in their tone Harold Monro's opinion that Ford was "too serious to take himself seriously." All three record "the pleasure of his company" in much the same spirit as had that other poet, Richard Aldington, with a bit of the same tincture of patronage:

> a human, lovable, absurd, vain, mendacious, gifted creature well worth the attention of the world. Though I steered clear of him after I got my second wind as an adult, I wouldn't have missed him for anything. He was more like the great Sir John Falstaff than any human being I have ever known, with touches of that kindred spirit, the legendary Marius of Marseilles.[6]

The Williams poem, "To Ford Madox Ford in Heaven," was written with both Ford's "On Heaven" and his last years in Provence in mind. Williams foists upon Ford too much of the Williams–Henry Miller brand of puritanism, one feels, for Ford's comfort.

> Is it any better in Heaven, my friend Ford,
> than you found it in Provence?
>
> A heavenly man you seem to me now, never
> having been for me a saintly one.
> It lived about you, a certain grossness that
> was not like the world.
> The world is cleanly, polished and well
> made but heavenly man

---

[6]*Life for Life's Sake* (New York: Viking, 1941), p. 150.

is filthy with his flesh and corrupt that
loves to eat and drink and whore—[7]

E. E. Cummings's tribute is more occasional and leads into an exploration of Ford's humanity, particularly of the paradoxes inherent in his nature.

a (vastly and particularly) live
that undeluded notselfpitying

lover of all things excellently rare;
obsolete almost that phenomenon
(too gay for malice and too wise for fear)
of shadowy virtue and of sunful sin

namely (ford madox ford) and eke to wit
a human being
—let's remember that[8]

None of these poets was able to forget Ford's humanity, but Robert Lowell's poem is the most conspicuously intellectual and shows the most detailed and intimate acquaintance with Ford's writings. Part of his "material" appears to be drawn from Ford's books of reminiscence: the poem opens with an interpretation of an anecdote Ford told in *Return to Yesterday.*[9] Part could easily be drawn from his own memories of Ford—Ford giving one of his stupendously unsuccessful lectures in Colorado and gasping for breath in the high altitudes, Ford in New York "heaping the board for publishers." The muscular *vers libre* bristles with wit, with explosively insulting friendliness, though a friendliness further beneath the surface than in the Williams and Cummings poems. Lowell asks the question that has plagued every Ford enthusiast:

But master, mammoth mumbler, tell me why
the bales of your left-over novels buy
less than a bandage for your gouty foot.[10]

The first concerted action of the Ford "revival" was the Ford symposium in *New Directions: Number Seven,* published in 1942 as a book. This was a very impressive but very miscellaneous collection of personal and literary tributes

[7]*Furioso* I (1940): 4–5.
[8]*Xaipe: Seventy-One Poems* (New York: Oxford, 1950), p. 9.
[9]New York: Liveright, 1932, p. 246.
[10]"Ford Madox Ford: 1873–1939," *Encounter* 2 (1954): 32 (republished in *Life Studies,* 1959).

in brief comments and considerable essays from friends and acquaintances and from some who knew Ford more in his books than in his person. Among the twenty-four contributions were three important reprintings, the 1930 essay by Granville Hicks, quoted earlier, and the obituary essays of Ezra Pound and Joseph Brewer, who was responsible for organizing the "symposium." The articles of particular interest include a warm personal reminiscence by Richard Aldington, who concludes by calling for "a Collected Edition of all his work, including the best of his literary journalism. This seems to me the best memorial to a writer, the only one he would really care about" (pp. 456–58). A collected edition of Ford's works has yet to appear, but Aldington's words encouraged the reprinting in this bibliography of excerpts of much of Ford's "literary journalism" never republished elsewhere.

Partly through the efforts of Caroline Gordon and those of another novelist-teacher, Mark Schorer, many college teachers have been persuaded to open a course in the modern English novel with study of *The Good Soldier.* Mark Schorer's essay "The Good Novelist in *The Good Soldier*" was the first important essay on that novel, appearing first in another "Ford symposium" and later as the preface to the 1951 American republication of *The Good Soldier.* This influential interpretation concluded with an implied injunction upon teachers of the novel: ". . . if it is a kind of archetype of the processes of fiction, if . . . it can demonstrate his craft to the craftsman, then it can also help all of us to read."[11] Schorer's essay did not pretend to be an "exhaustion of aspects" but an interpretation, and this interpretation has been challenged by later critics. Schorer finds the focal interest of the novel in its narrator, whom he is convinced the author views with disguised contempt—this view leading to an interpretation of the novel as "a comedy of humor, and the humor is phlegm." The tendency of Schorer's interpretation is toward viewing the narrator as bathetic rather than pathetic or tragic, "the major theme of the book being that appearances have their reality." Although Schorer finds that "it is in the comedy that Ford displays his great art,"—and comedy seems to be intended if the main theme is the reality of appearances—he concludes with the judgment that *"The Good Soldier* describes a world that is without moral point, a narrator who suffers from the madness of moral inertia." A similar judgment on Ford's moral intention was pronounced by another novelist-critic, Walter Allen, who also greatly admired Ford's technical achievements: "Human life, as Ford reveals it in his novels, is meaningless, and his values are purely stoic."[12]

One defense may be offered in Ford's own terms, for he believed that ideally every word should "count" in a novel, every word should contribute

---

[11]*Princeton University Library Chronicle,* April 1948, pp. 128–33.
[12]*The English Novel* (New York: Dutton, 1955), pp. 394–95.

to the progression of effects. "Of course you must appear to digress. That is the art which conceals your Art. . . . not one single thread must ever escape your purpose."[13] One of the strengths of modern criticism of Ford's writing is its growing realization of how far Ford put that principle into practice. The troublesome point is in determining to what extent Ford's words carry moral as well as artistic meaning. He was certainly capable of thinking in terms of allegory. One of the most interesting and most forceful of his periodical contributions was an essay on Conrad's *The Nigger of the "Narcissus,"* printed just five months after *The Good Soldier.* Ford treats the book as "a great allegory," a lesson for England in time of war could the English but read that lesson there. The embattled English are also "a ship's crew" whose solidarity is menaced less by the storm than by the Donkins in their midst: "In the height of the gale, in the softest of soft winds, Donkin, the eternal Cockney agitator, the eternal Yellow Press journalist, with his hideous accents, his hideous voice, and his mean personality, moves through the book as the writings on the wall."[14] The allegorical intention and impact of *Parade's End,* as interpreted in Robie Macauley's 1950 preface, would likewise seem justified. Yet those acquainted with the protean personality of Ford in his great body of work will be hesitant to fix definite and absolute meanings upon his words, or even upon whole novels. An impressionist, according to Ford's critical dogma, it must also be remembered, does not use words as counters for abstract conceptions. H. G. Wells once epitomized the difference between the impressionistic method and that of the writer of the "thesis novel" or allegorist. Although his representative of impressionism in this anecdote is Conrad, it might have just as well been Ford.

> I remember a dispute we had one day as we lay on the Sandgate beach and looked out to sea. How, he demanded, would I describe how that boat out there, sat or rode or danced or quivered on the water? I said that in nineteen cases out of twenty I would just let the boat be there in the commonest phrases possible. . . . He wanted to see it with a definite vividness of his own. But I wanted to see it and to see it only in relation to something else—a story, a thesis.[15]

The publication of Douglas Goldring's biography of Ford in 1948 almost simultaneously with republication of the Tietjens novels in Penguin paperbacks occasioned provocative speculations by Edward Crankshaw on Ford's literary reputation.

[13]*It Was the Nightingale* (Philadelphia: Lippincott, 1933), p. 212.
[14]*Outlook* 36 (1915): 110–11.
[15]*Experiment in Autobiography* (New York: Macmillan, 1934), p. 528.

Certainly the new generation stumbling across *Some Do Not* . . . will want to know what possessed its parents to leave out of consideration the work of so consummate an artist. The possible justification for Mr. Goldring's book is that it offers part of the answer to that question. . . . His book is offered as an act of piety; but there is only one way to make up for the wrongs done to a dead writer in his lifetime, and that is to clear the ground about his *work*. This Mr. Goldring does not do. . . . It would be truer to call them [Ford's novels] revolutionary prototypes than experiments; all the tears and striving lie behind them. . . . Ford was rejected not, as so many thought, because he had nothing new to say, but because he had too much and with new accents which most readers took for the old.[16]

The critic of Ford criticism may be allowed one final appeal, to point out one continuing deficiency in the writing about Ford: the five novels of Ford's that have most preoccupied critics in the past twenty years should not continue to preoccupy them to the exclusion of Ford's other writings. The attention of critics and laymen might be drawn once again to test the fine emotion of William Carlos Williams's concluding essay in the 1942 *New Directions* Ford symposium.

The arts are the repository . . . where the genius of the races of mankind has deposited its secret—to draw us all together. In the arts, in the great treasure of international letters, man must sooner or later drive himself to discover his redemption. When this shall be begun Ford Madox Ford will be found to have been an old worker there, a persistent refiner of that gist, a sort of radium, which most men never bother their heads to be concerned with though they plainly show its lack. [Pp. 490–91.]

[16]*National Review* 131 (1948): 160–67.

WILLIAM GASS
The Neglect of *The Fifth Queen*

The style is stagy, melodramatic, artificial, even quaint; themes are packed into paragraphs like fish in tins; individuals are addressed as though they were crowds; terms are dragged from their graves and put once more in the line of fire like ghosts given rifles; qualifying phrases are repeated like Homeric epithets; scenes are set the slow deliberate way posts are sunk in concrete; there is such a high tone taken you really might believe you were at court . . . but are these merely history's playing cards—these characters? Do they stand precariously in their designs like figures in *Alice?* History, that great fictitioner, surely did not create the honest, stubborn, beautiful, and saintly Katharine Howard, so richly realized she might have had some other life outside imagination, yet so near perfection we could not wish for her a lesser world to drag a dress in. The pouf of an unbeliever could not make its way against the pure gale of her talk, for indeed she is a soul made out of passionate speech. As for Thomas Cromwell, Lord Privy Seal, a man both duplicitous and dedicated, murderous and admirable, and one who well knows he has outlived three queens and a thousand plots—is he simply another slick and painted surface? does the shaded tablelight slide like frightened water from his smoothly insinuated shape? And Nick Throckmorton, whose golden beard is the devil's mane, or Magister Udal, wrapped in his furs like a ferret—are they only as thin as pasteboard, flat as any knave, although of the suit of diamonds? Then there's Lady Mary, as cold to the King as ice is to itself—is she of no account, to be sloughed off in a losing trick? Perhaps Thomas Culpepper, the Hotspur of this piece, has taken too much of his nature from his name; but consider, instead, his royal grace, the fat, beleaguered King, who, because he is the King, must use everyone in the service of the crown, and whom everyone, because he is the King, would use in the smaller service of themselves—does he not weigh upon his horse as heavily as his armor, and heavier on history? is he not even wider than his portraits? does he not clot every entrance like a wound?

Will the value of these characters simply vary with the course of play, though their stiffly posed and tinted images remain vividly the same? There

25

will be a critical fuss about this. Why, in a world of change, don't these people alter something other than their loyalties? And we might answer by asking how the stream of time might run but between unyielding banks, or how we might measure its motion except in the eddies it makes about rocks. Or do we prefer illusions, and like to fancy people grow new characters like their beards and bellies, whereas, in fact, by the time the bosom has budded and the first blood run, even the sweetest maid is beyond shaping. Again we might answer by saying that conditions change apace because people won't vary theirs a jot, though Lady Mary grows a little warmer, I remember—later —in a warmer room.

The Fifth Queen resembles the maze at Hampton Court. Meanings multiply among the corridors its sentences suggest. When a torch flares, they return like luminous echoes from concealed corners, cul-de-sacs, and distant doors. In fact, the work is so intensely visual, so alternately light and dark, you might think the words were being laid on the page like Holbein's paint.

> Whilst the maids sewed in silence the Queen sat still upon a stool. Light-skinned, not very stout, with a smooth oval face, she had laid her folded hands on the gold and pearl embroidery of her lap and gazed away into the distance, thinking. She sat so still that not even the lawn tips of her wide hood with its invisible, minute sewings of white, quivered. Her gown was of cloth of gold, but since her being in England she had learned to wear a train, and in its folds on the ground slept a small Italian greyhound. About her neck she had a partlet set with green jewels and with pearls. Her maids sewed; the spinning wheels ate away the braided flax from the spindles, and the sunlight poured down through the high windows. She was a very fair woman then, and many that had seen her there sit had marvelled of the King's disfavour for her; but she was accounted wondrous still, sitting thus by the hour with the little hounds in the folds of her dress. Only her eyes with their half-closed lids gave to her lost gaze the appearance of a humour and irony that she never was heard to voice.[1]

The style of this novel cannot be escaped, and readers who prefer their literature to be invisibly literary should shun it.[2] There are no merely workmanlike words here, anxious to get the job done so they can suds themselves up at some pub on the way back to the dictionary. Even the common people —Badge, the printer, or Margot Poins—aren't ordinary, nor is their lan-

[1]Page 365. The pagination of The Bodley Head edition, London, 1962, and the Vanguard edition, New York, 1963, is the same. This description is clearly inspired by Holbein's portrait of Anne of Cleves in the Louvre.

[2]In *The March of Literature* (New York: Dial Press, 1938), Ford says of Scott, a competitor, "His literary merits are almost undiscoverable" (p. 711) and again, that "perhaps the main characteristic of writers like Jane Austen and Trollope is their complete non-literariness" (p. 789).

guage, nor any of the spaces they inhabit: cottages, inns, attics, ingles.

The Fifth Queen constructs the secret theater of history. There are laby-rinthine hallways here, bewildering forests of passages and pillars through which the darkness whispers as though through parted teeth. There are secret and spiral stairs, low dupes, cats' paws, double agents, devious aims, false alarms, unreported catastrophes. Characters are caught in their own schemes like ants in honey. They move no more, then, than the patient queen. Wide Venetian velvet surcoats, ceremonially embroidered, jeweled, furred, do more than hide a corpulence like Henry's. There are cold wet walls, weeds pushing up through pavements like unmentionable desires, chills which can't be overcome. Chimneys smoke. Innuendoes slip past like drafts impossible to trace. Yet there is much lip service, courtly talk, and rumors as impossible to slap as gnats. A barge carries Cromwell quietly down the Thames, but there is noise and turmoil in the street. And lies . . . lies both petty and prodigious: those which are bald-faced, arrogant, and inept, and those subtle, careful, clever lies which lie so near the truth they might be lovers taking warmth from one another's intermingling limbs. In a world where trust is as provisional as loyalty, and loyalty as provisional as its profit, there are more than many spies. Faith stiffens character while it warps the mind, and treason (justified by citations from the Good Book, and by arguments pilfered from the philosophers, and by examples extracted from divines) enters and exits in every contentious breath. Speech is dangerous—speech of any kind. Your most innocuous opinions may be used to indict you, and the written word is like an incriminating print. There are purloined letters, falsified docu-ments, peep holes, sleeping potions, bribes. There is blackmail, whoring, theft, torture, threats, and countless other machinations. And there are also bearded, moist-mouthed villains straight from the great age of Webster, Tourneur, John Ford, and Machiavelli.

The Fifth Queen, then, is like Eisenstein's *Ivan:* slow, intense, pictorial, and operatic. Plot is both its subject and its method. Execution is its upshot and its art. *The Fifth Queen* is like Verdi's *Otello:* made of miscalculation, mismaneuver, and mistake. Motive is a metaphor with its meaning sheathed like a dagger. It is one of Shakespeare's doubtful mystery plays. Even though it includes clowns who berate one another, they make no successful jokes, and *The Fifth Queen* remains relentlessly tragic. It must be read with the whole mouth—lips, tongue, teeth—like a long slow bite of wine. For prose, it is the recovery of poetry itself.

This last effect is clearly Ford's intent. He has not been brought up in a gray thread, black bread, Protestant world. The studied emblems, the romantic longings, the medievalisms of the Rossettis, Hunts, and Ford Madox Browns—their sentimentalisms, their garish overcoloring, too—were part of his inheritance. He had no desire to write like Defoe just because he was writing prose. The novelist did not have to assume a severe, undecorated, screwed-down style, as if weakness were a show of strength, as if only the simple were sincere, or the plain ennobling; it was not necessary to adopt a false modesty for your talent as if it were a mark of virtue to write as though you hadn't any. Besides, he fancied himself an English gent.

> To put it roughly, we might say that the great periods and cadences of the seventeenth century had, by the eighteenth, deteriorated into a sort of mechanical rhythm and that by the nineteenth century, in the avoidance of the sort of pomposity and the dry rhythm of the eighteenth century, the language became so timid and indefinite that it was impossible to use it for making any definite statement.[3]

The struggle which *The Fifth Queen* represents—between the Old Faith and the New Learning—occurs at the stage of style and literary theory, as well as within the local practice of the genre, and not merely at the level of political, religious ideology or historical event. And the loss to later English life which Katharine Howard's fall signifies to Ford is regained by the writing itself. Rather than butt helplessly against the conventions of that coal-stove Realism which stands for the triumph of the Puritan business spirit,[4] *The Fifth Queen* seeks a language which springs from the traditions of the land and can be cultivated like another crop; so that Ford's return to the historical romance, despite its dubious popularity and retinue of pleasing scribblers, is intended to recover and release the word.[5]

To call a novel historical is nearly always to accuse it of something. Even among unreal objects, where fictions are said to belong, the "historical" has a special place; for if any history, by the necessity of its nature, is already full of unreliable representations, then its further reflection in fiction has to be wavering and dim indeed. The curious conjunction which makes up the name (historical facts in their causal connections as against the manifold misdirections of invention and dream) indicates that its very creation is suspect, as if a shadow were to be wrapped in further shadows until the smoking semblance of some enemy's cigar were ominously shaped, or a daggered figure in a cloak suggested . . . the looming bulk of a battlement, perhaps . . . a fluttering drape.

In historical fiction a superficial sense of antique reality can be easily

---

[3]*March of Literature*, p. 512. Unfortunately this charge, itself, is very poorly put. The cadence of *The March of Literature* is frequently slack and uneven, as are the qualities of its judgments.

[4]At least in Ford's mind, it does.

[5]Not all were scribblers quite, and not quite all were pleasing, but there was Scott, Hugo, Dumas *fils* and *père*, Stevenson, Bulwer-Lytton, Cooper, Hewlett, Haggard, Verne, Doyle, Quiller-Couch, Ainsworth, and Monro, among others. There is a good account of Ford's relation to his forerunners in H. Robert Huntley, *The Alien Protagonist of Ford Madox Ford* (Chapel Hill: University of North Carolina Press, 1970). Huntley calls appropriate attention to the historians who influenced Ford, although he misses Clarendon for some reason, and also discusses, usefully, Ford's physiognomic types.

achieved, but what is obtained is frequently felt to be facile and cheap, like the glib alterations—the blatant vulgarity—of masquerades. It is an amusement—an escape—and melodrama is its mainspring. Thus its tick is loud just because the time it pretends to tock for is far away. Unlike history, what the fiction recounts is rarely sordid or simply stupid, nor is it often tragic, because its heroes and heroines pass through the most terrible events unscathed, like driftwood down a rapids.

Where the historian looks for laws and regularities, patterns and steps, the novelist admires what merely decorates the dance. He prefers the exotic, colorful, and unique. He measures quirks and curiosities like a tailor, but cuts no cloth to the true weight and temporal figure of things. He shuns the normal, the plain. It has no zap. He dotes on gossip, slander, hearsay, anecdote, lies. He wants to recreate the past, not understand it as a historian should. The contents of constitutions and the import of decrees are tedious to get through; congresses are too boring to attend; committee reports too dry to report upon. Figures fill his heart with horror. He turns his back on bills of lading, tables of organization, and balances of trade. He wants amusing conversation—clever, witty, perceptive—and conversation is as out of place in history as a count of our morning cups of coffee.

So the novelist floats happily about on the edges and in the eddies of events and rarely moves in the mainstream. He habitually goes beyond the evidence, oversteps the bounds of probability, and invents occasions, speeches, feelings, thoughts, and scenes, which no doubt never were nor could have been, simply to enliven his narrative and entertain, rather than instruct, his readers. If it would further the drama to have minister and field marshal meet—no matter that their lives at no time touched—he need only scribble a few more paragraphs and the impossible deed is done.

The novelist's point of view tends to become passionate and heedless at the exact point the careful historian should become cold and cautious. Human decisions always seem supreme to him, and he does not suffer his characters to be vast natural forces like climate and disease, or even complex, indifferent social orders, or ponderous and mysteriously moving bureaucracies. He is customarily precise and fussy about trifles, but vague about the central and most effective matters, liking battles basically because there is much movement, excitement, noise, and blood, since it is the courage and fate of the hero that counts, not the cost or consequences of victory.

When Romance mates with History to fertilize fairy tales with the seed of the real world, they beget Myth. We are given young Abe Lincoln on the one hand, reading by log-light, and Robin Hood on the other, splitting infinity with an arrow as neatly as Abe's rails. The form of the swashbuckler, the border tale, the costume romance seems essentially unserious, and in our day it has become just another popular genre, not more significant than the thriller or the sitcom, the western or the soap. Ford Madox Ford contributed to the neglect of his great Tudor trilogy by remarking, in his book on Conrad, that "an historical novel even at best is nothing more than a *tour de force,* a fake more or less genuine in inspiration and workmanship, but none the less a fake."[6] If all of these heavily prejudicial and, indeed, greatly misleading words ("none the less," "even at best," "nothing more," *"tour de force,"* "fake") suit Ford's real feelings, then his ghost cannot complain when even critics rather well disposed to him paste the word "pastiche" across *The Fifth Queen* like a warning.

Ford led an unwise life, as Walter Allen has observed.[7] An unwise life, indeed. For one thing, he wrote simply too much sheer "stuff," and his best books got submerged in the accumulated glib. He badly mismanaged his divorce, and in the incredible confusion forfeited the sympathy of writers like Galsworthy and Wells, whom he should never have allowed to enjoy a moment of superiority at his expense, while also losing the friendship of stiff-necks like Henry James, who recoiled from impropriety as though it were snot on a custard. Ford's "Germanness" had always troubled him (he wanted to be French—what decent writer does not?), but his change of name didn't help him, and later, because he was unfortunately gassed during the war, so that afterward he always heaved and huffed, his original name returned to his lungs to taunt him. His habit of altering the facts to make the truth more truthful than it had been on the "real" rather than the "related" occasion, didn't help either, nor did his tendency, quite kind in itself, to condescend (according to Pound, even to God).

Ford's collaboration with Conrad, of which he was proud, nevertheless hurt his reputation, because Conrad was older, had had the flattering good sense to choose to write in English rather than in Polish or French, and was clearly an exotic genius; consequently Ford's account of their relationship seemed to many just so many self-serving lies, dependent as it was on the assumption that the two writers were equals, and that, when it came to the English language, Ford naturally knew a good deal more.

Ford was a sort of Don Juan with ideas, too, and it was difficult for him to sustain his interest in a project once it was obvious he had conquered it; thus he was inclined to finish up quickly in order to run after another— possibly prettier—notion.[8] He often needed a gimmick to get him going (the train wreck which propels his hero into the fourteenth century, for example, in *Ladies Whose Bright Eyes*),[9] but these mechanicalities invariably

---

[6]In *Joseph Conrad: A Personal Remembrance* (Boston: Little Brown, 1924), p. 186. Ford is saying, rather fatuously, that before forty, he had done little more than exercises.

[7]*The English Novel* (New York: Dutton, 1954), p. 396.

[8]Ford says that Conrad often grew weary, and "would occasionally try to rush a position. . . . That is why the ends of his books have sometimes the air of being rather slight compared with the immense fabrics to which they are the appendages." He, on the other hand, worked more nearly "to contract." *Joseph Conrad,* p. 185. The fact is that Ford's fictional "schemes" were frequently silly.

[9]By now, surely, some critic or reviewer has called it a "Twain wreck."

betrayed him, and their thin elaborations defied even splendid writing.

Ford was a success with women, always a bad sign, since they are certain to see that you fail somewhere else to prove your dedication. It is furthermore unsettling to other men if you look, as Wyndham Lewis wrote, like "a flabby lemon and pink giant who hung his mouth open as though he were an animal at the Zoo inviting buns."[10] Ford was a success as an editor, too, so people knew where his skills really lay, and could put him in his editorial place. There he earned the gratitude of many excellent authors of every school, style, and age, who promptly repaid him with malicious slanders, vulgar innuendo, and other Hemingways. Gradually Ford became known as one of those who circle the great as buzzards do, a loquacious "hang about," padding his reputation by dropping names, telling tales, and remaining bravely aboard foundering magazines until they disappeared beneath their debts. Oh yes. He wrote. Easily. Much. Fairy tales, biographies, travel, commentaries, criticism, memoirs and other states of mind, novels, poems. How could one eye keep such a dizzy flock of authors in view? Well, he had his small popular successes, his critical acclaim, but he was always broke. He retired to the country. He played, for a while, the gentleman farmer, embraced simplicity like another mistress, put on airs. He went on and on about Provence. Some claimed he was a conniver, a bounder. He got by on small change. He bragged by disparaging himself. He hated scenes and then arranged his life like a procession of them. He needed connections, though his family was widely known, and he had been raised to be the genius he was. He had also sat on Turgenev's knee, he said, or was it Tennyson's? Liszt's. Of Swinburne he had once caught a glimpse. He had an early romantic attachment to the Middle Ages. He liked Christina Rossetti. His form grew shapeless, his face puffy; he was always fairer than was a good idea. He had a wheeze. He formed strange ménages. He became minor.

Ford's greatest crime, however, was his migration to America. Not only did he come to the United States, he allowed us to discover him. Malcolm Lowry is another victim of our praise. *The Good Soldier* had to be stuffed down English craws like a pill poked down a cat's throat. Only Graham Greene (a man of amiable perceptions, and a Catholic capable of understanding Ford's obsessions), befriended his work.[11] Certainly the writers whom

---

[10]Quoted by Arthur Mizener in *The Saddest Story: A Biography of Ford Madox Ford* (New York: World Publishing Co., 1971), pp. 239, 240.

[11]This is not entirely true, of course. What was lacking was a *sustained* support. Rebecca West understood the greatness of *The Good Soldier,* yet when she wrote "It is impossible for anyone, with any kind of sense about writing to miss some sort of distant apprehension of the magnificence of his work," she was mistaken, for it was not impossible. When I talked to graduate students at the University of Leeds in 1966, they professed never to have heard of Ford. Perhaps it was because he was not in "The Great Tradition." Auden's defection was not easily forgiven either. From his critics, Ford has suffered more than most. Only a few of them even bother to spell his heroine's name—Katharine—correctly.

Ford so faithfully celebrated did not bang many pans in his behalf.[12]

Still, when Ford said that his historical novels were fakes, or when, in a badly bungled and widely misunderstood dedicatory foreword to *The Good Soldier,* he said that until that book he had not really extended himself and described his previous works as being "in the nature of pastiches, of pieces of rather precious writing, or of *tours de force,"*[13] then the critics believed him as they had never believed him before; believed as war departments believe in their weapons of war; and that word—*pastiche*—was cut on a stamp like EXPEDITE or AIRMAIL, and brought down on Ford again and again with a kind of coward's eagerness, and a now legendary stupidity.

Ford's modernist esthetic is derived from Flaubert, and it is based upon a formalism which is rarely popular with critics, while it fails even to come to the notice of the ordinary reader. It is a position, if taken, which requires some unpleasant reassessments of the Anglo-Irish-American literary tradition, and none of these alterations is likely to be tolerable to a history shaped largely by chauvinism and defended to schoolboys by bachelors and marms.

> It is to be remembered that a passage of good prose is a work of art absolute in itself and with no more dependence on its contents than is a fugue of Bach, a minuet of Mozart, or the writings for the piano of Debussy.[14]

The exceptional range of Ford's own writing allowed him to see the obvious (that fiction is written in prose) with a scarcely commonplace consciousness of the consequences: one being that the novelist must first of all be a master of the medium, and not merely a toothsome doughnut soaked in life.

> English, as we have said, is rather short in the item of great novels. It would, then, be almost a minor literature were it not for the prose writers whom we have been citing.[15] They, it will be observed, are none of them novelists. And, indeed, it was not until comparatively lately that the English novelist paid any attention whatever to his prose.[16]

The failure of the famous ruminative styles of Donne and Milton, Browne and Taylor to set the standard, and the consequent disappearance

---

[12]According to David Harvey "it was the confusing multiplicity of his literary personae coupled with the failure of his friends among the great to speak out in his behalf that most impeded Ford's critical recognition" (*"Pro Patria Mori:* The Neglect of Ford's Novels in England," *Modern Fiction Studies* 9, no. 1 (Spring 1963): 15. I have taken the West quotation from p. 14 of Harvey's article.

[13]It was, after all, a love letter to Stella Bowen, and he wanted to offer her his best.

[14]*March of Literature,* p. 512.

[15]Ford has been writing about Sir Thomas Browne, Clarendon, Pepys, Walton, and White, and will go on to cite Graham, Doughty, Hudson, Borrow, Beckford, and Thoreau.

[16]*March of Literature,* p. 520. He makes an exception of Dickens.

of rhetoric's art and rhythmic richness from English prose, beginning roughly and symbolically with the death of Swift in 1745 (as Ford marks it), is perfectly coincident with the progressive adoption of anti-Ciceronian models on the one hand, and the mounting influence of science, its societies, and its stylistic aims on the other. But the loss of that solemn periodic movement, that gay interior mime, which is the end and final music of the mind, is simultaneous, too, with the vast heady successes of colonialism, the increasingly thick and callused grip of Protestant ideals on the heart like a misplaced cold in the head, and the infectious spread of a crude monetary utilitarianism which would allow Art to flourish only if it were called Moral Education, and education to continue only so long as it could be shown to be suitable to the starchy new rulers of an empire.

Thus the decline of the ornate style commences at the conclusion of the late Renaissance. As the world's geography enlarges and men see strange new lands on which to fatten, its pretensions shrink. The spread of learning overlaps it, and the old grand manner is everywhere beset. Perhaps it is merely a "manner"—of scrapes and cuffs and laces—unmanly and impotent. So the self-assurance of this style weakens at a time when nation states are being set up like megaliths, crowds count, and crude is king. Commerce, manufacture—the sheer multiplicity of *things*—overwhelms its own opposing wealth of *words*. It is sickened slowly, done in by distribution, by vulgar masses and their love of sensation, by mindless duplication. The magazine serial becomes the madame. Lending libraries boss the block, and books are built like row houses, chapter connected to chapter, volume following volume, with a dreary sameness. The paragraph is replaced by the sentence; the sentence is shortened like a dress; the dress is moreover designed to be as plain as a Mennonite's nightgown; and that majestic, endlessly elaborating language, subtle and continuously discriminating, that joyful, private, yet publicly appointed prose, that mouthmade music, headlong, resonant, and roaring once, is reduced to a mousy squeak by the rising noise of the novel. That, at least, is Fordie's myth, and it is a myth he will live to write by.

It is not, of course, merely a myth. Robert Adolph's assessment of these matters is much more careful, scholarly, and discriminating than Ford's, who polemically lumps whole legions of differences together as you might melt old soldiers down to make fresh ones from the same lead. Still, Adolph's ultimate point is precisely the same:

> That we commonly regard Defoe, Richardson, and Fielding as the first important "real" or "modern" novelists is an admission that we, too, have lost the Elizabethan taste for the "qualitatively unique." We prefer to regard all action in fiction as part of a causal series. Like Burnet, we see things as "useful" only if there is an "argument" and a "pattern" both chronological and spatial. Here is another union of Truth and Utility. In the Platonically inclined Renaissance, truth was independent

of time and space, a reflection of some timeless and spaceless Ideal. With the triumph of the new nominalism, there are no more such Ideals.[17]

Ford knew, and knew he knew, and what's more (unfortunately combining the correctness of his conceit with an unmannerly candor), *said* he knew more about the strategies of the traditional novel than anyone writing in English. *The Fifth Queen* is a textbook of technique, a catalogue of resources, an art of the English fugue. The struggle it depicts is both historical and literary. But Ford is not an. innovator in the same sense that Joyce is, or Gertrude Stein, or Faulkner, or even Virginia Woolf. He is essentially a nineteenth-century novelist—the last of his line—with twentieth-century theories and a sixteenth-century taste on his tongue. His themes concern the conflict between periods, the dependence of principles (alas!) on times, our changing attitudes toward vice and virtue. Katharine Howard's sweet waist is grasped by the *Geist.* There is no future forward, yet there is no going back. Where rib confronts rib, Ford has none of the hope the lung has for its next breath. He has Hardy heavy on his one hand, Joyce will soon weigh down the other, Lawrence is standing on his chest. Ford will soon hail with regret that "finely sculptured surface of sheer words," as Wyndham Lewis wrote, which will protect the novel's center from the world, and constitute the main concern of much of the work to come.

So if, as Conrad declared, *The Fifth Queen* is the swan song of the historical romance, then *The Good Soldier* brings the Jamesian tradition to a close, just as *Parade's End* concludes the lifetime of its kind. There are other modes of English fiction for which Ford did not perform the last rites—the picaresque, for instance, the Wodehouse, the Waugh; but what serious artist would want to imitate, now, the beautiful bloat of late James? desire to create that particular world of hesitation and concern again, or become obsessed once more with the unsaid, the distantly implied, the cleverly concealed design, as if the carpet weren't there to receive a tread or please the eye, but to entrap the mind? who would willingly attempt still another time those elegant weekend garden parties which were always so richly walked, sedately tea'd, astir with clever conversation and subtle avowals, so abloom with intricate plans and genteel betrayals, that everyone was soon in vexation, doubt, and moral uncertainty as though lost behind a high meandering hedge? who would wish to impale themselves upon that impossible appointment? especially since Ford Madox Ford inherited the whole wealth of fictional capacities which Henry James spent a career amassing for the once impoverished novel of marriage and manners he had initially taken up and

---

[17] *The Rise of Modern Prose Style* (Cambridge, Mass.: M.I.T. Press, 1968), p. 267. We should not imagine that Ford's enemies had been overthrown by Cardinal Newman's Oxford victories at the time he wrote *The Fifth Queen.* If one thinks only of the enlightened, liberal, no-nonsense obtuseness of Wells, it will not be necessary to go on to Arnold Bennett and Galsworthy.

brilliantly brought out, the way those avuncular European villains of his take up some well-to-do, young, innocent American to sadden her into scintillation; consequently, *The Good Soldier,* with such funds at hand, could realize the genre's accumulated powers beyond any penny of further purchase.

The Tudor trilogy is a muscle show, all right, a strut, a flex of force, but it is not a simple deceptive flourish like General Beauregard's marching the same small squad round and round his camp to simulate the nick-of-time arrival of a rescuing army. Its surface is more accessible than that of *Pale Fire;* it plays no games with its readers and is never facetious like *Lolita.* There is no parody like that which sends the humorless reader away from *At Swim-two-birds.* It is not as exotic and apparently "worked up" out of history as *Salammbô,* nor is it as narrowly focused as *The Awkward Age,* although equally and severely scenic. It is tragic, but not as fanatically gloomy as the writing of Samuel Beckett. Unlike John Barth's *Letters,* it wears its learning lightly, and even lets its Latin sound like Oscar Wilde. The linguistic difficulties are minor, and its length does not exceed that of *Ulysses* or many of Thomas Mann's novels, or George Eliot's *Romola,* for that matter. It is a virtuoso performance—the first of Ford's great shows—and closes out the historical novel like an emptied account. Later he will try for a similar triumph over the realistic novel by inventing Christopher Tietjens, a truly good "good soldier." In an arrogant display of literary genius, Ford Madox Ford brought the nineteenth-century novel, in each of its principal areas of excellence, to its final and most complete expression. For this he has not been forgiven.

The Fifth Queen's ambitions, if we have understood them correctly, require it to be quintessentially historical. Yet there remains a real uneasiness, and Ford feels it. Like dust, there is so much accumulated death in history, whereas the novel has always been dedicated to life—life of every variety—often, indeed, to crowds, to the multiplicity of kinds, to cities, to human vitality itself.

Of course, a novel may be called historical simply because it is set in the past, with real times and places serving as exotic color—props and scenery—for the invented action; or it may be historical because, whatever the story it tells, its language is of another age; or it may be considered so because its characters are actual historical figures, even if they sit on stools in hell and calmly read out conversations, or are otherwise lifted from their period and milieu like dolls from decorated rooms. A novel may be *about* history—have history as its theme—or it may be epical in the old way by purporting to be a true account of times beyond our ordinary knowing and claiming to tell us of the Trojan War or about how Rome was founded, or what happened to certain knights on some crusade. Naturally enough, a fiction could be historical in several of these ways at once, just as a dish may be a disaster because it has been overcooked, as well as badly sauced and seasoned.

Any novel set in the present will shortly become historical. We need only wait. It is not the subject so much that matters as it is the author's attitudes and resources, for the principal difference between the historical novel and any other kind lies in the former's reliance upon texts, rather than upon the author's direct experience of events. Joyce knew the shops that lined the Dublin streets; he had looked in their windows and entered them, chatted, bought; but Ford knows Greenwich or the London of Henry VIII's time only through documents, paintings, and prints. Historical novels are thus almost purely linguistic, because they are derived from the author's knowledge of books, although these books may be understood entirely in terms of contemporary life—whatever that mishmash might be at any particular moment.

The belief that an author ought to write from experience—from experience, indeed, of a deeply personal, challenging, even agonizing kind—rather than contrive its effects at second hand: from books about the bullfight, for instance, whorehouse, Great War, social scene, or local wine, because otherwise the work will smell of the lamp, seem forced, lack life—is a ninny's notion; but it is firmly established, and as hard to discourage as a fungus. Conrad's career is such a distinguished and romantic example of the principle: live, then write, that who could fail to feel the impulse to follow it? and Henry James's desire that the novelist render an impression of life comes from such an august source, such perfect practice, who would want to refuse it? and so it is not surprising that Ford suffered from the itch of the idea, even to the point of denying his first masterpiece, and playing Judas to his muse; although he knew that Flaubert, to invoke another model, very carefully "worked up" his novels from books and papers, drew on his diaries, more than on the days they represented, to put a written Egypt down over a real one. We write about what moves us—that's true—and that is why poems are daily addressed to Dutch interiors and antique statutary as well as handsome men and lovely women, and composed both in rowdy taverns and solitary towers. Anyway, if you want to write about great deeds and grand events, you will have to read or hear about them first, for whom do you know who is great enough? and what have you gone through yourself that has such height? Ford understood perfectly well, too, that among the most important and powerful experiences for all serious authors would have to be figured those intensely significant sentences which pierced them as Saint Sebastian was, as well as those the wretched writer put down in despair (it might have been a day the sun delayed its dawn to warm one page like a winter field), and then was grateful and amazed to read what had been written there: such large and living lines the soul was reshaped by their weight.

Reshaped, rescued, rewarded . . . because, although one's life may be most heavily oppressed, and sorrow, docility, suspicion, hang like diver's weights about it, the spirit is elevated easily even by bibelots of beauty, exquisite ivories and glistening enamels, too, or other pretty *objects d'art—*

presumably emblems of an over-lacquered life. It can be carried off just as readily by a portrait, a paragraph, an image which takes it unaware, as you once might have been beset by a sudden ring of changes on a Sunday walk, so your soul sang the phrase, itself a bell; or remember how, in rivers of red and yellow light, you struggled like a salmon toward Christ's image streaming from the tall cathedral windows, or how you were briefly made brave by brass bands bombulating in a summer park, or how you shrank inside a grave and holy silence when, Othello dead, Emilia down, and Iago struck, the curtain slowly closed on the sight of Desdemona's desecrated bed.

These moments of mild-mannered sublimity have their rights. They are not less than life, but life sharpened sweetly—given purpose, value, substance, point—and so are more than mere experience, as a ballet is more than simple dance.

Nevertheless, if Ford Madox Ford had known Katharine Howard as a schoolgirl, rather than as a set of texts, he would not have referred to her novel as a pastiche.

When Madame Bovary sets forth on her adultery, she is not already dead; however, when Katharine Howard arrives at the King's court; on a mule, as is appropriate to her religious role; in the midst of a riot, which signifies the quarrel in the realm; with the hot-tempered Thomas Culpepper whose love shall be her ruin; and buffeted, injured by the crowd, weary with the journey, says: "I would find my uncle in this palace"; the head that speaks has been buried beside that of Anne Boleyn's for several centuries.

Because Katharine Howard is a character in history, she is never able to move toward her own death in the same free way an invented character does. Katharine, indeed, has her fate, and we know what that fate is, not because we have read reviews, or the book, before; but for reasons which lie outside it, in past space, former time, other works. The notion that the author must revivify history is not an empty or an idle one. Katharine Howard must be brought back from the grave before Henry can cast his eyes upon her, love her, make her queen, and toss his hat down like a soft blow upon her hopes. Ford's account is openly inaccurate in many ways, but the path he has chosen narrows as he strides it, because if he keeps, as a historian should, to the facts, he loses the heroism of his heroine, the villains fail of real villainy and become petty and mean, Henry's majesty is gone, and no clear straight line can be drawn through the story's cloud of lies; whereas, if he departs from the truth, as the novelist must, immediately a more satisfying development or dénouement is seen, then the reader rightly wonders why he chose to write about history anyway.[18]

The important historical novel must remove history from history the

---

[18]Francis Hackett calls Katharine "a juvenile delinquent" in his *Henry the Eighth* (Garden City, N.Y.: Garden City Publishing Co., 1933), p. 352.

way Colette removed her mother from her life to resettle Sido again in *La maison de Claudine.* Ford's success at liberating Katharine Howard from *her* texts, for service in *his,* seems effortless and nearly instantaneous.

> 'Where be we?'
> They had entered a desolate region of clipped yews, frozen fountains, and high, trimmed hedges. He dragged the mule after him. Suddenly there opened up a very broad path, tiled for a width of many feet. On the left it ran to a high tower's gaping arch. On the right it sloped nobly into a grey stretch of water.
> 'The river is even there,' he muttered. 'We shall find the stairs.'
> 'I would find my uncle in this palace,' she said. But he muttered, 'Nay, nay,' and began to beat the mule with his fist. It swerved, and she became sick and dizzy with the sudden jar on her hurt arm. She swayed in her saddle and, in a sudden flaw of wind, her old and torn furs ruffled jaggedly all over her body.[19]

The perception is exact, the final phrasing perfect, and there the real woman is—in the ruffled features of a few words. Her reality will remain relentless; she will not fade.

The history that is taken from history takes on the status of myth. Anyone who wishes may place Katharine Howard in a fiction, and fill her mouth with words, just as Gide may write of Oedipus as rightfully, if not as well, as Sophocles; but no one may reasonably remove Madame Bovary from her book, and only her author might essay another version.[20]

The figures which move so magnificently through *The Fifth Queen* are quite properly more luminous than life, because they are no longer mere men and women in the world. Men intend, and act, but rarely mean, while characters signify, and their vows and desperate ventures are simply little curvatures in the creation of the larger sign.

It is morning when Katharine Howard arrives at Greenwich in her raddled furs and old mule, in the middle of a riot, but Thomas Cromwell, Lord Privy Seal, has slid down the river the night before through pages which are pure evocation. Udal has come too, foolish young Poins, the King preceding. We have seen the spy, Throckmorton, lean near Privy Seal's ear and fear form like frost on the Chancellor's beard. Lies flicker in time to the torchlight on the dark water. Careers bob up and down like boats. Ford is peopling his scene, setting his situation in motion. The rumor is already about that the King has turned sick at his sight of Anne of Cleves, and Cromwell,

---

[19] *The Fifth Queen,* pp. 38–39.
[20] It is likely that Beckett regards many of his novels as a reworking of the "same story." "my life last state last version ill-said ill-heard ill-recaptured/ill-murmured in the mud brief movements of the lower face/losses everywhere" is the fifth verse of *How It Is.*

whose hopes hang about the neck of this Protestant Queen like a locket, is given to us, in a typical passage, arriving at his quarters:

> He entered his door. In the ante-room two men in his livery removed his outer furs deftly so as not to hinder his walk. Before the fire of his large room a fair boy knelt to pull off his jeweled gloves, and Hanson, one of his secretaries, unclasped from his girdle the corded bag that held the Privy Seal. He laid it on a high stand between two tall candles of wax upon the long table.

Cromwell enters, not his room, but his door, which we must presume is held open for him. His entrance is as swift and terse as this simple, yet remarkable, first sentence. Cromwell's position, his power, his tenacious grip on things, is presented through a rapid series of possessives, each the same: it is *his* door; the men are in *his* livery; they remove *his* outer furs, deftly, for they do not wish to hinder *his* walk. The room is *his,* the jeweled gloves, the girdle, and the secretary too.

"In," "out," "before," "off," "between," "upon": spatial prepositions predominate, and the actions are those which specifically rearrange things in space: "enter," "remove," "pull off," "unclasp," "held," "lay between"/ "upon." Many of the adjectives are spatial, too ("ante-," "outer," "large," "high," "tall," "long"), and often held against their nouns by an unstressed syllable: "ánte-róom," "óuter fúrs," "jéweled glóves," "córded bág." We see the action of removing the furs just as we might see it on the stage.

> The boy went with the gloves and Hanson disappeared silently behind the dark tapestry in the further corner. Cromwell was meditating above a fragment of flaming wood that the fire had spat out far into the tiled fore-hearth. He pressed it with his foot gently toward the blaze of wood in the chimney.

Again we begin with an ambiguity. As blouse with skirt, the boy does go well with the gloves. We understand the point of this paragraph when we remember that a beefeater, guarding the ardently Catholic Lady Mary's door, had spat upon the ground as Privy Seal passed. By this time everything has been put in its place: clothes have been removed, the Seal is resting between its two candles, the page and the secretary have retired, and the fragment of wood gently returned to the fire with a foot which knows how easily it may be scorched, even though its gesture is also a sign for the ruthless exercise of power.

Nor do we find any fear in Ford of the letter *f*'s faintly whiscular puff. Then:

> His plump hands were behind his back, his long upper lip ceaselessly caressed its fellow, moving as one line of a snake's coil glides above another. The January wind crept round the shadowy room behind the

tapestry, and as it quivered stags seemed to leap over bushes, hounds to spring in pursuit, and a crowned Diana to move her arms, taking an arrow from a quiver behind her shoulder. The tall candles guarded the bag of the Privy Seal, they fluttered and made the gilded heads on the rafters have sudden grins on their faces that represented kings with flowered crowns, queens with their hair combed back on to pillows, and pages with scolloped hats. Cromwell stepped to an aumbry, where there were a glass of wine, a manchet of bread, and a little salt. He began to eat, dipping pieces of bread into the golden salt-cellar. The face of a queen looked down just above his head with her eyes wide open as if she were amazed, thrusting her head from a cloud.

This passage, because of the way Ford is able to embody in it the many themes and oppositions of the book, is exemplary; but it is not an isolated instance; rather it is a perfectly fair sample of the style and quality of the work as a whole. The *mise en scène* is the Tudor tongue. The language depicts a situation which functions at once as symbol; there are no idle gestures here; arms do not flail, legs kick, to make the puppets look alive. We see in the text what Cromwell sees in the fire, and the world of the work rises up around us from the first page.

As pictorial as *The Fifth Queen* is, and as frequently static, it is not stitched the way Rilke's Cluny unicorn is, or his carefully posed outcasts, walls, his ghosts and nervous dogs, because the mind of Malte brings all things to a standstill, whereas Ford's castle corridors contain thieves, murderers, maidens, metaphors in motion.

Cromwell's snakelike lips are repeatedly invoked, as is the roundness of his face, an un-Homeric use of epithet which Gertrude Stein found effective in writing *Three Lives,* a work, like *The Notebooks of Malte Laurids Brigge,* strictly contemporary with *The Fifth Queen.* Cromwell's lips slide as his mind slides—in coils of continuous cold calculation. We have felt his power, seen his self-control. The wind, like a rumor, lends the illusion of motion to the chaste Diana and her hounds, while fluttering candles do the same for the carvings of kings and queens. Appropriately, Cromwell approaches an aumbry, a cabinet for keeping things. It is a meat safe, sometimes, but alternately, it is a chest, in churches, for sacred utensils. He stands, in short, in a system of relations, the perfect politician, since his meal is spare, yet the flour of his bread is expensively fine; the salt is such a simple substance, yet it lies cupped in gold; facts are in front of him, myths behind, though both waver; above, kings crowned with flowers seem to grin, while around this pious Protestant, Papist trappings suggest the blasphemous character of his frugal snack: a secular ritual carried out with Christian symbols against a background of pagan gods and severed heads.

The writing is as ritualized and formal and rich as the scene. Ford repeats the word "quiver"; he rhymes "round," "hound," and "crowned"; he follows a phrase like "where there were . . ." with "manchet," one of his favorite antiques; he rolls around in his vowels, throws out lines of alliteration, risks outrageous puns (hiding a "hind" in "behind" to go with the stags and hounds); and has, generally, a great good time.

Finally:

> 'Why, I have outlived three queens,' he said to himself, and his round face resignedly despised his world and his times. He had forgotten what anxiety felt like because the world was so peopled with blunderers and timid fools full of hatred.[21]

"His round face resignedly despised his world. . . ." It is roundly said; and one senses that Cromwell possesses the world's roundness as thoroughly as his full face possesses its phases.

The trilogy is composed of a series of great confrontations: moments which represent Katharine Howard's passage to the block. One of these is Katharine's visit to Anne of Cleves, whom we have already seen sitting in her painted gallery at Richmond. I have tried to suggest that the narrator's general point of view is one with the language of the time, but Ford does more than give the writer leave to play the sedulous ape to Burton and Sir Thomas Browne. He gives his invented historical creatures a tongue of sometimes Shakespearean splendor. The mouth is full again, as it should be, as it once was, and words rest on a breath which would otherwise be idle, since characters need to speak but not to breathe.

Katherine addresses the Queen in German, which surprises her; it is the form of Anne's replies, however, that counts with us:

> 'I learned to read books in German when I was a child,' Katharine said; 'and since you came I have spoken an hour a day with a German astronomer that I might give you pleasure if so be it chanced.'
>
> 'So it is well,' the Queen said. "Not many have so done.'
>
> 'God has endowed me with an ease of tongues,' Katherine answered; 'many others would have ventured it for your Grace's pleasure. But your tongue is a hard tongue.'
>
> 'I have needed to learn hard sentences in yours,' the Queen said, 'and have had many masters many hours of the day.'

Anne of Cleves has not learned her German from books, because she cannot read. She has in consequence, Ford tells us, a memory she can rely on, and reply with.

> 'You seek my queenship'; and in her still voice there was neither passion, nor pity, nor question, nor resignation. . . . 'You have more courage than I. . . .'
>
> Suddenly she made a single gesture with her hands, as if she

---

[21]The preceding passages have been quoted from pp. 28–29 of *The Fifth Queen*.

swept something from her lap: some invisible dust—and that was all.

The Queen knows that in England they slay queens. She also knows—well remembers—what she wants in her swept-out lap. And through that knowledge, we know Anne of Cleves, her cautions, and her comforts.

'I am neither of your country nor for it; neither of your faith nor against it. But, being here, here I do sojourn. I came not here of mine own will. Men have handled me as they would, as if I had a been a doll. But, if I may have as much of the sun as shines, and as much of comfort as the realm affords its better sort, being a princess, and to be treated with some reverence, I care not if ye take King, crown, and commonalty, so ye leave me the ruling of my house and the freedom to wash my face how I will. I had as soon see England linked again with the Papists as the Schmalkaldners; I had as lief see the King married to you as another; I had as lief all men do what they will so they leave me to go my ways and feed me well.'[22]

The neglect of this novel, the critical obtuseness which the Tudor trilogy has had to endure, the indifference of readers to an accomplished art, and a major talent, the failure of scholarship even to disclose the real clay feet of the real Ford, even the esteem in which *The Good Soldier* is held, as if that book were being used to hide the others, but, above all, the unwillingness of writers to respond to a master, constitute a continuing scandal which hushing up will only prolong; yet one does wonder what is to be done. Certainly no adequate history of the recent English novel can be composed that does not recognize the door through which that novel passed to become modern.

In a typical piece of polemic, Wyndham Lewis outlined what he called the taxi-driver test for fiction. One is simply to imagine inviting a cab driver into the house and asking him to open some literary work at random. Then *"at whatever page he happened to open it,* it should be, in its texture, something more than, and something different from, the usual thing that such an operation would reveal."* He goes on to reproduce, in facsimile, the opening pages of *Point Counter Point* and *The Ivory Tower* with predictably decisive results. In Ford's version of this game,[23] one picks the first substantial paragraph to be found on page 90. Let us do so, and take Ford's chances for him. We find ourselves in the middle of one of *The Fifth Queen*'s greatest set pieces: the

---

[22]I have somewhat abridged these passages from chapter 6 of *Privy Seal* (the second book of the trilogy), pp. 365–72.

[23]Wyndham Lewis, *Men without Art* (London: Cassell, 1934), p. 295. Ford carries out this test on Sir Thomas Browne, in *The March of Literature,* p. 513, with the success you would expect. One taste will not tell you how a whole dinner may be shaped, but if the cook is incompetent, it scarcely matters what the order of his dreadful dishes is.

revels given by the Lord Privy Seal in honor of Anne of Cleves. Men dressed as Roman gladiators are using a mannikin in mock combat with a lion. Lewis is satisfied simply to point his pen at his specimen page of Henry James, and so, at Ford, shall we.

> The ladies pressed the tables with their hands, making as if to rise in terror. But the mannikin toppling forward fell before the lion with a hollow sound of brass. The lean beast, springing at its throat, tore it to reach the highly smelling flesh that was concealed within the tunic, and the Romans fled, casting away their shields and swords. One of them had a red forked beard and wide-open blue eyes. He brought into Katharine's mind the remembrance of her cousin. She wondered where he could be, and imagined him with that short sword, cutting his way to her side.
>
> 'That sight is allegorically to show,' Viridus was commenting beside her, 'how the high valour of Britain shall defend from all foes this noble Queen.'
>
> The lion having reached its meat lay down upon it.[24]

---

[24]Katharine's cousin is Thomas Culpepper, with whom she arrived at court, and because of whose love she shall be condemned. The defense of the Queen is ironic in several directions at once. Master Viridus is in the pay of Privy Seal, has changed his name from Greene, and is a worshipful student of the Italian tongue.

DENIS DONOGHUE
Listening to the Saddest Story

Begin at the beginning. Let us suppose that we are reading the book for the first time, starting with the title page which has Ford's name, the title *The Good Soldier,* a subtitle "A Tale of Passion," and in quotation marks the words "Beati Immaculati." Let us assume that we recognize the Latin as the first words of the Vulgate version of Psalm 119, in the Authorized Version, "Blessed are the undefiled in the way, who walk in the law of the Lord." The meaning of these several phrases is merely virtual at this stage; they promise to mean something, but only in the future and therefore in retrospect. We do not yet know who the soldier is, or what is the form of his merit. "A Tale of Passion" is another promissory note, nothing more. The allusion to Psalm 119 is as distant as Latin from any local reference. These phrases will signify, but not yet. So we turn the page and find a "dedicatory letter" to Stella Ford, signed F. M. F. and dated New York, 9 January 1927. We are reading not the first edition (1915) but a text warmed by Ford's affection: "I have always regarded this as my best book." The letter tells us that Ford sat down to write the book on his fortieth birthday, 17 December 1913, and that he wanted to do for the English novel what Maupassant had done for the French in *Fort comme la mort.* We are also told that Ford originally called the book *The Saddest Story* and that he changed the title only because the publisher found its reference to sadness inopportune, sadness being already universal in 1915. *Ford comme la mort?* In any case we have come to the end of the letter and are ready for part 1:

> This is the saddest story I have ever heard. We had known the Ashburn-hams for nine seasons of the town of Nauheim with an extreme intimacy —or rather, with an acquaintanceship as loose and easy and yet as close as a good glove's with your hand. My wife and I knew Captain and Mrs. Ashburnham as well as it was possible to know anybody, and yet, in another sense, we knew nothing at all about them. This is, I believe, a

This essay, written for *The Presence of Ford Madox Ford,* was first published in *Sewanee Review* 88 (Fall 1980).

state of things only possible with English people of whom, till today, when I sit down to puzzle out what I know of this sad affair, I knew nothing whatever. Six months ago I had never been to England, and, certainly, I had never sounded the depths of an English heart. I had known the shallows.

I don't mean to say. . . .

And so on.

A first reading of that paragraph would pick up such things as the following: a story, to be told by a voice peremptory about its role if a little helpless about its knowledge: a tone which commands attention even while it confesses itself bewildered. Not "the saddest case I have ever known" but "the saddest story I have ever heard"; as if the narrator were telling you a story he had heard from someone else; a story, then, as such, to be told for its interest. But it is odd that the narrator is already making such a fuss about the insecurity of knowledge: he knows something, presumably, but insists that he does not know it securely. On a first reading we hardly stop to count the number of occasions on which the verb *to know* is invoked—seven, in fact, high frequency for a short paragraph—but we register the narrator's nervousness in the presence of knowledge. He says something, and then he qualifies the saying, as if the words pushed him further than he cared to be pushed, his scruple being what it is. "Or rather. . . . And yet, in another sense. . . ." The business of England and the English is also odd. The kind of knowledge in question is based upon social meetings, society's seasons rather than nature's, but the narrator has adverted to another kind, the depths of an English heart to be sounded. Depths, distinguished from the shallows, if not further plumbed. We do not measure those depths; we do not know how deep the narrator thinks they are. For all we know, the depths of an English heart may be a contradiction in terms: no heart, no depth. Already we have caught the narrator's misgiving: the relation between words and what they claim to know seems confused. It is not that the words cannot rise to a real knowledge, but that they presume upon it. They are premature, pretending to know in advance what the narrator cannot even claim to know in hindsight. The sentences seem explicit, but what they explicate is far darker than their syntax implies, and so the narrator must confound their lucidity, intervene on behalf of truthfulness. Truthfulness, rather than truth, since truth refers to the facts of the case and truthfulness to the spirit in which they are to be declared; his truthfulness, the narrator's.

The experience of a first reading is more telling than criticism has recognized. When we write a critical essay on a text, we read the text over and over and look at it every which way in the hope of seeing something aslant that we could not see directly. Every further reading has to deal with our previous readings: we write, then, from impressions which are already a palimpsest. We assume that the latest reading is best, richest, issuing from

45

a greater experience of the text. I do in part believe it. Every book asks to be read. Johnson: "That book is good in vain which the reader throws away." Most books are content to be read once, they do not claim to be worth reading twice. Literature claims to be worth reading twice. If you can bear to read a detective story twice, it is because the book has aesthetic interest over and beyond its detective interest. Even so; a first reading has at least this privilege, that we can ask ourselves what keeps us turning the pages. With later readings, that question cannot arise; we keep turning the pages to verify or qualify what we recall from earlier readings.

What am I talking about? Only this: the privilege of a first reading not because it is likely to be better than any subsequent reading—there is no evidence for this—but simply because it is first, like our first meeting with someone who becomes a friend. Ideally, a critical essay would be written directly after the first reading of a text, to gain all the advantages of firstness, ignorance, contingency. Later readings should issue in marginalia, addenda, perhaps corrigenda, but should not suppress the first report. I recall one of William Troy's essays on Virginia Woolf which produced his several accounts of the same body of fiction, accounts written at different times over a period of many years. I do not recall that the earliest account was based upon a first reading, but I hope it was. I mention the matter now mainly because its merits are impossible. I wish I could report upon my first reading of *The Good Soldier,* but I cannot; it is lost in a mass or mess of several readings. My account of a pretended first reading of the first paragraph is merely formal, a conceit devised from regret that the real first reading is gone from me. What follows is drawn from the welter.

In the first paragraph, beginning with "This is the saddest story I have ever heard," the narrator presents himself as a storyteller, though he appears to take little pleasure in that role. He tells the story because he is the only one left to tell it or with an interest in telling it. Edward and Florence are dead, Nancy is mad, and Leonora is pursuing her new life by putting the old one behind her. The narrator, Dowell, is fated to tell the story, and he tells it with an air of fatality. But his genre is necessarily talk, garrulous enough to roam and digress, raise hares, engage in speculation and surmise. Ford is writing a book by pretending that Dowell is telling a story to a silent listener:

> So I shall just imagine myself for a fortnight or so at one side of the fireplace of a country cottage, with a sympathetic soul opposite me. And I shall go on talking. . . .

The pretense is insistently oral. "But I guess I have made it hard for you, O silent listener, to get that impression," he says at one point, one of many. The terminology of print and paper is voided. In part 3, Dowell describes his wife as "a personality of paper," in the sense that "she represented a real human being with a heart, with feelings, with sympathies, and with emotions only as a bank note represents a certain quantity of gold." The true element is air, breath: the story is given not as so many pages of print but as a mouthful of air. The pretense is maintained until twenty pages from the end. At the beginning of the fifth chapter of part 4, Dowell gives up all pretense of storytelling and insists upon the work as writing. "I am writing this, now, I should say, a full eighteen months after the words that end my last chapter. Since writing the words 'until my arrival,' which I see end that paragraph, I have seen again," and so on. The reason is that Nancy, who is with him ("sitting in the hall, forty paces from where I am now writing") is gone far beyond dialogue. No conceit, no romantic fancy, could allow Dowell to think of her any longer as his "dear listener"; she is "not there." So he gives up the pretense of speech and hands over the ending of his story to loneliness and print. And, worse still, he makes his written words turn upon Nancy, accusing her of cruelty comparable with Leonora's, a sinister conspiracy of the two women against Edward. Till that point, Dowell had taken the dear listener as a surrogate for the still dearer Nancy. Now that the pretense has to be dropped, Nancy is replaced by the severity of the written word, and punished for her absence; she is beyond speech, beyond hearing.

Going back to the first paragraph for a second, third, or fourth reading: Dowell's gestures are now familiar to us, especially his trope of correction and his trope of ignorance. For the first, we hear with now greater emphasis his revisions, when he says something and then backs away from its commitment. In the first paragraph, having said that the Dowells knew the Ashburnhams "with an extreme intimacy," he immediately qualifies the saying: "or, rather, with an acquaintanceship as loose and easy and yet as close as a good glove's with your hand." Intimacy seems to be vetoed by acquaintanceship, but the acquaintanceship is then warmed, like fingers in a good glove. A few pages later Dowell has a grandiloquent passage about the intimacy of the two couples as a minuet, and he leads the dance for half a page only to wave it away: "No, by God, it is false! It was not a minuet that we stepped; it was a prison. . . ." Much later he says, "And yet I do believe that for every man there comes at last a woman . . . ," and he changes the form of his belief even before the sentence is complete: "or, no, that is the wrong way of formulating it." When he says something, the saying makes it feel wrong, too much more often than not enough. A paragraph ends, "So, perhaps, it was with Edward Ashburnham," and the next paragraph begins, "Or, perhaps, it wasn't. No, I rather think it wasn't. It is difficult to figure out. . . ."

As for Dowell's trope of ignorance, I would not blame a reader who finds tedious his constant insistence that he knows nothing, that nothing can be known. "I know nothing—nothing in the world—of the hearts of men."

"Who knows?" resounds through the book. Questions are posed, two alternative answers offered, but neither of them is an answer, and the whole episode is voided with an "I don't know" or "It is all a darkness" or "Perhaps you can make head or tail of it; it is beyond me." Facts are recited as if they were significant, but then the official significance attached to them is prised away, first with revisions and modifications, then with a gesture of ignorance. Why?

Think again of Dowell as narrator, or rather as storyteller. The question of reliable and unreliable narrators has often been raised in reference to him, but it is not the real question. Reliable or not, he is the only narrator we have, and we must make the best of him even when he makes the worst of himself. The real question is: What remains, now that nearly all the ostensible significance of the facts has been drained from them by Dowell's scepticism? And the answer is: Dowell himself remains. If you are listening to a storyteller, and he is telling the story subject to constant interruptions, his backward glances, revisions, corrections, and protestations of his own ignorance; these interrogations may damage the confidence with which you receive the story, but not the zest with which you attend upon the storyteller. The more he disputes the significance of the facts he recites, the more indisputable he becomes. We accept him precisely because he is evidently more scrupulous than we would be, in the same circumstances. Accepting him does not mean that we think him infallible but that we think him honest: he may still be obtuse, slow to sense the drift of things. No matter; we listen to his voice. Nothing in *The Good Soldier* is allowed to escape from Dowell's voice, until in the end he disowns voice itself and goes over to the cold fixity of print. It does not matter what he says, as distinct from the saying, which matters all the time. The force of the story, whether it is maintained, deflected, or subverted, returns intact to the teller. It is here that the story is performed; the unity of the tale is in the teller, not in the facts he recites. With Dowell, the tropes of correction and ignorance which seem to warrant our discounting in advance nearly everything he reports, or at any rate our subtracting from its authority, have an entirely different effect; they keep him immune to his subject, or superior to it. The gestures by which he answers contingency make him immune to it. No wonder he survives its attack.

Dowell cannot defeat contingency in its own terms. He survives not only because, as the narrator, he must, but because he converts everything that happens into his own gestures, which are all the better for being his trademarks. Let me explain. Fredric Jameson argues in *Fables of Aggression* that Anglo-American modernism has been dominated by an impressionistic aesthetic rather than by Wyndham Lewis's externalizing and mechanical expressionism. The most influential formal impulses of modernism, he continues, "have been strategies of inwardness, which set out to reappropriate an alienated universe by transforming it into personal styles and private languages."

Such wills to style now seem "to reconfirm the very privatization and frag-
mentation of social life against which they were meant to protest."[1] Jameson
does not discuss these strategies of inwardness in detail, but I assume he
means, mostly, the impulses common to Joyce's early fiction and Eliot's early
poems. Call those strategies Stephen Prufrock, for want of an official name.
Is it not clear that Dowell's way of dealing with crass contingency is by
transforming it into a personal style and private language? His apparently
obsessive themes (heart; Catholicism; good people; knowledge; service)
should be construed, like Prufrock's fancies and Stephen's murmurs, as his
poetic diction, a specialized vocabulary significant only in relation to him; his
private language to which he resorts not only when he has nothing else to
do but when a strategy of such inwardness is the only device he can practice.
The chief attribute of such a diction is that it is self-propelling; that is (so far
as the disinterested reader receives it), repetitive. A diction is that in our
language which seeks to establish itself by repetition; it acts in a poem or a
novel as a cell acts in politics, a clique, a party of like-minded people. In a
poetic diction the words are not the same but similar in their origins, affiliations, let us say in the ideology they sponsor. What, besides the narrator, is
John Dowell? He is an ideologist who deals with a flagrantly alienated
universe by forcing it toward the inwardness of his diction. We say the diction
is obsessive, but we really mean that it has established itself in advance of any
contingency that might threaten to overwhelm it. Dowell, not a strong
character in other terms, has the strength of the voice he is given, the strength
to draw every event toward himself. If his voice remains unanswered, it also
remains unanswerable; his style is answerable to contingency by virtue of
being, in Jameson's sense, private.

Impressionism is as good a word as any to describe this device. Dowell
is like Ford in this respect: the truth of an event is always the accuracy of his
impression of it. He despaired of ever achieving an autonomous truth, independent of his sense of it; and he converted despair into scruple. The words
he needs and uses are those which, with maximum resource and accuracy,
convey his impression of a fact or situation, and they release themselves from
further obligation. So the direction of force in *The Good Soldier* is always from
the outer event to the inwardness which receives and transforms it. Tropes
of correction and ignorance arise from Dowell's sense that the event and his
impression of it do not necessarily coincide; but this is misgiving congenital
to idealists. Meanwhile his speech is an exercise of the only power he commands, the power to draw every event into himself and convert it into privacy
and inwardness.

Why do we speak? The question is reasonable when asked of a Dowell,
who has nothing but speech. We speak to exercise the faculty and power of

[1] Fredric Jameson, *Fables of Aggression* (Berkeley: University of California Press, 1979).

49

speech. Again we speak from need, the need to recognize our need, including especially our sense of the inadequacy of speech. We speak to be completed and fulfilled; meanwhile to be appeased. In *The Good Soldier,* Dowell's speech is the only power he commands, and what speech commands is mostly the space of its presence, its resonance. Dowell's voice has every power in the world except the power to change anything or forestall it: it can do all things, provided that they are all the one thing, the conversion to inwardness by repetition. So there is no contradiction in referring to the power of Dowell's voice and recognizing that, for himself, he insists only upon helplessness. Up to the end and more especially at the end, Dowell insists that he is feeble, effete, a mere shadow of greater men: specifically, he insists, "I have only followed, faintly, and in my unconscious desires, Edward Ashburnham." As Prufrock says "No! I am not Prince Hamlet, nor was meant to be"; a Polonius, perhaps. But voice, in Dowell, is more powerful than anything he knows in himself: in his mere person he has nothing to match it.

That is to say: the power is in the role of storyteller. It does not matter that he is obtuse, if he is obtuse; slow to grasp what Leonora knows when she rushes from the room at M— and speaks of "accepting the situation"; and naive generally about Ashburnham and Florence. No matter; the beauty of the book arises from the ironic relation between two factors—the primacy of Dowell's voice, if for no other reason than that it is the only voice we really hear; and his persistent effort to direct all our attention and nearly all our sympathy toward Edward, who has wronged him in every way that seems at first to matter but finally does not matter, since Florence was already bogus. The book draws every event or fact toward Dowell; while he insists that, by comparison with Ashburnham, he is nothing, a shadow at best of a greater self.

Much of our understanding of storytelling is due to two studies, Albert B. Lord's *The Singer of Tales*[2] and Walter Benjamin's "The Storyteller," in *Illuminations,*[3] a collection of his essays edited by Hannah Arendt. *The Singer of Tales* is a study of oral narrative, the epic construed as an oral art. Particularly we note the formulaic element in epic narrative, phrases which make a breathing space for the singer and establish the provenance of epic poetry as such: they correspond to Dowell's recurrent themes or motifs, which otherwise look like nervous tics and allow some readers to refer, too casually, to obsession. *The Singer of Tales* also supports, only less specifically, the notion of our attention, as listeners, being drawn always to the singer, the storyteller. The narrative always remains a mouthful of air, enacting not only ostensible events in a world at large but the proximity of the singer to his voice. Benjamin's essay mainly distinguishes between novel and tale; between

---

[2] Albert B. Lord, *The Singer of Tales* (Cambridge: Harvard University Press, 1960).
[3] Walter Benjamin, *Illuminations* (New York: Schocken Books, 1969).

fiction as a function of the printing press and fiction as story, oral narrative. The novel is meant to be read in solitude, and it features an elaborately detailed psychology. The tale is meant to be heard in common, it is a function of speech and, equally, of listening; its psychology is general rather than specific, more interested in the sort of thing people do than in any particular thing a particular person has done. In the tale, the explanation of the events is left loose, open-meshed; in the novel, the explanation is inscribed. We are discouraged from offering our own reasons to account for what people have done or failed to do. The events narrated in a novel generally proceed in accord with the linear, sequential form sponsored by pages and print: in the tale, the storyteller is free with the circuit of his story; he delivers things in the order in which he forms impressions of them, he remembers and forgets, he adverts to the slack of his narrative and stops to take it up. *The Good Soldier* has often been read as a precociously modern novel that anticipates many of the procedures of more recent French fiction in the fractures of its narrative. A simpler explanation is that it is what its subtitle says it is, a tale told by an amateur storyteller who does the best he can and takes every latitude offered by that genre.

Northrop Frye has pointed out in *Anatomy of Criticism* that a genre tends to be mixed rather than simple, and that fictions tend to result from mixtures of generic elements.[4] Very few fictions are single-minded instances of their genres. So it is not an embarrassment to say that *The Good Soldier* is a mixture of novel and tale; though I would maintain that it is a tale incorporating, often with only a show of interest, some elements from the novel. The novel tends to place its events in society; its art is politics so far as its themes are evident; it concerns itself with the human relations provoked by a given society. These elements are active in *The Good Soldier,* but not as active as a list of its ostensible themes would suggest. We hear a good deal about property, travel, love-affairs, the season at Nauheim and other places, but the social atmosphere is notably thin: we are not encouraged to sense, beyond the four chief characters and the various women whom Edward loved, a social world densely wrought, going about its business. The social atmosphere is thin for a book that seems to present itself as an account of such things. But the explanation is that in its scheme of organization and judgment, *The Good Soldier* is only nominally a novel. The novel supplies only its decor, not its judgments. The judgments issue far more directly from the tale, in which characters are more types than individuals and psychological explanations are felt to be beside the point. Why does Edward do the things he does? Because he is the type to do them: that is Dowell's pervasive implication. His actions are not explained, as a novel would offer to explain them, by reference to his early circumstances, and so forth. Again: where blame must be laid,

---

[4]Northrop Frye, *Anatomy of Criticism* (Princeton: Princeton University Press, 1957).

Dowell does not lay it upon society, but upon Fate. The ordinances of society are not invoked. The main conflict is not between self and society but between type and morality, and finally the blame is laid upon Fate, the force of nature that ordained the type in the first place. In Dowell's account of Edward and the Kilsyte girl, only Edward's nature is blamed, and thereafter the God of his nature. "There is no priest that has the right to tell me that I must not ask pity for him, from you, silent listener beyond the hearthstone, from the world, or from the God who created in him those desires, those madnesses. . . ." The same page has a rather Conradian passage about "that inscrutable and blind justice" which punishes you "for following your natural but ill-timed inclinations." A few pages later we hear of "the shadow of an eternal wrath"; later still, of "the ingenious torments that fate prepares for us" and our drifting down "the stream of destiny." Bad coincidences are attributed to "a merciless trick of the devil that pays attention to this sweltering hell of ours." And so forth. Dowell's accusations become more extreme as the story goes on, and in the end Fate becomes a neo-Darwinian mutation by which vivid organisms are suppressed so that ordinary, normal, prudent organisms may survive.

Since this development brings the major judgment of the book, I should round it out. The crucial passage comes at the beginning of part 4, chapter 5, where Dowell, thinking of Edward and Nancy and Leonora, says that events worked out "in the extinction of two very splendid personalities—for Edward and the girl *were* splendid personalities, in order that a third personality, more normal, should have, after a long period of trouble, a quiet, comfortable, good time." That last phrase, which refers to the married life of Leonora and Rodney Bayham, is enough to show what Dowell feels about the dispositions of Fate which have issued in a good time for such trivial people; and about the cost to other people. Dowell reverts to the point a few pages later:

> Conventions and traditions I suppose work blindly but surely for the preservation of the normal type; for the extinction of proud, resolute, and unusual individuals.

And again, later, mocking the happy disposition of blessings and punishments:

> Well, that is the end of the story. And, when I come to look at it, I see that it is a happy ending with wedding bells and all. The villains—for obviously Edward and the girl were villains—have been punished by suicide and madness. The heroine—the perfectly normal, virtuous, and slightly deceitful heroine—has become the happy wife of a perfectly normal, virtuous, and slightly deceitful husband. She will shortly become a mother of a perfectly normal, virtuous, slightly deceitful son or daughter. A happy ending, that is what it works out at.

Indeed, he cannot leave the point alone. On the next page he refers to the sinister conspiracy of Fate and Society:

> Mind, I am not preaching anything contrary to accepted morality. I am not advocating free love in this or any other case. Society must go on, I suppose, and society can only exist if the normal, if the virtuous, and the slightly deceitful flourish, and if the passionate, the headstrong, and the too-truthful are condemned to suicide and to madness. But I guess that I myself, in my fainter way, come into the category of the passionate, of the headstrong, and the too-truthful. For I can't conceal from myself the fact that I loved Edward Ashburnham—and that I love him because he was just myself.

The Byronism of these passages is of course odd, except that it is a Byronism of desire and not of deed. Society has nothing to fear from such desire, unless it forces itself into action and calls itself Edward Ashburnham. *The Good Soldier* is not "a novel without a hero," it is what it claims to be, a tale of passion in which passion is found in Edward and only its desire in Dowell. And since the ground of Edward's passion is his nature, the force that destroys it and destroys him can only be called Fate. If the force were contingent or conventional and not categorical, it could be called Society. But the book is a tale because its conflicts are social only betimes and by the way; the true conflict is aboriginal, it has to do with natures and principles. Fate is what we call Nature when its dealings with us are sinister not by chance but by design and malice. Society is a cultural term, and it arises in *The Good Soldier* only at the last moment and, even then, misleadingly; it is nothing more than the visible form of Fate, Fate's conspirator on the daily surface of life. The chief irony of the book is that these warring principles are narrated and invoked by a storyteller who knows them only in shadow and by the intermittent knowledge of his own desire. "I don't know why I should always be selected to be serviceable," he muses at one point. He seems born to be in attendance; diversely upon Florence, Edward, Leonora, and Nancy, but more fundamentally upon passions that he cannot feel in himself but only through others, especially through Edward. If he is superior to the events by being immune to them, he gains this immunity by being fated to know only indirectly and at several removes the passions that made the events. No wonder we recall him as rueful and sedentary, when his own feelings are present; and as rising only to the occasions provoked by others.

There is no contradiction in thinking of Dowell as Byronic in desire and again, in the way he thought of himself, as a nurse if not a poodle; because his Byronism is a value asserted in the modern world but known, and known well enough by him, to be archaic and belated there. It is precisely because the value is archaic that it has to be asserted, and may be. Dowell's Byronism remains nostalgic so long as it is doomed in practice

53

and archaic in every form of itself short of practice. If it had the slightest chance of being embodied successfully and at large, it could be invoked and would not need to be asserted. So it stands for all those "lost values known to be lost" which R. P. Blackmur has ascribed to Ford's novels as the substance of their unmoored sensibility. "Each of these books," Blackmur remarks, "has something to do with the glory of an arbitrary prestige resting on values asserted but not found in the actual world: values which when felt critically deform rather than enlighten action in that world, so that the action ends in the destruction of the values themselves."[5] In Edward Ashburnham the destruction of Byronism is complete; it survives only as a pale shadow of itself, and only as a virtual value, in Dowell, where it never reaches further than mockery. Who are mocked? The "beati immaculati" who walk in perfectly normal, virtuous, and slightly deceitful ways which they appropriate as the way and the law of the Lord. But the mockery, valid enough in the usual anti-bourgeois tone of modern literature, is itself mocked by being ascribed to a man whose criticism of life is, in every limiting sense of the phrase, merely verbal. Dowell says of Edward and Nancy at the end:

> So those splendid and tumultuous creatures with their magnetism and their passions—those two that I really loved—have gone from this earth.

What does Dowell know, we may well ask, of tumult and magnetism, except as his own unconscious desire, carefully suppressed from the field of action and belatedly incited into words? For him, and not for him alone, the words become a substitute for the action that cannot otherwise be taken. If we forgive him, it is because he has not quite forgiven himself.

We return to our starting point: Dowell as narrator, reciting the deeds of others and the suffering which in part he shares with them. His reliability is not the problem. He is central to the story because he is the storyteller. The pathos of the book is that the passion to which Dowell appeals has no continuing place in the world. In many senses, we have approved its loss; in a residual sense, our approval is itself compromised. We do not want Byronism back, but we cannot be sanguine about the ease with which we have repudiated all such desires.

[5]R. P. Blackmur, "The King over the Water: Notes on the Novels of F. M. Hueffer": *Princeton University Library Chronicle,* 9 (3); reprinted in *Modern British Fiction: Essays in Criticism,* ed. Mark Schorer (Oxford: Oxford University Press, 1961), p. 141.

ROGER SALE
Ford's Coming of Age: *The Good Soldier* and *Parade's End*

I want to begin with a series of propositions, all true, arranged to move from the widely accepted toward the little believed, and toward the heart of the argument of the following essay.

1. Ford's reputation as a novelist rests almost entirely on *The Good Soldier* and *Parade's End.*

2. Ford is more admired in America than in England, and the English often take this as a sign that Americans are sentimental Anglophiles when it comes to good soldiers and the Last English Tory.

3. *The Good Soldier* has been continually in print for a generation; *Parade's End* has twice failed to remain in print during the same period. This indicates something about how and why books are taught in American classrooms, and about the way pedagogical intentions can shape critical taste.

4. The intricacy and value of the technical ingenuities of Ford's major novels have been overrated, which may help explain nos. 2 and 3 above.

5. The fancy narration of *The Good Soldier* blinds many to the fact that it is a shabby little shocker.

6. Ford is not well served by those who are content to make no critical statements stronger than no. 1 above. He is best served by those willing to be critical at every turn, even to the point of entertaining the proposition that his work is all a pack of cards.

7. Stella Bowen, Ford's mate in the decade following the war, is humanly the most important person Ford had known by the time he wrote *Parade's End.* Valentine Wannop, who is based on Stella Bowen, is the best heroine in English fiction created by a man.

8. As a result, *Parade's End,* though chockablock with faults, is his great mature achievement, and one of the few irreplaceable novels of the century.

Whatever else *The Good Soldier* is, it is not even close to being the saddest story any of us have ever heard. Placed next to Troilus and Criseyde, Adam and Eve, Clarissa, Pip, Lydgate, Tess, or Jude, Edward Ashburnham is re-markable for arousing little feeling at all. It may be the saddest John Dowell ever heard, but then, he seems to have heard no others.

The Good Soldier is a horror story, and the long debate about the relation of Ford the novelist to Dowell the narrator and of both to Dowell as character is really only an attempt to say what the horror is. The words are the same whether read as the permanent inability of Dowell to understand himself and others or as a cunning confession by the narrator of his blindness during the years of his marriage. The effect is much the same, too, regardless of anyone's precise calibration of the degree of Dowell's knowingness or blindness. Everyone remembers the brilliant opening two parts where Dowell con-structs the minuet of the Ashburnhams and the Dowells: Nauheim, the trip to "the ancient city of M—," the scratching of Maisie Maidan's cheek, the piquant pose of her corpse, the "revelation" scene where Florence watches Ashburnham and Nancy Rufford through the shrubbery. The first-time reader, like Dowell as we imagine him to have first experienced it, sees very little; the rereader, like Dowell looking back, sees it all. Dowell tries hard to get Florence's mind off "things" and onto culture, and culture persists in offering analogues to what is happening in the minuet: Ludwig the Coura-geous, who wanted three wives; Peire Vidal, the troubadour who pays his court dressed in wolfskin and so is taken for one and torn apart by the dogs of shepherds.

This last story is followed by Dowell's description of the good soldier's arrival in Nauheim, Ashburnham as the wolf dressed like a man:

> And there he was, standing by the table. I was looking at him, with my back to the screen. And suddenly I saw two distinct expressions flicker across his immobile eyes. How the deuce did they do it, those unflinch-ing blue eyes with the direct gaze? For the eyes themselves never moved, gazing over my shoulder towards the screen. And the gaze was perfectly level and perfectly direct and perfectly unchanging. I suppose the lids must really have rounded themselves a little, perhaps the lips moved a little too, as if he should be saying, "There you are, my dear." At any rate the expression was one of pride, of satisfaction, of the possessor. I saw him once afterwards, for a moment, gaze upon the fields of Branshaw and say, "All this is my land!"

Ashburnham as grand seigneur is followed by the second of "the two distinct expressions":

> And then again the gaze was perhaps more direct, harder if possible— hardy too. It was a measuring look; a challenging look. Once when we were at Wiesbaden watching him play a polo match against the Bonner Hussaren I saw the same look come into his eyes, balancing the possibili-ties, looking over the ground. The German Captain, Count Baron Idi-

gon von Lelöffel, was right up by their goal posts, coming with the ball in an easy canter in that tricky German fashion. The rest of the field were just anywhere. It was a scratch affair. Ashburnham was quite close to the rails not far from us and I heard him say to himself: "Might just be done!" And he did it. [P. 29.][1]

The first-time reader, like Dowell at the time, can only notice. The rereader, like Dowell the narrator, knows Ashburnham is moving in on Florence Dowell, first with a "There you are, my dear," then with a "Might just be done!" The grand seigneur, the daring polo player, the good soldier, the sentimentalist, and above all, the accomplished lecher. As rereaders we see the words as a kind of double entendre, Dowell as dupe, Dowell as sad narrator.

It is all trick writing, exquisite of its kind. What strains our credulity is not so much the fact that Dowell was once so colossally dense, but that someone so dense could, the moment he understands the sad joke that has been played on him, write it all so cleverly so that first-time readers take it one way and rereaders a different way. We must grant the cleverness to Ford and not to Dowell. But mostly what Ford wanted was an effect and, very clearly, he achieved it. It is worth noting that what most people remember of this novel is bits from the first two parts, which end with Florence running from spying on the conversation between Ashburnham and Nancy Rufford, running into a man named Bagshawe. Bagshawe then tells Dowell that this Florence was Florrie Hurlbird "Coming out of the bedroom of a man called Jimmy at five o'clock in the morning." After this, Florence is found dead. We may as first-time readers feel "ahead" of Dowell the character, knowing more about what is going on than he did, but here, in this night Florence dies, Dowell and first-time reader become one. These are the terrific sections of the novel, where illusion is constantly offered up, and even as rereaders we love it, and then the illusion is cunningly withdrawn, the minuet becomes a prison, and we love that too.

One reason these early scenes are most vivid for us is that they were for Ford himself as well. A good deal of his effort here is to gain some kind of revenge on Violet Hunt, the "cold sensualist" who had given Ford so many Dowell-like illusions during the five years before he began *The Good Soldier.* The editing of the *English Review,* which began in 1908, had been continually entangled because Ford wanted to handle the magazine with the indifferent largesse of an Edward Ashburnham about financial matters. He did not have the income to do this, and he did not have the stature among his peers to convince them that a journal of the best writing cannot be commercially successful. Friend and foe alike pushed him from pillar to post, and so of course he longed for the lazy, stupid life of the good soldier, and of course

[1](Vintage edition, 1951).

he reeled to Violet Hunt and South Lodge for whatever consolation they could provide. As Dowell intones, so Ford earnestly believed in those years: "For, whatever may be said of the relation of the sexes, there is no man who loves a woman that does not desire to come to her for the renewal of his courage, for the cutting asunder of his difficulties" (p. 115). Many have believed that heart-rendingly innocent and dangerous sentence; many may still do. But five years after coming to Violet Hunt for the cutting asunder of his difficulties she appeared as Florence Dowell. In creating her, and in creating a Dowell who could naively trust her, Ford created the parts of the novel everyone remembers vividly because the shift in his relations with Violet Hunt was most vivid to him as he was writing the novel.

Yet it was not Florence who could stand as villain of the piece. She is altogether too silly and shallow, too much a sign of Dowell's will to believe, to be that. And so, after she dies, Dowell says: "From that day to this, I have never given her another thought." He hasn't, and one doesn't. She is fit enough to victimize Dowell, but to victimize Ashburnham, Ford needed someone more formidable, because it was central to the feelings he was uncovering that someone besides Ashburnham be to blame. And so, if not Florence, then Leonora, and the real horror of the novel lies there, in the suddenness with which Ford and Dowell turn, after Florence dies, to look for some other woman to blame. For men are not finally to blame for anything—that is what the battered, confused, and still childish Ford clung to in 1915. Saving the good soldier's hide is what the book turns out to be really about.

The operation begins with a passage near the opening of part 3, the end of which I have already quoted:

> As I see it, at least, with regard to man, a love affair, a love for any definite woman, is something in the nature of a widening of the experience. With each new woman that a man is attracted to there appears to come a broadening of the outlook, or, if you like, an acquiring of new territory. A turn of the eyebrow, a tone of the voice, a queer characteristic gesture—all these things, and it is these things that cause to arise the passion of love—all these things are like so many objects on the horizon of the landscape that tempt a man to walk beyond the horizon, to explore. [P. 114.]

This exploring, this walking beyond the horizon, is not what Ashburnham did with Maisie Maidan, certainly not what he did with Florence or Nancy Rufford, unless we isolate the telltale phrase about "acquiring of new territory" and remember the earlier passage about Ashburnham walking into the dining room and spotting Florence Dowell. No, for Ashburnham it is all old territory after awhile, and old much before that for Florence and Leonora.

Having said this, Dowell must then say it is not the sex that is important:

"It is a thing, with all its accidents, that must be taken for granted, as, in a novel, or a biography, you take it for granted that the characters have their meals with some regularity. But the real fierceness of desire, the real heat of a passion long continued and withering up the soul of a man, is the craving for identity with the woman that he loves." That, I suspect, is a passage that lies closer to Ford's heart than to Dowell's, but in any event, it allows Dowell to praise Ashburnham endlessly as he acquires his new territory, explores beyond the horizon, but then does not end up in bed, as with Mrs. Basil, Maisie Maidan, and Nancy Rufford. It also allows some woman to be blamed when it does not work out well.

Dowell follows this long homily with his account of the early married life of the Ashburnhams, which focuses on what Dowell believes is Leonora's excessive response to her husband's profligacy about both women and money: "Leonora was worrying about his managing of the estates. This appeared to him to be intolerable." Well might she worry, and well might he find that intolerable. But after his affair with La Dolciquita, which costs about fifty thousand pounds, all that language about being so afraid and needing assurance from women of one's worthiness to exist seems like iniquitous moonshine. Such women can offer no such assurance, and neither Ashburnham nor Dowell nor Ford is going to ask Leonora to offer it; in addition, the Ashburnham income, though ample, is hardly able to stand another blow like La Dolciquita, and by himself Ashburnham is helpless in such matters. "But it was old Mr. Mumford—the farmer who did not pay his rent—that threw Edward into Mrs. Basil's arms." As though Edward caused nothing and could cause nothing, and so was a mere victim the moment Leonora pensioned off old Mr. Mumford.

Earlier in the novel Dowell often speaks of his wife as "poor Florence" just as he is about to submarine her; so too, later on, as he begins to mount his assault on Mrs. Ashburnham in earnest, he starts referring to her as "poor Leonora." When she fails to do the decent thing: "But, at that date, poor Leonora was incapable of taking any line whatever." Then, when she does the decent thing and suffers for it: "poor forlorn woman." But lest we extend any compassion toward her, Dowell follows up with word of Rodney Bayham, the man who is presumed to be unimportant because he likes Leonora.

The climactic episode thus is assembled with Leonora, exhausted from dealing with Florence Dowell at Nauheim, rewarded with Nancy Rufford at Branshaw; with Edward mooning with self-pity because he loves Nancy uncontrollably but does not try to seduce her; with Nancy herself unable to see why anything is wrong. Since Edward does the "right thing" by getting drunk and staying drunk, by trying to get Nancy sent away, by praying desperately, by thinking of no one but himself, Dowell, Ashburnham, and Ford can understand this by seeing it all as a conspiracy:

> For, though women, as I see them, have little or no feeling of responsibility towards a county or a country or a career—although they may be lacking entirely in any kind of communal solidarity—they have an immense and automatically working instinct that attaches them to the interest of womanhood. [P. 244.]

Lest this lead one to think there is anything decent about this working instinct, Dowell then must discover that Nancy is really Leonora under the skin: "And, no doubt, she had her share of the sex instinct that makes women be intolerably cruel to the beloved person."

Women start by tempting men into exploring territory. They continue by trying to save men from their worst follies, which is an intolerable infringement. They then cruelly conspire against the men they love: "It was as if Leonora and Nancy banded themselves together to do execution, for the sake of humanity, upon the body of a man who was at their disposal. They were like a couple of Sioux who had got hold of an Apache and had him tied well to a stake. I tell you there was no end to the tortures they inflicted upon him" (p. 239). By this point Dowell has given up considering what either Leonora or Nancy actually did to earn such language.

All sense of doubleness, of some gap between the understanding of Ford and Dowell, or between Ford and Ashburnham, has disappeared by now. All three plunge into an immolation of victimage: "Thou hast conquered, O pale Galilean," Ashburnham sneers at his wife, and Dowell follows that up with passages like this:

> Leonora, as I have said, was the perfectly normal woman. I mean to say that in normal circumstances her desires were those of the woman who is needed by society. She desired children, decorum, an establishment; she desired to avoid waste, she desired to keep up appearances. She was utterly and entirely normal even in her utterly undeniable beauty. But I don't mean to say that she acted perfectly normally in this perfectly abnormal situation. All the world was mad around her and she herself, agonized, took on the complexion of a mad woman; of a woman very wicked; of the villain of the piece.

And this:

> She was made for more normal circumstances—for Mr. Rodney Bayham, who will keep a separate establishment, secretly, in Portsmouth, and make occasional trips to Paris and to Buda-Pesth. [P. 240.]

Worse than that, Rodney Bayham will buy his clothes ready-to-wear.

Vengeance is Dowell's. The bright, nervous, volatile first two parts give way to the revenge of the victim left alive in the name of the victim who goes off "for a bit of rest." Since it must be revenge, the novel ends up shabby, hysterical, a victim itself of Ford's worst instincts.

The point is not that Ford was "good about" or "not good about" women. He certainly meant to be "good about" women, as his 1913 pamphlet for the Women's Suffrage League, *This Monstrous Regiment of Women,* can show. It is a trivial and irrelevant little piece, all about how England was really England only under the rule of women monarchs, but even so, it shows Ford trying to be on "the right side." But perhaps this contributed to his being so vindictive in *The Good Soldier.* He knew better, as it were, but felt worse. After the collapse of the *English Review* his life got increasingly messy. He was separated from his wife, he was trying to keep up the pretense that he and Violet Hunt were not lovers, and he was poor at handling such matters. "You will find yourself at forty with only the wrecks of friendship at your feet," Conrad had warned him in 1909, when Ford was thirty-six, and by the time he was forty and beginning *The Good Soldier,* that was pretty much true. He had a ten-day stint in jail for contempt of court. He made a long, silly, and futile attempt to insist he was a German citizen so he could obtain a divorce from Elsie Hueffer in Germany. That was followed by lies, to himself, to Violet Hunt, and to the world, about what actually happened, what his rights were, what morally should have happened. He was driven to give loftier, purer, and more fantastic versions of himself with each setback. He hated scenes with a passion befitting Edward and Leonora Ashburnham, yet for a number of years got himself in the middle of scenes, nasty and messy ones too.

While Ford was working on *The Good Soldier,* his relations with Violet Hunt were getting very frayed, yet he could count on no one more than her. The early scenes in the novel, however, show her in a very unattractive light. She seems not to have been altogether the trifling twittering figure Florence is made out to be, yet Ford took quite a few episodes out of their chaotic trip to Germany and brought them into the novel for her and everyone else to see. She had no Edward Ashburnham in her life, though Ford seems to have had one or more Maisie Maidans in his. She must have felt betrayed by the book, and could have continued her relation with him only because she too was driven by desperation and self-deception not to face up to what otherwise was perfectly obvious.

Having begun, however, to scrape away at all that baffled and defeated him about women, Ford rediscovered that it was not really Violet Hunt but Elsie Hueffer who maddened him. Hunt was "one of us," a loser, a victim of sharp tongues and innuendo, whereas Elsie Hueffer could be made out to be the one with the sharp tongue, the symbol of all that embittered Ford about English society. "The heroine," Dowell calls Leonora at the end, "has become the happy wife of a perfectly normal, virtuous, and slightly deceitful husband. She will shortly become a mother of a perfectly normal, virtuous, and slightly deceitful son or daughter" (p. 252). And so, through his portrait of Leonora, Ford could implicate his wife, the friends who had sided with her, the publishers who balked at granting him his terms, and the country that was, in his eyes, going to ruin. Which is not to suggest that Elsie Hueffer was a saint, or that one should try to defend what Ford was attacking. *Parade's End* will show there was ample room for satire. It is to say, however, that this "best French novel in the language" is a poisoned book. It achieves by its cleverness a horror that Ford was well aware of, and it also achieves horrors he could only partly acknowledge or understand. His is really a much sadder story than Ashburnham's. The good soldier had money and status and ease, and he squandered and pilloried his inheritance; Ford had none of these advantages, his inheritance was a different one entirely, and he was in his way trying to honor it.

Most of that inheritance was the novel as art, the Flaubertian tradition of Turgenev, James, Maupassant, Crane, and Conrad as opposed to the English popular tradition that Ford called the nuvvel. Whatever else Ford might question, he never questioned the idea that those who might admire him must admire his masters, and admire the storehouse of techniques Ford worked from and in. It is an art of control, of concealment and revelation —"Above all, to make you *see.*" Like anything else that can fascinate human beings, the art of making a reader see is easily employed for its own moral value. Thus one understands why Ford called English fiction before Henry James "fairy tales for adults," though even if the term is in some way accurate, *Pride and Prejudice, Great Expectations, Wuthering Heights, Barchester Towers, Middlemarch* and others are great novels whose art is very admirable indeed. Furthermore, when one asks what one sees when the labor of the novelist is to make one see, even James found Frederic Moreau of *L'Education sentimentale* someone of less than enduring interest, and one might well find the revelations of the shabbiness or cruelty of Gilbert Osmond or Chad Newsome not quite worth the art it takes to bring the candle toward them. But these perspectives were not available to Ford as he was writing *The Good Soldier.*

Of the writers in the Flaubertian tradition, it is James that Ford most resembles in this novel. For Ford as well as for James, concealment and revelation are exercises in seeing how it can best be done, and for both what is revealed is a sexual horror that will, in turn, conceal a deeper sexual horror the reader is left to imagine more than see. The besetting weakness of the Flaubertian tradition is that artfulness is often mistaken as an end in itself, and concealment and revelation, when not informed by something really worth seeking, can seem either empty gesture or striptease. Ford had tried, in *The Call* and *The New Humpty-Dumpty,* to get the materials that he works with in *The Good Soldier* into focus; what makes *The Good Soldier* superior is not so much superior art as a stronger and deeper relation with these materials. Finally, it seems to me, the art of this novel serves a real, urgent, powerful but ignoble goal. It is superior to other Ford novels, and indeed to much of James and Conrad, because of the reality and power of its feelings. Their ignobility, however, is what is really concealed by the intensity of the feeling and the deftness of the art.

Parade's End is another matter entirely. Each time I begin this huge work, it is with a kind of dread that I will discover that its detractors are, alas, right. I remember the first time very distinctly, because I read it one summer twenty odd years ago along with a group of other novels I had never read: *The Red and the Black, Madame Bovary, The Brothers Karamazov, Anna Karenina.* I emerged saying, perhaps somewhat over-confidently, that *Parade's End* was better than all these except the last. Shortly thereafter I read "The King over the Water," in which R. P. Blackmur makes this strong and persuasive argument:

> And this is to say that Hueffer is a minor novelist in the sense that his novels would have little existence without the direct aid and the indirect momentum of the major writers on whom he depended. He dealt with loyalty and the conflict of loyalties like Conrad, he dealt with fine consciences and hideously brooked sensualities like James. But all the loyalty he did not find heightened by Conrad was obstinacy, and all the conscience and sensuality he did not find created by James were priggery and moral suicide. Adding to this what has already been said of the chief novels, makes a terrible simplification: it says that Hueffer supplied only the excesses of his characters' vices and virtues, and only the excesses of their situations; and it suggests that his sensibility was unmoored, or was moored only in the sense that a sensibility may be moored to lost causes known to be lost.[2]

That seemed, and still seems, much more intelligent and sensitive than most praise I have read of Ford; it also seems a fair judgment of *The Good Soldier.* To pick up *Some Do Not . . .* with this from Blackmur in mind—surely, I have felt with the beginning of each rereading, I must finally abandon my love for this novel.

But no. I continue to find myself succumbing to the charm of the whole enterprise and continue to feel as I get into it an exhilaration that comes from knowing that what lies ahead is in the hands of a writer of great skill, his materials and his life finally worthy of the lavish technique being expended upon them. *Parade's End* always seems in danger of being a piece of sentimental fakery, but very seldom is that. It is charming throughout, as long books so seldom can be. It is much funnier, much more piquant, much more amusing about its own quirkiness than I have ever seen it given credit for. It is, finally, especially but not exclusively because of Valentine Wannop, a work of strength, health, and joy, moored to much more than lost causes known to be lost.

Some Do Not . . . is a full-scale historical novel, its landscape indeed very much like that of one of Ford's medieval romances, and that works entirely to Ford's advantage. It was only ten years between the 1912 with which the

---

[2]*Modern British Fiction,* ed. Mark Shorer (New York, Oxford University Press, 1961), pp. 140–41.

novel opens and the 1922 in which the writing of it began, but a great deal had happened in between, to Ford and to England. Ford had been through the war, had been gassed, had been afraid his memory had failed, and had been afraid he could never again be a writer. He also had found, near the end of the war, a woman who could help him through these crises, who could give him a kind of emotional and domestic stability he had never known. The England of 1912 on which he looked back was the ghastly England of the critical years before *The Good Soldier,* but from his newly found position of security and hope he could create an England that need never have been in order for it to fuel and fuse Ford's comic, eager, ironic imagination. It is not a lost cause known to be lost that Ford is writing about, but a lost world reclaimed by an imagination so free that because of it, comedy and nostalgia harmonize so each can delight the other.

Parade's End, but *Some Do Not . . .* especially, is a book filled with utterances, proclamations almost, about the way people are, or should be, about facts and conventions, about what one does or does not do, about what has or has not happened. The story, in one sense, is our discovery of the large number of these utterances that are not true or not true as originally alleged. Ford loved utterances himself, loved people who could make them, and therefore, perhaps, understood their folly as well. One of the richest of these utterances is offered in the title—Some do not—and Ford begins working with it early on, when Vincent Macmaster is watching Christopher Tietjens toss his kit-bag into the window of a train just leaving for Rye. As Tietjens lumbers after it and swings on the foot-board of the train, the station-master shouts after him, "Well caught, sir," for "it was a cricketing country." Macmaster thinks to himself that if he, the son of a Scottish grocer, had done the same thing, the station-master would have shouted "Stand away, there." He then thinks of a couplet:

> The gods to each ascribe a differing lot:
> Some enter at the portal. Some do not!

Christopher can do what Macmaster cannot because he is a Tietjens of Groby; he enters at the portal as his route by right.

A good deal of the novel is then taken up with showing either that there are no more portals in Edwardian England, or that the gods have changed the rules. Macmaster seduces the wife of a mad clergyman, welches off his friend, writes a bad book about Dante Gabriel Rossetti, and yet ends up Sir Vincent Macmaster, indispensable aide to Sir Reginald Ingleby, Imperial Department of Statistics. Tietjens's portal is into no empyrean: he is shipped off to the trenches of France, hounded by his wife, bankrupted, discharged from his club, doubted by his father and older brother, dished by Macmaster and his wife, and accused of having gotten Valentine Wannop with child, though she is a virgin and he has not so much as kissed her.

This irony, though, is easily offered: there are no more portals, and no more gods, just as there will be no more parades. The use to which Tietjens himself puts the phrase is richer: some seduce the woman they love, some do not. At the climax of the novel, on the night before Christopher is to leave for France a second time, he and Valentine end the evening carrying her drunk brother into her mother's house:

> Tietjens' mind said to him: "Now when they came to her father's house so nimbly she slipped in and said: 'There is a fool without and is a maid within. . . .' "
> He answered dully: "Perhaps that is what it amounts to." [P. 282.][3]

Who knows, though, what it amounts to? It might amount, as he has just thought, to "Why don't you kiss the girl? She's a *nice* girl, isn't she? You're a b——y Tommie, ain't cher?" Or it might amount, as Valentine then says, to "Yes! yes. . . . Ugly. . . . Too . . . oh . . . private!" Or it might be, as Christopher goes on, "But obviously. . . . Not under *this* roof . . ." because "We're the sort that . . . do *not.*"

Christopher is pleased with himself for this utterance, because he enjoys being "the sort that" something or other. But what is it they are not doing? They are not going to bed, yes, to be sure, but why? Because he is married? Because she is a virgin? Because this is her mother's house, or because it is too . . . oh . . . *private?* Yes, Macmaster and Edith Ethel Duchemin are the sort that do, and Christopher and Valentine are the sort that do not. The distinction is clear, yet Ford has given us an England, a Christopher, a novel, where all distinctions and utterances are subject to "story," to a what happens next that can mimic, or make cloudy, what someone making an utterance once thought was clear, obvious, or right. Thus, by the end of *Parade's End,* Christopher and Valentine become those who do, or at least do go to bed, live with each other, have a child.

Ford loves working with these large ironies, but he has many smaller and perhaps more interesting ways to deal with utterance and utterer. The Rye scenes, which occupy most of the first half of *Some Do Not . . . ,* make one of the great openings in English fiction because Ford feels free to cast Christopher and Valentine, those he loves, loose in great comic sequences of utterance. In the scenes on the golf course and at the Duchemin breakfast, Ford lets six, eight, ten voices loose at once, to denounce each other, make assignations, have fits, be helpful, demand help, wonder what has become of England if *that* is what help is nowadays. I offer here a fairly long series of quotations, but it is not long enough to show how charming and free-floating it all is. The scene is at the country club. Present are Tietjens, Macmaster, General Campion (who has just told two City men not to discuss their Hungarian whores in public), Campion's brother-in-law Paul Sandbach (who is currently suspended from the House of Commons for having called the

---

[3](New York: Alfred A. Knopf, 1950).

chancellor of the exchequer a "lying attorney"), and the Rt. Hon. Mr.
Waterhouse, Liberal MP, who is being hounded by suffragettes:

> "Hullo! Sandbach! Enjoying your rest?"
> The General said: "I was hoping you'd take on the job of telling these
> fellows off."
> Mr. Sandbach, his bull-dog jaw sticking out, the short black hair on
> his scalp beginning to rise, barked:
> "Hullo, Waterslop! Enjoying your plunder?"
> Mr. Waterhouse, tall, slouching, and untidy-haired, lifted the flaps of
> his coat. It was so ragged that it appeared as if straws stuck out of the
> elbows.

Sandbach is a Tory and Waterhouse a Liberal, but their duet shows that that
distinction, however important in a different context, is only cause for celebration here. In this context, each man's hair and Waterhouse's jacket seem
pointed at, as if they might be as significant as the men, or what they say:

> "All that the suffragettes have left of me," he said laughingly. "Isn't
> one of you fellows a genius called Tietjens?" He was looking at Macmas-
> ter. The General said:
> "Tietjens . . . Macmaster. . . ." The Minister went on very friendly:
> "Oh, it's you? . . . I just wanted to take the opportunity of thanking
> you."

The distinction between the appearance of Tietjens and Macmaster, crucial
for Macmaster earlier, is uninteresting to the Rt. Hon. Minister. But Tietjens,
the youngest there, hates being thanked by a mere minister, and Ford delightedly shifts and shifts about:

> Tietjens said: "Good God! What for?"
> "*You* know!" the Minister said. "We couldn't have got the Bill before
> the House till next session without your figures. . . ." He said slyly:
> "Could we, Sandbach?" and added to Tietjens: "Ingleby told
> me. . . ."
> Tietjens was chalk-white and stiffened. He stuttered:
> "I can't take any credit . . . I consider. . . ."

I consider . . . it merely my duty? I consider it impertinent to be thanked by
a man I've never met? I consider it outrageous to have official business
spoken of at a country club? But Tietjens, to whom no thought is too lofty
or unlikely, cannot finish this one:

> Macmaster exclaimed: "Tietjens . . . you. . . ." He didn't know what
> he was going to say.
> "Oh, you're too modest." Mr. Waterhouse overwhelmed Tietjens.
> "We know whom to thank. . . ." His eyes drifted to Sandbach a little
> absently. Then his face lit up.
> "Oh! Look here, Sandbach," he said. "Come here, will you?" He

walked a pace or two away, calling to one of his young men: "Oh, Sanderson, give the bobbie a drink. A good stiff one." Sandbach jerked himself awkwardly out of his chair and limped to the Minister. [Pp. 59–60.]

Enjoying his position, Waterhouse dispenses with Tietjens with politeness, turns to the disgraced Sandbach, remembers to be good to the bobbie who is saving him, if not his jacket, from the feminists. And Tietjens is left sputtering: "Me too modest! *Me!* . . . The swine. . . . The unspeakable swine!" Reading such a scene, one understands why so few writers after Jane Austen attempted scenes with half a dozen and more speakers, and only Ivy Compton-Burnett is Ford's equal in this regard among those who have tried.

Ford was tentative and insistent in his handling of Ashburnham because he could not afford to have him not be the good soldier. With Tietjens, by comparison, he seems to be in open air, loving him, loving all his utterances, yet so assured in that admiration that he can easily make Tietjens seem a fool, as in the scene above, and, at other times, even know himself to be one. His investment here is not in Tietjens but in being able to render 1912 England as though it were medieval, absurdly long gone. In a brief brilliant discussion of this novel, William H. Pritchard calls this pastoral:

> The whole of *Parade's End* in its creation of heightened and simplified characters—fabulous monsters of one sort or another—is a very well produced pastoral play with an imagination behind it which yearns to breathe freer than life's complex circumstances permit.[4]

In *Some Do Not . . .* the imagination can be freer than it is later on, because the point about it all, the point about the ironies that leave no utterance unchallenged, is that it is all going to go. In the going the real yearning to be freer than life's circumstances permit will be more deeply felt and more sternly tested.

Thus, while Sylvia Tietjens is "evil," Macmaster a "villain," and Campion a "meddling fool," these labels never really seem useful. Thus Edith Ethel Duchemin, for whom Ford has only unmitigated contempt in one frame of mind, can dream of her pre-Raphaelite tryst with Macmaster:

> "Yes! Yes!" she said. "There's a little white gate from the lane." She imagined their interview of passion and mournfulness amongst dim objects half seen. So much of glamour she could allow herself.
>
> Afterwards he must come to the house to ask after her health and they would walk side by side on the lawn, publicly, in the warm light, talking of indifferent but beautiful poetries, a little wearily, but with what cur-

[4]*Seeing through Everything* (London: Faber and Faber, 1977), p. 98.

rents electrifying and passing between their flesh. . . . And then: long, circumspect years. [P. 104.]

This is trashy sentimentality on Edith Ethel's part, posed scenes and posed passions and posed circumspection that she wants in a sufficiently low way that she cannot in fact sustain for more than a few months after her first tryst with Macmaster with any circumspection, and she cannot become Lady Macmaster without being passionately hateful to Christopher and Valentine. But if all illusion is going to go, if all utterance is going to become irrelevant or foolish, then we cannot simply judge Edith Ethel and have done.

Furthermore, the tryst we do get instead of the one Edith Ethel imagines here comes that very night, not by a white gate from the lane but in a horse cart, and the participants who have their "interview of passion and mournfulness amongst dim objects half seen" are not the ones who "do," but the ones who "do not," Christopher and Valentine. The point of the parallel, to repeat, is not to define the hero and heroine but to modify and obviate our need to judge the other, the "wrong" lovers. No parallel, indeed, can begin to describe what is so magical about the day and night enjoyed by the gallant youth and fair maid. Here Ford does what his Flaubertian masters would not have dared to do, namely, he enjoys a youthful passionate romance in first bud; it is fun, unsolemn fun such as most writers of romance are too scared or too solemn to attempt; it is as far beyond the capacity of Dickens or Wagner as it is beyond James or Conrad. Here the sexual bitterness of *The Good Soldier* is cast off because Ford's own life in the early postwar years with Stella Bowen had given him enough of the essential validity of the romance without making him eager to avoid making fun of it.

Christopher and Valentine leave the breakfast at the Duchemins to walk to lunch at Mrs. Wannop's:

> Walk, then, through the field, gallant youth and fair maid, minds cluttered up with all these useless anodynes for thought, quotation, imbecile epithets! Dead silent, unable to talk, from too good breakfast to probably extremely bad lunch.

Christopher, as he often is, is wrong, because lunch when it comes is admirable. But the useless anodynes for thought do indeed put him in God's England:

> " 'Land of Hope and Glory!'—F natural descending to tonic, C major: chord of 6-4, suspension over dominant seventh to common chord of C major. . . . All absolutely correct! . . . Pipe exactly right. It must be: pipe of Englishman of good birth; ditto tobacco. Attractive young woman's back. English midday summer. Best climate in the world! No day on which man may not go abroad!" [Pp. 105–6.]

The night is even better, because now Valentine has her chances to poke fun at Christopher even as she says how delighted she is with him, and to be with him:

> Tietjens let the cart go another fifty yards; then he said:
> "It *is* the right road. The Uddlemere turning *was* the right one. You wouldn't let the horse go another five steps if it wasn't. You're as soppy about horses as . . . as I am." [P. 135.]

She has been chaffing him a good deal, about his Latin pronunciations and his misquotations especially, but she had said "I'm loving it all," so he could bring himself to answer, "I'm rather loving it too!" Thus, instead of making a pronouncement about how soppy Valentine, or women, are about horses, he relaxes into remembering his own soppiness, and Valentine can then relax and carry on about how and why the name is Udimore, not Uddlemere:

> "Why, Tietjens said, "are you giving me all this information?"
> "Because," the girl said, "it's the way your mind works. . . . It picks up useless facts as silver after you've polished it picks up sulphur vapour; and tarnishes! It arranges the useless facts in obsolescent patterns and makes Toryism out of them. . . . I've never met a Cambridge Tory man before. I thought they were all in museums and you work them up again out of bones."

We have already had four or five examples of the way Tietjens arranges useless facts and makes Toryism out of them, and Tietjens has had to say to himself earlier that evening that Valentine's objections to him closely resemble his wife's:

> "That's what father used to say; he was an Oxford Disraelian Conservative Imperialist. . . ."
> "I know of course," Tietjens said.
> "Of course you know," the girl said. "You know everything . . . And you've worked everything into absurd principles. You think father was unsound because he tried to apply tendencies to life. You want to be an English country gentleman and spin principles out of the newspapers and the gossip of horse-fairs. And let the country go to hell, you'll never stir a finger except to say I told you so."
> She touched him suddenly on the arm:
> "*Don't* mind me," she said. "It's reaction. I'm so happy. I'm so happy."
> He said: "That's all right! That's all right!" But for a minute or two it wasn't really. All feminine claws, he said to himself, are sheathed in velvet; but they can hurt a good deal if they touch you on the sore places of the defects of your qualities—even merely with the velvet. [Pp. 135–36.]

Christopher must learn later that Valentine, beautifully and tartly spoken though she is, has no claws. He really knows it already and is only hurt that she is right and that, with her, he need not and must not lapse into reticence as he always has with Sylvia, the only other person who is right about him. He does not speak as well as she does here because he is so much more accustomed than she to dispensing with life by uttering. He knows that too, or is learning it as she reveals it.

One wants to continue quoting from this beautiful scene forever; it is probably Ford's finest moment. That Christopher does not kiss Valentine when he wants to is as it should be, but it does mean that the scene, the novel, and the tetralogy all are denied the sex that should follow this marvelous romance beginning. Given the poison that sex brought to the Ford of *The Good Soldier,* however, one perhaps can say that just this much maturing release was a great deal, and that the need, if that is what it was, to keep the romance from its sexual fulfillment is really only a minor, if real, limitation on Ford's achievement. Lawrence, who does give us the sex, seldom can do it without bringing in some poison too, and he knows nothing of this exulting intelligent first falling in love; how moony some of his lovers are, how insistent are some of his others, by comparison.

Ford faces a formidable task as he finishes the first part of *Some Do Not. . . .* It is not just to bring Christopher and Valentine to the scene at the end of the novel from which I have quoted earlier, but to return them to the world they seem to have left this holiday night, to Tietjens's strange awful marriage, his downfall as a rising young man, to the war. And he must do it without wistfully repudiating this scene by means of the nostalgic groan that it was all in another world. What helps him is that his relation with Stella Bowen, on which this one is based, was not all gone by but was present in the postwar world to sustain him and his novel. Little is clear on the record about whether Ford was planning more volumes as he was writing the first. The death of Proust in the fall of 1922 was the titular inspiration for *Parade's End;* what Proust had done, though Ford knew it only by reputation, Ford would try to do. Being quite capable of utterances, he could have intended as he began *Some Do Not . . .* to write a multivolume novel about what he knew of England between 1912 and 1922, and he could have changed his mind within a few months. My sense is that as long as his relation with Stella Bowen was good, he could go on, and keep his investment in Christopher and Valentine central to his investment in the whole work. When that relation began to fade, therefore, so did his abiding interest in the work.

The dates work out as follows: Ford began *Some Do Not . . .* late in 1922 and finished the book in a year; it was published in 1924. *No More Parades* was begun in October 1924, when Ford was tangling himself in his affair with Jean Rhys, and the novel and the affair were both mostly finished by May 1925. Ford told Stella Bowen "nothing could ever upset us again," but she

knew better: "The desire for freedom," she wrote later, "was already beginning to work in me, and what he really needed was another mate." *A Man
Could Stand Up—*, which opens with Valentine's Armistice morning, was
begun in the winter of 1926 and finished within a few months; it was published in America about the time Ford arrived in New York for a lecture tour
the following October. He began *The Last Post* in the winter of 1927, and
it was published early in 1928, when Ford was back in New York and in love
with a woman named René Wright; it was because of that love that Bowen
finally decided she wanted to separate. Thus, during the writing of the last
three novels Ford and Stella were not on the footing they had been for the
few years ending with the period in which *Some Do Not . . .* was written. The
affair with Jean Rhys was painful and embarrassing, but probably less so for
Ford than for either of the others; the structure of his life with Stella remained intact. But she learned from it how vulnerable Ford was, "tragic
because the scope of his understanding and the breadth of his imagination
had produced an edifice which was plainly in need of more support than was
inherent in the structure itself. A walking temptation to any woman, had I
but known it." Which she soon knew full well, and so she could interpret
what was happening when Ford later lingered in New York long past his
announced dates of return. The structure still needed support, but Bowen
was tired of providing it.

By his own admission, Ford had intended to end *Parade's End* with *A
Man Could Stand Up—* and it was only the "stern, contemptuous and almost
virulent insistence" of Isabel Patterson, Ford wrote later, to learn "what
became of Tietjens" that led to the writing of *The Last Post.* One presumes
money had something to do with it as well, since the middle volumes of the
series were more popular than anything Ford had yet written. In any event,
The Last Post is an afterthought and reads like one too. Ford manages to pay
homage to his years in Sussex with Stella Bowen, but that relationship was
fading for him as he wrote it. I like the book because I, like Isabel Patterson,
want to know what became of Tietjens, but it is very much a "done" book,
a skillful performance of the sort Ford could bring off without asking himself
very hard why he was writing it. It has a great climactic scene in which Sylvia
appears to announce the fall of Groby Great Tree and to rescue Valentine
from humiliation, but the rest is given over to studied indirection.

The question, then, is what to make of the middle volumes, *No More
Parades* and *A Man Could Stand Up—.* Although by common consent they are
not as good as *Some Do Not . . . ,* they are not, therefore, appendages, which
The Last Post turns out to be. Pritchard describes his sense of the matter this
way:

Regretfully, since there are fine moments in them, I would have to agree
that the last three volumes of *Parade's End* are agreeable, minor litera-

ture; a way of suggesting how this is evidenced would be to examine their increasingly lengthy concentration on Tietjens' or Valentine's or Sylvia's internal narrative, well-punctuated by ellipses and other breakings-off.[5]

The distinction seems important: on the one hand the marvelous, deadpan, sympathetic wit of the Rye scenes in *Some Do Not . . .* and the more relaxed internal narratives later on, when Ford can just write on and on, saying what someone thinks, feels, figures; the most obviously defective of these are the places in each of the last three books where someone reviews the past to fill in readers who are picking up the series in the middle.

It should be pointed out, however, that much the longest of these internal narratives is Valentine's in the fourth and fifth chapters of part 2 of *Some Do Not . . . ,* over fifty pages in which Valentine sorts out her relations with Tietjens, Edith Ethel, Sylvia, and her mother in the years between the Rye scenes (1912) and this meeting with Christopher and Mark Tietjens in front of the War Office (1917). It is written relaxedly, without much regard to shape or form, and I find it all wonderful, the part I would point to first to show why Valentine is one of the great heroines of English fiction. Stella Bowen, knowing Valentine was modeled on her, called her "so beastly normal." What astonishes me is how appealing Ford can make this image of virtuous young womanhood, bathing herself in the memory of her two "love scenes" with Tietjens in which love is never mentioned, exploring her admiration for and jealousy of Edith Ethel and Sylvia, delighting in her own physical fitness, getting dressed to walk twelve and a half miles so she can have another meeting with Tietjens and save a few coppers, delighting then again in thinking how absurd such savings are after Mark announces that he is making a settlement on Valentine's mother.

One quotation can show only a bit of this beastly normality. Here Valentine first remembers that when Tietjens did not openly make love to her before he went to France the first time, she had "restored to her her image of the world as a place of virtues and endeavours." That goes smash when she concludes that Edith Ethel's hatred of Tietjens must have been caused by her having been in love with him, having been his mistress, as Sylvia told Valentine over the phone that morning:

> For Mrs. Duchemin she still had a great respect. She could not regard her Edith Ethel merely as a hypocrite, or, indeed, as a hypocrite at all. There was her achievement of making something like a man out of that miserable little creature—as there had been her other great achievement of keeping her unfortunate husband for so long out of a lunatic asylum. That had been no mean feat; neither feat had been mean. And Valentine knew that Edith Ethel really loved beauty, circumspection, urbanity. It

[5]*Seeing through Everything,* p. 99.

was no hypocrisy that made her advocate the Atalanta race of chastity. But also, as Valentine Wannop saw it, humanity has these doublings of strong natures; just as the urbane and grave Spanish nation must find its outlet in the shrieking lusts of the bull-ring, or the circumspect, laborious, and admirable city typist must find her derivative in the cruder lusts of certain novelists, so Edith Ethel must break down into physical sexualities—and into shrieked coarseness of fishwives. How else, indeed, do we have saints? Surely, alone, by the ultimate victory of the one tendency over the other! [Pp. 267–68.]

This is not like the Rye scenes at all; here Ford is immersed in the straightforward admiration for the decent workings of Valentine's mind.

As a result, one must find the mind as admirable as Ford does or the writing will not work. And I do. Valentine is sexually innocent, but as she thinks about sex she is shrewd, sympathetic, and generous. It is not weakness or vanity that makes her persist in taking Edith Ethel seriously but the knowledge that there are saints, and strong doubled natures among the failed saints. There is no need for feats of technical virtuosity when considering the clean straight lines of Valentine's passionate intelligence. I find her goodness satisfying and exciting, and I am convinced that Ford's ability to create her is a major sign that he had come of age in this novel; as long as the relation that underlay her creation sustained him, the novel rings true.

What Ford wanted was to have the stylized deadpan wit be his way of creating the prewar world, and then to take that away for the most part and to put his characters through the long tunnel of the war itself, letting them loose in the long interior monologues. The danger here is indulgence, justifying the characters, especially Tietjens, merely because they think and feel in a certain way. The way out of indulgence is balance, where the outside world does not simply jump up to endorse some private wish. One marvelous moment of such balancing comes early in *A Man Could Stand Up*—when, on the morning of Armistice Day, Valentine is reflecting on the headmistress Miss Wanostrocht's meandering about whether there will be any more Respect after the war is over. Everyone remembers, because it plays such a large role in clarifying the title, the moment in *No More Parades* when Tietjens announces there will indeed be no more parades. Ford then has a similar utterance put in Miss Wanostrocht's mouth, and here is Valentine's reply:

No more respect. . . . For the Equator! For the Metric System! For Sir Walter Scott! Or George Washington! Or Abraham Lincoln! Or the Seventh Commandment! [P. 511.]

Valentine *will* keep Christopher engaged in the business of living rather than cluttering his mind up with useless anodynes for thought. Not that Christopher's utterances about the Kitchener battalion and "Land of Hope and Glory" are contemptible, any more than was his refusal, on whatever grounds, to break the seventh commandment. But Valentine knows him, knows what they should do, which will include breaking the seventh commandment, and as long as a voice like that is available to Ford, he will not simply indulge his love of Tietjens, his love of Tietjens's lost causes known to be lost.

So too can Ford use Sylvia Tietjens. Having Valentine in the book, having Stella Bowen in his life, meant that Ford could be much more tolerant of and therefore much more incisive about Violet Hunt in *Parade's End* than he could be in *The Good Soldier.* Ford is clear that Tietjens's insistent "Neither do I condemn thee" practically by itself creates Sylvia's desire to strike back and punish him; this is what Ford could not see when he created Edward and Leonora Ashburnham. Sylvia's sense of Tietjens is fixed, as if he were a target, but that is because Tietjens offers her a fixed target, as he does not with Valentine. The presence of Valentine makes it seem perfectly natural for Sylvia to want to attack Tietjens, just as it is in its perverse way natural that Tietjens will behave so Sylvia will want to attack; they are not fixed in a prewar world, but their relationship is. And in this book the original presence and the later memory of Father Consett, who offers his scathing judgments of Sylvia in a most forgiving way, means that judgment does not here lead to a hounding down, as it does in *The Good Soldier.* Because of Stella Bowen, Valentine; because of Stella Bowen, the forgiveness of Violet Hunt and even of Elsie Hueffer, and thus the careful and flexible creation of Sylvia.

One triumph of this letting in of air around Sylvia comes in the comic, grotesque, yet touchingly romantic scene at the end of part 2 of *No More Parades.* At Sylvia's hotel, which is near Tietjens's transport depot, Lieutenant Cowley drunkenly keeps trying to offer eulogies to Tietjens as soldier, not knowing they are precisely what Sylvia does not want to hear. Tietjens himself, bone weary and trying to keep up appearances about his marriage, stumbles through the evening, never imagining how much pain he could spare himself and Sylvia if he would just give her a sign of caring and respect —and it is much easier to sympathize with him here than it is with Ashburnham in a similar situation. Sylvia, nerves neurotically taut from lack of sleep, terror of war, and loathing of her own scheming, wants somehow to seduce the lonely buffalo that is her husband. She remembers that the Duchess of Marlborough wrote, after visiting her own soldier husband near the field of battle, "My Lord did me the honour three times in his boots." The scene is mostly Sylvia's, but the others provide balancing and clarifying presences, topped off by the drunken General O'Hara who wakes from a stupor to exchange sexual innuendoes with Sylvia, which drives her into Tietjens's arms as they dance and she hums Venusberg music. She is not forgiving him, but she is feeling almost uncontrollably giddy and heated, and so is willing to be decent to him if he will be her husband. But because Tietjens can be her husband only in a lofty and impenetrable way, her sexual excitement—

though we learn this only quite a bit later—must resolve itself back into revenge.

Ford needs Sylvia just as he needs Valentine, as major alternative sources of energy and complication to set off against Tietjens. Where I always do see Ford being indulgent about Tietjens is in the war scenes themselves, the supply depot and the trenches. If Stella Bowen had given Ford herself, and thereby his ability to create Valentine and Sylvia, nothing could save him from wanting Tietjens, as his surrogate, to be the great leader of men at arms that he, Ford, clearly had not been. There are splendidly vivid moments in these sections—Tietjens writing his sonnet for Captain McKechnie, Tietjens listening to the larks outside the trenches, Tietjens diving into the mud to find his subaltern Aranjuez—and Ford is excellent at conveying a sense of muddle and clutter as the essential experience of soldiers. But it is clear too that McKechnie and Levin and Campion and Cowley and the unnamed colonel and Aranjuez all exist as instruments to validate Tietjens, to applaud him, to come grudgingly to admiration for him, to set themselves up as blackguards by opposing him. The war becomes Tietjens's war in a way that limits him: if he is stubborn, it must be a noble stubbornness; if he thinks, it must be a thought no one else could have; if he is a fool, it is a divine fool. Ford may not have been driven to defending Tietjens at war as desperately as he was to defending his earlier good soldier, but he is nonetheless careless, soft, and daydreaming here as he never is when Tietjens is with Valentine or Sylvia. Here is the kind of thing I mean, at its worst, but therefore clearly able to expose an insistent tendency:

> There were all these inscrutable beings: the Other Ranks, a brownish mass, spreading underground, like clay strata in the gravel, beneath all this waving country that the sun would soon be warming; they were in holes, in tunnels, behind sack cloth curtains, carrying on . . . carrying on some sort of life, conversing, breathing, desiring. But completely mysterious, in the mass. Now and then you got a glimpse of a passionate desire: "A man could stand up on a bleedin' 'ill"; now and then you got —though you knew that they watched you eternally and knew the minutest gestures of your sleep—you got some sort of indication as to how they regarded you: "You are a law unto yourself!"
>   That must be hero-worship: an acting temporary regimental sergeant-major, without any real knowledge of his job, extemporising, not so long ago a carrier in an eastern county of remarkable flatness does not tell his Acting Commanding Officer that he is a law unto himself without meaning it to be a flattering testimony: a certificate, as far as it went, of trustworthiness. [P. 570.]

As though the Other Ranks existed as creatures who exist to certify Tietjens's sentimental desire to be, and to be thought of as being, a law unto himself, a man standing alone on a hill, the Last English Tory, the soldier equivalent of George Herbert of Bemerton. Ford had come of age in this novel, but in these places he shows himself still a little boy.

In a different kind of book about war this indulgence would loom as a much larger defect than it does in this one. *Parade's End* is a novel about private experience, understood historically and often expressed as public emblem, but essentially a matter of its three major characters. The history, the public emblem is mostly a matter of having the characters utter and having the story show what becomes of the utterance and the utterer. Those who do not become, in a modestly triumphant way, those who do. No more parades is no more respect for Sir Walter Scott and the seventh commandment. The gallant youth who becomes the man who stands up on a hill reels through empty rooms on Armistice Day, lunges into the street, trying to sell a piece of furniture. The fair maid stands in her room, pregnant, helpless, as Sylvia, Edith Ethel, the tin Maintenon, General Campion, and young Mark Tietjens invade her Sussex retreat, and only her putative mortal enemy, Sylvia, can rescue her. The ironies work both to support as well as to deflate, but their presence is the sign that Ford had tested his materials and made his history. If this were a novel that made its claims differently, that staked itself on its ability to render war and other public events, the last three volumes would seem more pulpy than they in fact do. Part of Ford longed to say "I was there, damn you, and this is what it was like." Part of that part, indeed, really had been there and can tell us much, but Ford was a braggart warrior too. Fortunately, Ford had been battered and tested, and had emerged with a new life, and he was able to write most of his novel before that new life faded. He earned his idealization of the beastly normal Valentine, his incisive perception of the defeated Sylvia, his bemused love of the lonely buffalo.

Knopf has recently brought *Parade's End* back into print, in a one-volume paperback, and so we, in America at least, have a chance to show some small part of a generation of readers that it is a great book. Its length is a pedagogical inconvenience; a course with *Ulysses* and the major Lawrence in it may seem weighted down enough already without it. But, for me at least, it is those books that it should be placed alongside, better than Conrad or Woolf or Forster or Huxley or Waugh, and it should never be allowed to disappear again. It is a genuinely rereadable book, one that can be freshly enjoyed—and not merely studied and reread selectively—as much or more on the fifth time through as on the first. Ford's was not an angry spirit, or an insistent one; for all his restlessness and fears he came to accept life as fascinating, sad, funny, and humbling. He cannot guide anyone anywhere. But in *Parade's End* he made his experience not just fascinating, sad, funny, and humble, but gloriously so, and few books do that.

ANDREW LYTLE
A Partial Reading of *Parade's End*
or
The Hero as an Old Furniture Dealer

Parade's End is Ford Madox Ford's second masterpiece. *The Good Soldier,* using a smaller scene, is a more intensive rendition of a common subject. The actors in *Parade's End* make a microcosm of the enlarged drama, whose enveloping action is the end of European civilization. It is a tetralogy. The first book, *Some Do Not . . . ,* divides English society between those who will sustain the inherited manners and mores and those who will not. The Tories (not just the political party), that is the king's men, that is those who uphold and defend the traditional English ways, once ruled the kingdoms according to feudal codes and the empire at least by means of the ceremony and regalia and the discipline of a long-standing public service.

This belief and habit have been increasingly threatened by the *arrivistes,* especially during the nineteenth century, men who think first of their private interests and afterwards of the public good, or even regard the *res publica* and their interests as one and the same thing. They occupy government bureaus and financial institutions. They infiltrate society. This has been a slow but continuous process ever since the fifteenth and sixteenth centuries, when the prospering merchants felt they wanted more than the countinghouse and the odors of their trade. It was natural to want to share the rule of England. The feudal world, though changing, was able to absorb them. After all, they were merely shifting their knowledge of craftsmanship to another occupation, Christendom being an agglomeration of crafts, from king to yeomen.

In time the newcomers were indistinguishable from the gentry. But the industrial revolution and international banking introduced a new kind, an abstract, irresponsible kind of power. A population settled on the land, where the seasons set the pace of work, could and did without impairment take in outlanders without changing too fast its cultural habits. But the new money was a different matter. Its control was outside the county communities and often England itself.

Christopher Tietjens, the hero, is an example of the indigenous manner of change. The Tietjens came from the Netherlands with William. The head of the family got Groby, a rich country estate, from an English Roman Catholic family, in a way which put a curse upon the place. In time the Tietjens were absorbed in the usual way. They are now all English and all county family, with coal mines as well as land. And they are Yorkshiremen. To emphasize this, Macmaster, Christopher's roommate and friend from his college days, stands for the initial phase of infiltration, but with a difference. He is in a sense a foreigner, that is, a Scotsman. His birth is low; Christopher's is not. But the specific difference is his attachment to those who administer the state, and these administrators lack the sense of feudal honor or care for the public thing. He and Christopher are in the same bureau of statistics, but their attitudes are not the same. In their persons, beliefs, and associations the two men contain the antitheses which operate throughout the entire action. For the sake of truth and proper rule, Christopher complains of the hypocrisy and dishonesty of his superiors, as they manipulate statistics. Macmaster feels that his friend is needlessly throwing away his opportunities, as he did at school in mathematics. Although the best head at it, he came in second. He did not want to be known only for this skill. Macmaster would not dare contradict a superior or refuse to obey. His hope is to be accepted as a man close to the inner workings of rule, with the end of being safe. His interest is selfish; Christopher's is not.

No More Parades, the second book, is largely placed in France during the catastrophic world war. No more parades means no more ceremony, no more formal behavior either in public or private, no more religious rites, workable conventions, all those forms which confine the natural man's instinctive and intuitive behavior towards Christian order. This war goes beyond professional armies. Entire populations, unlike the close-order tactics of the eighteenth century, are subjected to slaughter. The millions of casualties will assure the selfish men who played it safe at home their places of political and economic power. The dead do not protest. Those who still ruled before the war fought it and died; the administrators at home manipulated their interests. It is they who resisted the single command for the allies. Had they succeeded in this, Christopher feels the Germans would have won. In explaining to General Campion why he will not be able to return to his job after the war, he says that those who remained safe at home will penalize those who fought for their country. Not only will they resent the better manhood; they will want the women and the jobs.

It is France rather than England that is the epitome of European culture. The French are practical. They understand money and know its limitations. A Frenchman will put a penny in the poor box at night to have a penny to spend in the morning.[1] Few would confuse industry with progress. On the verge of the war the population was largely peasant, at least with a peasant understanding. Mark's French mistress is petty bourgeois, but she could as easily fit into a peasant's life, which for a while she does in the Tietjens's household after the war. A peasant will put hard money in his sock and hide it when times get perilous.

Christopher tells Valentine Wannop in their intimate tête-à-tête why he despises the oncoming war. Since his private life is ruined, he had thought of joining the foreign legion as a private. "One could have fought with a clean heart for a civilization: if you like for the eighteenth century (France) against the twentieth. But our coming in changed the aspect at once. It was one part of the twentieth century using the eighteenth as a catspaw to bash the other half of the twentieth." He goes or rather returns to the war and there exhibits how a man could stand up, the title to the third book. The fourth and last, *The Last Post,* indicates with a devastating irony the price he and his beloved, Valentine, must pay to do so. What they pay is the measure of what England has lost.

The action itself is the concrete incidents which reveal this enveloping action, that is, the universal truths which underlie this fiction. It has to do in a seemingly simple way with the loves of men and women. And how historic change, through war, exemplifies publicly the same tensions. To oversimplify: the hero, Christopher Tietjens, resists and is ruined by those powers which bring to an end an ancient Tory's idea of England. For Christopher so sees himself. More discursive than *The Good Soldier,* the scenes are interspersed with panoramic summaries, often in the reflections which comment upon or elaborate the drive of the action.

The conflicts are all set forth in the first book. Sylvia Tietjens, his wife, is the antagonist. At once almost we discover that she has married Christopher to give a name to another man's child. And afterwards, bored by her husband, she goes to France with a lover. She soon discovers that this is not what she wants and writes to her husband that she is willing to return to him. Her mother, Mrs. Satterthwaite, has followed to prevent an open scandal. She waits with Father Consett, the family priest, at a remote spa in the Black Forest of Germany, which Father Consett suggests is haunted by evil spirits. Indeed, the last Crusade was directed here towards a Christian conversion. The hotel is a grand duke's former hunting lodge. The priest comments on the wall decorations, gore and globs of blood of the huntsmen's kills. Nothing sporting, only the bloody kill. This bloodlust controlling industrial might contains the threat to civilization, as it stands for the destructive forces in

---

[1]Djuna Barnes, *Nightwood* (New York: Harcourt, Brace & Co., 1937).

private life. It is here Sylvia, leaving her lover, joins her mother and the priest.

There is a singular history belonging to mother and daughter. They both married good men, and they both hate them. The mother did; the daughter does. This also is an English Roman Catholic family, which means that their place, since Henry's assumption of both mitre and crown, has been restricted. The history of the English Roman Catholic differs from that of the rest of the English. He cannot have the same understanding of his past. For a long time he was deprived of his political rights; he does not forget the persecution by the Cecils, the calculated injustice in the courts, by which Groby was lost to the Tietjens; most of all the prohibition of the mass, the sacrament crucial to Christian worship. By the time of the action of this book, the social position of the English Roman Catholic is secure. Why then do mother and daughter hate their husbands and Sylvia complain of boredom? I suggest this: since the English Roman Catholic cannot exercise all his rights, his sovereignty is to that extent impaired. If what a woman wants of her man, according to the Wife of Bath, is his sovereignty, she in this instance cannot have it whole.

Father Consett knows man's imperfection and with charity toward this imperfection ignores the schism by advice which could mend it, at least for those in his care. He tells Sylvia to be a good wife, look after her husband, and bear him children. This is what she would like to do, have a man to respect and share domestic felicity. But in her confusion, she cannot at first see her husband in this light. A man secure among his peers would be for her one belonging to the very group Christopher detests, the *arrivistes.* Although Christopher is an Anglican Catholic, his plight is not unlike that of the Roman Catholic gentry whom the Cecils persecuted. Without the physical torture, he throughout will be put to all the ways of being ostracized and so exiled at home. And so she will not receive him in the full pledge of matrimony. And when she would like to, it is too late. So she is bored . . . bored . . . bored. She does not know why, but her priest does.

Christopher agrees to take her back on his own terms. She accepts because she intends to torture him the rest of his life. She tells the priest that, if necessary, she will corrupt their child—it turns out to be his. At this Father Consett threatens to burn her with holy water, and she comes to her senses. The extent of her misdirection has brought her with certain of her intimates to tamper with black masses. Father Consett does not take this seriously. It's not much more than fortune-telling or table-thumping. He says: "It's volition that's the essence of prayer, black or white." When she leaves the room, he tells her mother that her hell on earth will begin when her husband (since they will not be living together *maritalement*), a young, full-blooded man, will go running head down after another woman. And she—"the more she's made an occupation of torturing him the less right she thinks she has to lose him." This proves to be true, with complications not stated by the priest.

Ford does not intend this fiction to prove anything historically. He is rendering the given moment of history as people make it and, in peace time, the cultural conditions through which and by which all human beings are effectively moved. The affections, the biological needs, make the greatest effects. By no means, however, do they shape the full-rounded meaning of what happens to the hero and the heroine in their persons and as they reflect the matters common to what was Christian Europe.

There are constants we all recognize: betrayal, envy, the dishonesties of appearance. General Campion, the hero's godfather and of like caste, sees largely as a professional soldier. To him men go wrong in three ways—sex, money, and drink. Certainly sex and money have to do with the complications of this book, but not quite in the oversimplification an institution like the army would make. Seeing behavior in platitudes delays General Campion's understanding of Christopher. It is never quite clear that he fully solves the behavior of this Tietjens.

Earlier in life Christopher has wanted to be a saint, an Anglican saint like his mother. Of course saints are not made this way. The name Christopher means he who bears Christ, from a legend of a gigantic saint who carried the Christ child across a river. The word was originally applied by Christians to themselves, meaning they bore Christ in their hearts. And it seems that this is what this Tietjens wanted to do and what he meant by being a saint. By the nineteenth century England had so fallen away from religious worship that a follower of Christian beliefs subjected himself to a kind of martyrdom, as an earlier saint of the same name suffered. Christopher himself thought of his aspiration as being sentimental; he might have thought anachronistic. He tried to practice the cardinal virtues of justice, prudence, fortitude, and temperance. To those who were carnally disposed this was unforgivable. In one of the most moving scenes in the book, after he has assured Sylvia that she is honorable and did the right thing to find in him a father for her child, a thing any woman should do, she says to him there is only one man "from whom a woman could take 'Neither I condemn thee' and not hate him more than she hates the fiend." At this point she has come to love him and knows it is too late. That a man could act out of principle her experience of her physical charms will not let her believe: this is the affront direct. She knows who the other woman is.

Christopher makes a kind of pilgrim's progress. The two ways are not theological, not up or down. They are middle class and genealogy: money or family as the basic structure of the state. The middle class belief is in money as power and as the ultimate good, even though belief in it must be variable. Genealogy is the history, the persistence, and the description of family, that force for stability and prudence in a continuing order. The predominance of one or the other, on the public scene, has to do with history. Personally, it is what a banker can do to evict a man from his place in society. A small check Christopher has given to his club is returned for no funds. He resigns from the club. The funds have been manipulated by the banker's nephew to ruin Christopher, as he lusts after Christopher's wife. The banker, when confronted by his nephew's perfidy, relies at first on a technicality—the account was overdrawn. He is not a bad man; he likes Christopher and the way he has acted, and he promises to rectify the abuse. Christopher tells him it is too late. The news will be all over the city. He is ruined. This is a clear instance of how the power of money specifically can destroy. It can have no morals. The immorality of the act, the nephew's act, can always be disguised by the technical, amoral laws of banking.

When Christopher refuses to allow the banker to explain to his club and reinstate him—it is too late—the banker is shaken. Where will it end and what will be the repercussions? For a man to resign from his club under a cloud, that masculine assurance of social standing and intimacy, means his exclusion from those houses that have always received him. Because he has not been untrue to his beliefs and principles, Christopher is willing to abide by this ruin. It is this that alarms his wife and the banker and misinterprets him to those who should know better. The returned check is merely an instance of how Christopher's character is sullied. All the offensive charges in politics and human behavior are attributed to him: socialism, selling his wife for pay (apparently not too uncommon), seducing the daughter of his father's friend.

The failure of belief in a divine order of the world established, of necessity, materialism as the ultimate support of the English nation. Earlier Calvin had defined this change most cogently. As God's minister, he became the sole interpreter of God's will and God withdrew into some inner chamber. Who were the elect? Obviously those who prospered in a material way. Business as a total definition of man supplanted the Christian man as image of what he should be. Charity gave way before the selfish will. Practically, the ministry played Calvin's role to the Crown. This is what Christopher meant when he told Campion that his loyalty as an antique Tory was so old that nobody would understand it.

The succession to and opposition to this old view of England are intrinsic to industrialism, scientism, and international finance, et cetera. This tension clearly shows itself in the distinctions between Macmaster's point of view and that of the Tietjens. This egocentric view of matter tends to separate man from nature. Of all the attendant ills of industrialism, et cetera, this fact is the most vicious. It makes pre-eminent that which dies as man lives, that is, the ego, and neglects that property which is eternal and survives matter as dust. At least this is the Christian promise. Mrs. de Bray Pape, the woman who has inherited the Maintenon's soul, is the archetypal example. She lays flat with her skirts the Tietjens hay, ignorant that she is walking through hay or that it will make it hard to cut.

This is done easily, without making a point of it, as the county landlords and farmers are shown with intimate knowledge of, as they care for, growing things and animals. Mark's one passion is following the races and we do not get the sense that he does so just for betting. He studies the forms assiduously, that is, the genealogies of the thoroughbreds. This interest comes from his county background. But it is Christopher who shows most clearly the attachment to and understanding of animals. He has lived with them and by them. He whipped one of his father's grooms for turning the horses loose in pasture with curb bits on, making it painful to eat. He gave advice to a cabman about feeding his horse; he saw what made Mrs. Wannop's animal seem vicious and corrected it. Later, when General Campion ran into the same horse in a fog, as he and Valentine were returning to her mother's, he knew what to do to save its life, if not its usefulness. In the army he was asked to handle a captured horse. He violently protested against the officer in command of a depot of horses. This involved the action of sending him to the front, which seemed to be death, as he could not be put under the officer's charge.

Sent by the cabinet minister to persuade the policeman not to pursue Miss Wannop, Christopher not only carried out his mission but mended the broken leg of the policeman's wife's canary. He also learned to distinguish a dog otter's spoor from a gravid bitch's.

More directly the dog cart and the horse and the fog, animal nature and nature, gave harmony to the night journey that Christopher and Valentine, human nature, took to deliver the suffragette to safety. The clop of the hooves, the smell of animal and harness and the noise, quiet, natural to the two human beings being driven, instinctively (their wills at first protesting) drew them together. Their bodies kissed without kissing with an instant transferral of this knowledge of mutual feeling. Riding through the invisible fields and orchards led the man to renewal of his deep love for the country-side of England, the nostalgic setting for English maid and man. The fields, the moors, the animals grazing, the orchards became to Christopher parts of his being. It is this a man fights for, when it is threatened.

Macmaster had no interest in, knowledge of this close intimacy between man and beast and growing things. He was a townsman, with little experience beyond the cobblestones of certain streets. He is not a bad man. His actions (or the motives for his actions) are based on nothing more profound than ambition and private needs. The inadequacy of this the action judges. He thinks no further than his anger at Sylvia for her adultery. He urges his friend to divorce her, calling her the cruelest beast. This advice ignores the institutional and sacramental aspects of marriage. It is all feeling. Christopher rebukes him, reminding him that he is talking about his friend's wife. "You can relate a lady's actions if you know them and are asked to. You mustn't comment. In this case you don't know the lady's actions even, so you may as well hold your tongue."

He tries to instruct Macmaster about monogomy. The stability of society depends upon it. Adultery embarrasses intimate social gatherings, formal ones too, by intruding a too private matter, making public private intimacies. He defends monogamy even after his own private struggle with anger, humiliation, and the temptation to do what Macmaster suggests. But his sense of justice prevails. And when he tells his wife that she is honorable, he also rebukes her, not for the white lies she has let her son tell but for teaching him bad manners. The boy is heir to Groby, and he should not put a frog in his nurse's bath. She is an old and familiar retainer whom he should respect and treat with respect. County manners against the private will, which Sylvia understands but Macmaster cannot.

With no family behind him, a solitary in town, Macmaster must have something outside himself (he is not religious) to sustain him. He takes to literature, not out of any love for it but for what good it will do him in his competition for place in the statistical bureau. His choice was Pre-Raphaelite. This suited the circumspect, that is, the cautious middle class to which he belongs. He is doing a monograph on Rossetti, and it is this which brings him to adulterous dealings with the woman whom he will later marry, as he seeks her husband, an intimate of Ruskin's, for help in his research. Ruskin was the popular writer of the late nineteenth century. He also told his wife as they drove to their honeymoon that they would live as the angels. His disciple, whom Macmaster sought, imitated the master too literally, and so led Macmaster to his involvement with his wife.

Christopher has argued that both adultery and war threaten the peace. Macmaster, parroting his superiors, announces there will be no war. "We . . . the circumspect classes will pilot the nation through the tight places." Christopher answers him with war is inevitable, since his kind are such hypocrites. There is no country in the world which trusts England. "We're always, as it were, committing adultery—like you fellows—with the name of Heaven on our lips." And he quotes from Macmaster's monograph: "Part till we once more may meet/In a Heaven above."

The comparison throughout between the loves of Tietjens and those of his friend Macmaster is almost a little allegory. Duchemin, the familiar of Ruskin, is a rich and paranoid priest, who frequently turns to violence. He not only imitates, to the distress of his wife, his master's celibacy, but at a trying breakfast, given so that Macmaster might learn what he needs to know, Duchemin enters shouting *"post coitum triste"* and later quotes from the *Satyricon.* He is seated behind tall silver candelabra and heavy silver dishes, tall beautiful flowers, to protect the guests. This rich assemblage of artifacts of "culture" is largely for the enveloping action, since it removes from the ritual of food, a ceremony given to social amity, a mad priest who is a literary, not a religious, authority. To the same purpose the flora serve madness: art and nature abused. Under such conditions does Macmaster find his love, in adultery and later in marriage. A decadent literature and rich artifacts are no substitute, however, for divine and institutional guidance. This ornament becomes the pattern of their life together, first the masked meetings, after marriage her salon, this time surrounding her "celebrities" with her appointments, especially at the tea table. These celebrities of hers have accidental reputations. To make this evident, when Mrs. Wannop, the only real novelist since the eighteenth century, arrives, she is isolated and insulted by her hostess, in spite of the fact that her daughter, Valentine, is serving the tea. The moment comes, fortunately, when those who know gather about her, to the chagrin of the hostess, whose falsity is exposed.

The contrast to the love between Christopher and Valentine is almost too obvious. Like Mrs. Duchemin-Macmaster she is also her lover's feminine counterpart: she is the true English maid. Her acts are generous and loving and charitable. She comes as close to selflessness as is believable. Her father, an eminent professor and dear friend of Christopher's father, dies and leaves his family almost penniless. Valentine works for small pay as a domestic slavey so that her mother can keep at writing. She sleeps under the stairs because she will not sleep with the drunken cook. She sees depravity but remains untouched by it. She hates injustice and risks herself aiding a suffragette friend. Her courage contrasts visibly with the Englishmen, hangers-on of the *arrivistes,* some of them the great selfish themselves, who go about with sticks looking for suffragettes to attack.

She and her friend had merely disrupted a golf game, a purely masculine affair, as a symbol of protest. No other way could the women make it so clear that they were in earnest. This weekend pleasure and social climbing of Londoners coming down to the country already describes a decline. The county social hierarchy is openly threatened, but not by suffragettes. General Campion, along with his companions, is shocked at the loose and loud talk of the club's guests. As president he rebukes them for their manners, which had revealed in vulgar fashion their private affairs in a too public way.

The suffragette affair brought Christopher and Valentine together. She turns to him to defend her and she turns to a man. He trips the policeman who is pursuing her, and she escapes by hurdling the dyke. Afterwards, having persuaded the policeman to turn in a No Can Do—he was anxious to oblige—Christopher learns that she is a member of the community in high standing. For several years she has managed the constabulary's wives' and children's annual tea and sport. She is a good sport herself, holding various records in running and jumping. Her true kindness and interest act in the interest of others. This is the basic Christian and feudal virtue, especially when the act is sacrificial, as when she gives up, they both give up, their first try at concupiscence to bring home her drunken brother and put him to bed. The sacrifice is measured by Christopher's going out to France the next morning, perhaps to be killed. Lust would have ignored the brother.

It is obviously Valentine's nature to serve. The other property of her nature is innocence. It cannot be tarnished by the multiple sins and vices that perforce become the milieu of her movements. Although she is a witness, her idea of sex remains pure idea: men are brutes, insatiable, lustful. Her profound giving of herself to Christopher, without concupiscence, remains untouched. Nor does she understand her own sex too clearly, and this is because of her innocence. She has abetted Mrs. Macmaster in assignations, an abortion, cared for her in her afflictions imposed by the paranoid priest, served almost as a domestic, and was so treated, in the salon of marriage and ambition. The return was not what she had thought it, loving friendship, but the casual acceptance of her service as the due of patronage.

This continued until Edith Ethel (Mrs. Macmaster's given name) insulted Valentine's mother in her daughter's presence. Even then the daughter was slow to understand the cruel and brutal ego which her supposed friend was. There was a passage of frankness at which Edith Ethel reviled her with false accusations, one of which was that she had had a bastard by Christopher. In a subtle way the vilification described her own character and experience. Even under such an attack Valentine did not think of her own self-esteem. In charity she sought for the cause of this violent denigration of herself, decided it was from jealousy. Christopher had been Edith Ethel's lover, so little did she understand human behavior at this time. This allowed her at first to feel sympathetic towards it. She was thinking of what it was to love Christopher. When the crucial moment comes, however, and her own nuptials are threatened, she acts unhesitatingly to prevent interference. She resists her mother, thinking of her, and Sylvia thinking of herself. Christopher had wavered. This was the beginning of her acceptance of the realities of life, as opposed to her abstract ideas of war and men.

It is Armistice Day. The war is over and Christopher is back in London. She and he are trying at last to be alone together. Sylvia has stripped the flat of furniture, except for some books and a cabinet. In a sense this defines the two lovers' predicament; this emptiness of a dwelling place is society's abandonment of them. The ill will and bad luck which have afflicted Christopher at war follow him here. He has no money. They meet in parting as he rushes out to sell the cabinet to raise forty pounds. He tells her to wait. Her mother calls to dissuade her from their intention. Her mother talks with him to the same end. The Armistice intrudes and delays. The men who served him in the last months of war enter to celebrate. There is a frenzy of despair in the falsely festive mood from those released from the trenches, blemished, with marred bodies and minds. And with the ghosts of the dead misting their eyes.

At last she and he are alone together, abandoned to themselves. She wonders if he will murder her, and her courage is equal to the total risk. Of course there will be a murder: her virginity. This absolute innocence now will be lost in their predicament.

The greater part of the action of *Parade's End* takes place at war, with the exception of the last book. The action is largely scenic, long scenes inter-larded with panoramic summaries, just when such comment or reflection is needed to give greater substance to the dialogue. The scenes, discursive as they are, are among the best in the book. They give a rounded sense of the body of the world as it is afflicted by a power selfish and alien to Merrie England, or what is left of it. The confusion in the strategy of the Allied armies derives from a cynical political game, which threatens the French with a withdrawal of troops for another theater of war, towards English prestige in the Middle East after the disaster at Gallipoli: in other words, towards a selfish end. The French respond with railroad strikes to let the English know what to expect if they try to withdraw. The same ministers oppose a single command and so prolong the war and its casualties. This is the public evi-dence of the rule which Christopher protests.

The private intrudes its domestic wants into the military through Sylvia. She conceives of the front as one large bawdy house in which her husband, along with all soldiers, spends his time fornicating. She thinks he has brought Miss Wannop there: he has not written to Miss Wannop in two years. Sylvia becomes a disruptive core to military discipline. She descends upon General Campion's headquarters as if to a county weekend. She has come driven by a sexual obsession for her husband, with the constant aim to destroy or force him to return to her. It is not entirely sex. She has come to understand that sex is a part of the total man, which she finds her husband to be.

Being a whole person, Christopher has fixed beliefs and a large compre-hension of human affairs. Neither he nor Mark expected to inherit Groby. What transport came to mean to Mark, knowledge of English life and En-gland's role in the world was to Christopher. These were matters that those who ruled England should know. His private irony, or rather the irony of his role, showed how well he could serve, limited to small and scattered areas of performance. General Campion tells him he is no soldier. He does not look the part, but his commands are run in a military fashion, even to untangling general and specific confusions which attend this war. Trench warfare is like a siege that need have no end, because its rear is open to the transport of supplies and reenforcements. It is slaughter rather than war as professionally known. Crowding together underground, deep in mud, and the shattering sounds of artillery produce psychic shock on much of this civilian army. With patience and sympathy Christopher solaces and cares for these afflicted and still untangles contradictory orders, the perpetual waiting to move that allows the men to think of death—all of this to his exhaustion, which he cannot give in to.

There are two successions of scenes which reveal the disorder and its cause that are the heart of the action. The first results in the train of Sylvia's appearance. She brings with her the malignant gossip about her husband, and this damages military discipline. General Campion should have sent her home as soon as she arrived, but there were personal ties. She was thought to be his mistress; and so authority was corrupted at its source. The scandal she provoked involved her former lover, a general of police, and Christopher, representing two of General Campion's dicta, women and whiskey.

General Campion acts decisively and quickly. He sends Sylvia home and comes to Christopher, who is under arrest, to learn the truth. He is still offended by his godson's sloppy appearance, but he respects him and begins to see, or suspect, that he has been maligned. He comes dressed as if for parade. As a professional soldier he knows the value of regalia, medals, parades, shining boots and the wearing of a crop, his magical wand, to support men under fire. The colors to dress on in a charge sustained the effectiveness of close-order drill. When guns shot only a hundred yards, the line had to remain solid, closed up, to pass through that much lead. French warfare was another matter; nevertheless the General, slim and neat in all his formal dress, could be a symbol to citizen soldiers as he was to the profession. He signified not just a man fighting but a man in his office, where lay the command of life and death. His very neatness and frailty before the mud and filth in which his men struggled, their grossness, suggested a kind of purity of authority, impervious, stainless, and paternal. The French colonel often addresses his privates as mon enfant. He represents throughout, but particularly in this long scene, the feudal inheritance, the secular office which once was knighthood. In essence this is so. The changing conditions, which he will fight, have changed him. But, insofar as he can, so long as they do not interfere with discipline, he practices the cardinal virtues. He is just: he comes to Christopher to know the truth. He shows fortitude; he will resign and run for parliament, sacrifice his career for a greater purpose, if certain things take place. He is prudent, allowing neither scandal nor dereliction of duty to affect the efficiency of the army; nor will he disturb the balance prematurely. His temperance is less convincing.

If Christopher is an Anglican saint who practices the Christian disciplines to the point of martyrdom, or prolonged abuse, if martyr is too strong a word, then the meeting between the two joins the secular and the religious offices to withstand strained circumstances brought about by hostile forces. They see alike on public issues, the crucial one of the single command, even down to the same language; but Christopher will not discuss his private and familial affairs. His explanation of the personal attacks on his character he clarifies to the General's seeming satisfaction. The General had shown, as had his father and brother Mark, a too ready belief in his depravity.

At the end they part in understanding and agreement on General Campion's course of action, if certain things take place. The General makes it clear that the only decision open to him was to send his godson to the trenches, but with a promotion, to show that he was not to blame for the scandal. About to part, Christopher reminds the commander that officially he had come to inspect the kitchens. Sergeant-cook Case had been in the professional army with Campion. He remembers him as a good soldier broken to the ranks over desertion because of a woman. He came to live with her as his sister.

The inspection is referred to in religious terms. The kitchens are bright and clean, the cooks goggle-eyed at attention. The "cook-house was like a cathedral's nave, aisles being divided off by the pipes of stoves. . . . The building pauses, as when a godhead descends." With short steps he walks up to "a high priest who had a walrus mustache and, with seven medals on his Sunday tunic, gazed into eternity." The General taps a good conduct ribbon with the heel of his crop and asks, "How's your sister, Case?" Every ear is attuned to the question. We know at once here is a commander of an army that men will obey, even in his errors. To Tietjens "this was like the sudden bursting out of the regimental quick-step, as after a funeral with military honours the band and drums march away, back to barracks." It is the funeral of Tory England and Europe that he has in mind.

Christopher does not go to his death in his new command. The colonel has cracked up, and so Tietjens commands as second in command. The colonel and his major, McKechnie, have turned a public office into a private performance. They looked upon themselves and the regiment as pals. But they did not command pals, that is, friends, but a distinct part of an army. Their positions were official, not personal. Here again is the confusion between public and private. The soldiers recognize it when Christopher is actually in command. The pals had made no contact with the regiments to their regiment's flanks. Among other military needs Christopher attended to this. To act alone when you are a part of a whole is military disaster, which would have overtaken the regiment when the Germans made their push in the spring. This is a small incident and comments on the lack of a single command.

Self-interest against the common good, the confusion between public and private, operates throughout as the controlling impetus towards the undoing of civilized Europe. McKechnie, the nephew of Macmaster, feels that his uncle has betrayed him by not keeping him out of the army. He affronts Christopher with all the gossip Sylvia and London have spread against his character. He does this because his ambition is thwarted by having Christopher outrank him. Seeing everything from a personal interest, he can only believe that he is outranked because Sylvia is sleeping with Campion. To him there is no public good.

He took in college the Chancellor's prize in Latin, the very kind of thing Christopher refused in mathematics. To McKechnie, the prize is for use in the competition for place, his uncle's own kin. For Christopher Latin is a habit of reading. It is expected of one of his station in life. There is the memory, also, that Latin once was the universal tongue for the officialdom of Christian Europe. McKechnie forces Christopher, out of his by now paranoid necessity, to compete, to bet on who could write a Latin poem faster. It is easy for Christopher, but not until after the war does McKechnie come up with his. To insist upon it during the Armistice celebration shows him on the verge of cracking up. To reprove him, Christopher tells him to show it to Valentine, who is a fine Latin scholar. The point here is this: all the military who come to celebrate seek him out because he has been a good officer to all of them. Even the pals, ruined as they are, arrive. This is the final delay for the lovers' nuptials, which take place as the first three books end.

The Last Post was published after the first three books. Certain opinion holds that the three books were complete in themselves. It is true that parts of *The Last Post,* certain of Mark's long recollection, is repetitive and somewhat contradictory to the others, but without it the ending would have emphasized the union of the two lovers beyond the meaning of the whole. The lover gets his woman, but the obstructions remain. The bugle call, the last post, taps in this country, in this connection is the death salute. It is played badly by a younger brother of the bugler. The noise irritates Mark. The death salute should only be played ceremonially, on parade. The boggling of it, in a domestic situation, describes the nature of the death of England. An official sounding off has been reduced to the discords of an untrained child playing at home.

The end of England is the end of feudal Christendom, the war and Armistice being merely the final blow to what remained of its structure. Cast out from being a part of life in London, Christopher brings his mistress, now pregnant with his bastard, to the country. He has bought a cottage, a show-place of what an English cottage should be. There is some land to it, allowing for a garden, an orchard, and pasture, from which the household gets part of its living. Of the county, they instinctively return to the land. It is still there and some of its old structure remains, concretely shown in the persons of a fox-hunting landlord and his hind, who has been whipped and cast out for betraying his wife at a delicate time. He then serves Christopher in the old way. And so Christopher's household finds shelter and a living, but not quite. He is in the old furniture business, as partner with an American Jew. Macmaster, since it was fashionable at one time, took as a fad the pretended pleasure and understanding of old things. Unfortunately they were usually fakes, which Christopher pointed out. As for Christopher, the actual things were the furnishings of his life, by which he had always been surrounded. So it was that he could recognize and buy with authority.

This is the irony to which the action arrives: he must live, not by living among old and sound works of craftsmanship, but by selling them. His cottage was bought to live in, certainly, but not entirely. Being the fine example of a period, it displays his wares in a convincing setting. But the catch is, the furniture never remains the same. Valentine sorrows that her home is not her home. Will the marriage bed be taken from under them? Or more outrageous, will the cradle in which she rocks her child, her bastard child, be sold as she rocks him to sleep? And to make the situation unbearable, Sylvia has moved into the neighborhood to pursue her vendetta.

This revolves at its peak about the rental of Groby to a rich American woman, muchly set on sunshine and health. The woman has rented Groby, and she and Sylvia between them will cut down Groby Great Tree. But they have to get Mark's permission. The nephew, Christopher's son and heir to Groby, much against his will, at his mother's insistence, arrives with the woman. The renter is a preposterous caricature. She believes she is the spiritual descendant of the Maintenon, assured by the leader of a cult that the French king's mistress's soul has entered her body. The woman even as a caricature is hard to believe, except that she represents the kind of world that has triumphed: she is ignorant and believes that riches are all-powerful and give to the owner the sanction to instruct, judge any who enter her presence. The ignorance is so profound and dangerous it defines the last position of Puritanism. As the opposite to such a person there is Lady Tietjens (Mark, at his brother's suggestion, has married his mistress) with her firm grasp on the essentials of life.

The burden of the movement is Sylvia's descent upon her husband's ménage. Her curiosity about what goes on allows her to commit the vulgarity of talking to the wife of her husband's carpenter. "It had struck him [Mark] as curious taste to like to reveal to dependents—to reveal and to dwell upon, the fact that you were distasteful to your husband." She would like evidence that Tietjens, as the cottage is called, is a moral chancre in the countryside, to the end of having the local magnate, Lord Fittleworth, drive them away. She makes the error to impute to Mark's illness the sins of his youth. Lord Fittleworth is an old friend of Mark's, of the same cast and performance for the good of England, one of the old gentry, and a hard fox-hunting man.

Mark lies under a bush arbor with roof but no sides, day and night, near the cottage. He never speaks and is treated as if he has had a stroke. Whereas the post of observation of the first books might be called the Hovering Bard with its restricted omniscience, the view here is the Roving Narrator, the action opening in a stream of consciousness in Mark's mind, from which it roves to Lady Tietjens, and without a jar to Valentine and others. Mark never speaks after two happenings. The Armistice which ended the war without invading Germany he considered a betrayal of France by its Allies, a waste of his work in transport which stood for all the blood and treasure England had spent to no good end. He foresaw it had all to be done again. The other matter was his discovery that Christopher meant not to take any money or Groby from Mark or his father.

Refusing to speak put him in a perfect position for observation and reflection. His situation is almost godlike, observant but unreachable. He communicates by batting his eyes. It allows him, as he watches the action about him, to judge it but also to judge himself. Christopher with loving care had nursed him through pneumonia. They became very close. His younger brother showed his love but also that he would not forgive the betrayal. Mark's roommate, Ruggles, half Scottish and half Oriental, brought the gossip to Mark and he to his father. As the two were discussing the matter, Christopher entered the club. His father pretended not to see him. This was the betrayal, not to give his son a chance to know the rumor and hear him out. The shock of his brother's stubborn decision forced Mark for the first time to think beyond his selfish interests and pursuits. He did not blame Christopher. He came to accept that his own indifference had caused all the trouble that gathered about Christopher. And this allowed him to view with understanding and a Christian forbearance all the people who descended upon Tietjens.

Both younger sons, neither was prepared for the responsibility of Groby; yet both would inherit it. Mark refused to become attached to it. This was his way of not being denied what he could have loved. He withdrew into a life of his own from which grew an indifference to his kin and an ultimate betrayal of his brother. To repair somewhat the damage, he had moved into his brother's place to sustain him with his name and fortune.

Christopher as younger son, inheriting from his Southern mother a great capacity for love and being loved, not expecting to be master of Groby, looked upon the place with sentimentality. The proper sentiment of a landlord was to care for men and beasts, pay taxes, keep up his station, and hand it on unimpaired to the next generation. Christopher's sentimentality gave him the knowledge of old things from which he could make a living. It caused him, however, to attach his thoughts to a part, such as to Groby Great Tree or to the violation of renting Groby furnished to a stranger. The welfare of the whole estate should have been his prime consideration. He gave it to his son, falsely believing or forgetting that a man who cannot rule his family any better than he had, would be incapable of ruling an estate, which was a small community. He took to heart that his name was infamous. He forgot the ancestor who died in a whorehouse, another who, being drunk, killed himself falling from his horse. His father presumably committed suicide, unequal to disaster. (Mark in his reverie decided this was not so.) Christopher's sentimentality, a part of his sainthood, disallowed to himself the usual human frailties and vices, and this is the grimmest pride.

Sentimentality being more or less than the occasion requires misled Christopher in his basic responsibility to himself and his wife and child and his mistress. Making Valentine his mistress and giving her a bastard was not sentimentality, but to think that they could live as if legally married was a form of it. He seemed not to realize, he who pretended to all knowledge, almost supernatural guidance, the simple social misfortune he would bring upon his mistress and their child in gratifying the common needs of sexual congress. The bar sinister is nothing new in society. Armorial shields have its markings. That Christopher is willing to accept isolation from his kind is one thing, but what of the child? And what of the neglect of his legitimate son? Under his care would young Michael-Mark have said that Marxian Communism is the thing, a contradiction both to his religion and his responsibility as a landlord? Surely as he grew, the heir to Groby needed his father's counsel.

It seems, in a way, that Christopher was bitten by the snake whose poison had entered the common bloodstream. Under the most adverse circumstances he performed his public service with efficiency and kindness. War's violence did not undo him. But domestically he allowed his private feelings to neglect his office as heir to Groby. He forgot Groby was a large estate which the landlord did not own in fee simple but ruled as trustee in his generation, to be cared for and passed on to the next trustee. He refused it as if it were money, for a personal reason, and he had good cause. Yet it showed him acting like those whom he considered the destroyers of Europe. Ashburnham committed suicide; Christopher withdrew from society. Ashburnham's act drove his beloved to madness; Tietjens's act revealed how far his idea of an Anglican saint failed to resist the archetypal betrayal, upon which depended the salvation of mankind.

But this is Mark's book. Christopher does not appear until the end. Mark's self-examination under the aspect of eternity removes the core of selfishness and returns him to his humanity. And this takes him to his childhood at Groby. At the age of twelve he shot under his grandfather's eye, a fluke shot, several birds at once. These were encased at Groby, and the children of the family referred to them as Mark's bag. This he considered to be his claim to immortality. He meant by this, I think, that the family is the one thing which lasts and by which you can be defined in your fulness of being. Sylvia confesses to him the abandonment of her persecution of his brother. She has had Groby Great Tree, symbol of the family, cut down; but she will not cause harm to Valentine's child, any woman's child, and with tears she lets it be known that what she wanted was to feel again the softness of a baby in her arms. This is the family definition, its fructification and continuance. She will divorce Christopher, and this means to Mark that his brother and Valentine can be married and bring up their child as legitimate issue of a marriage. He pities Sylvia and speaks, he who had not spoken— "You poor bitch, you poor bitch, the Riding has done it."

The riding is an administrative part of a Yorkshire county; it is a legal and social communion of families of all degrees, the earl, Fittleworth, his hind Gunning, the carpenter, all, in spite of change, tenacious in their habits. Lady Tietjens, Mark's wife, makes cider in a French way, and the carpenter's wife feels she is a threat to the countryside and ought to be arrested. The inherited way seems at the end of the story to be hard to abolish. In Mark's reverie: "Well, if Sylvia had come to that his, Mark's occupation, was gone. He would no longer have to go on willing against her; she would drop into the sea in the wake of their family vessel and be lost to view."

The night before, "a great night, with room enough for Heaven to be hidden there," all the animals in the county stampeded and broke through hedges, it was said, because of an earthquake only they could feel. Mark knows better. It was God walking on the firmament. From this mysterious response of animals to the land that sustains beast, flora, and human beings, the supernatural makes a fusion of lasting things. Man is not capable of resolving the complications he brings about. Even Sylvia before her decision feels through Father Consett that God is on the side of the family and the good, else how could his creatures persist, if the family is not there to bear the young. The end seems to promise a reprieve from suffering. Fittleworth arrives before Mark with Marie Léonie at his elbow and says "I've driven all these goats out of your hen roost. . . ." Cammie sends her dear love. As soon as he was well to bring her ladyship down. He reassures him about Sylvia's intentions. They could all be a happy family. Anything Cammie could do . . . . And because of Mark's unforgettable service to the country. . . . Marie Léonie sees his sweat. Fittleworth says joy never kills, but so long, old friend. It is not joy that kills him but his release from the family responsibility, which he has taken up, but with the Tietjens stubbornness, a little late.

Then Christopher is at the foot of his bed, face white, eyes stuck out, blue pebbles, with a piece of aromatic wood in his hand. He tells the tree is down, half the wall, Mark's bedroom is wrecked, his birds thrown on a rubble heap. Then Valentine, breathing hard as if from running, appears and tells him where he has left the prints, but mainly with a desperate reproof, how are they going to feed the child if he does things like that. "How are we ever to live?" Christopher heavily, because he is exhausted in body and mind, slowly turns his bicycle around.

"Now I must speak," Mark said to himself.
He said:
"Did ye ever hear tell o' t' Yorkshireman.
. . . On Mount Ara . . . Ara. . . ."

His tongue is thick and his mouth twisted. This is a family saying which she knows. A Yorkshireman speaks to Noah and says it will clear up, in spite of the water. And then he tells her to put her ear near his mouth. He whispers an old song his nurse sang: " 'Twas the mid o' the night and the barnies grat/And the mither beneath the mauld heard that." "Never," he says, "thou let thy barnie weep for thy sharp tongue to thy goodman. . . . A good man!" He asks her to hold his hand, and quickly dies. Valentine tells the doctor it is too bad it could not have been his wife. "But she did not need them [his last words] as much as I."

The four books close on this. Pomp and circumstance, the confusion and sorrows of the world, family pride—all is reduced to the simple language common to all, a nurse's admonition, of bearing and forbearing for family amity and the love for the child, the inheritor of life.

HOWARD NEMEROV
Remembering Ford Madox Ford and
Parade's End

Beginning with two young men before The War,
Young men 'of the English public official class'
'In the perfectly appointed railway carriage'—
Lord Russell would say, a couple of worlds away
As usual, that he pitied his children
Because nobody born since Nineteen-Twelve
Could have known a moment's happiness; nobody,
He meant, save of the middle class and up,
Like your two young men, Macmaster starting out
On the social and sexual climb and Tietjens
The yeoman at statistics and sufferings—
Beginning your four gospels about a world
Threatened by nothing more than suffragettes,
As outward and as *there* as it had been
For Jane and George but showing its omens forth
In clerical madness, fog, and a fatal smash
Between the automobile and the horse;
Progressing as it had to do into mud and death
With but one memory of Bemerton's parish priest:—
    Sweet day, so cool, so calm, so bright,
    The bridall of the earth and skie—
And back to London in hysterical victory,
The adjutant's cry across the square: "There will be
No more parades;" and thence to England's remains,
The winding down in one poor dying mind
Not even the hero's, the great house sold away
And the great tree cut down—dear God, dear Ford,
It's like that earlier English myth of how
Before the Tudors it was all roast beef

And wassail ale and the Yule log and the boar's head
In hand bear I; yet we, who did the next
Big one entailed upon us at Versailles,
Read you and believe your word. They were,
As we are, a sorry lot; you made them good.

EDWARD KRICKEL
Lord Plushbottom in the Service of the Kingdom:
Ford as Editor

Everybody who knew Ford attested to his inveterate role-playing—H. G. Wells, Edward and David Garnett, Douglas Goldring, Violet Hunt, Ezra Pound, Richard Aldington, D. H. Lawrence, Stella Bowen, Ernest Hemingway, Robert McAlmon, and Robert Lowell, to mention the better-known ones. To many, he was offensive, a figure of ridicule. Robert McAlmon said he was a mythomaniac who looked like Lord Plushbottom in the funny papers, and Hemingway depicted him as a buffoon in *A Moveable Feast.* Yet most would have agreed with Lawrence's words: "Hueffer . . . was very kind to me, and was the first man I ever met who had a real and a true feeling for literature."[1] Ford's encouragement of young writers of genius and superior talent is one of the more attractive parts of the literary legend of the twentieth century. His grandfather had told him: "Beggar yourself rather than refuse assistance to any one whose genius you think shows promise of being greater than your own."[2] Perhaps it was in following this advice that he was, as Pound said, the best literary editor England ever had, though the attitudes toward the man colored the reputation of all his work, including the *English Review* and the *Transatlantic Review.* We have no trouble accepting Ford as a genius whose career touched much of the best literature in our century. Anything he did is of interest and worth. The reviews are of a piece with his other work in having the same large aims and many of the same qualities, including faults, in the details of the accomplishment. Ford's reviews have been well studied from several points of view by Douglas Goldring, who participated in one of them, by Frank MacShane, by Bernard J. Poli, and by Arthur Mizener. In the absence of new facts, I accept theirs, if

[1]*Phoenix* (New York: Viking, 1936), p. 253.
[2]*Memories and Impressions* (New York: Harper, 1911), p. 219.

not always their interpretations of them; but there is little point in repeating them in detail here. Ford's own versions appear in *Return to Yesterday* and *It Was the Nightingale.*

What Ford did, he told stories about, sometimes deliberately evasive ones for reasons we know (and for reasons we do not), and usually told them again and again, with no two versions identical and some contradictory. His friends did the same thing both with events and with his stories. At least he had a theory, which one must take as one can, for his reminiscences (he sometimes called them novels): "I don't really deal in facts; I have for facts a most profound contempt. I try to give you what I see to be the spirit of an age, of a town, of a movement. This cannot be done with facts."[3] Poli spoke the truth when he said these lines apply to Ford's editorship of the *Transatlantic Review* (and why not the *English* too?) as well as to his biography; "it is a spirit one has to catch; the facts are hardly relevant."[4]

Pound, who knew Ford well, said he was "almost an halluciné."[5] But most of Ford's anecdotes about himself were deftly sliced and pricked by his peculiar "Fordian irony," for which I have no technical name, but in which are an awareness and a self-mockery, and also in which what is said is meant not quite as stated—though it might be true; yet at the same time it is riddled with the awareness that his claim is too high. He would prefer that we make it for him, so he could deny it, including the component of truth in it, which is assuredly there. Richard Aldington took a tolerant view of Ford's tale to his father about meeting Byron and said there was probably "an authentic tradition which Ford over-dramatized in his devotion to artistic form."[6] The bearing of all this is the multiple awareness Ford held in regard to his work, his exploits, and his tales about them. The paradigm of his career holds true for his experiences as editor, and there is a consistency that never wavers, is never confused in the time shifts, the *progressions d'effets,* and the rest of it which he applied to his life no less than to his work. This consistency may be called a vision, a belief, a faith in regard to the value, the necessity even, of fine writing to a civilization. Without it, there was no civilization, he felt, and in the nationalized, industrialized, and commercialized world he lived in —that we still live in—literature was less and less efficacious, more and more needed.

One recurrent figure is that of "the only perfect republic and the only permanent kingdom. . . . The Kingdom of the Arts has many subjects who

---

[3]Ibid., p. xviii.

[4]*Ford Madox Ford and the "Transatlantic Review"* (Syracuse: Syracuse University Press, 1967), p. 144.

[5]In *Ford Madox Ford: The Critical Heritage,* ed. Frank MacShane (London: Routledge and Kegan Paul, 1972), p. 216.

[6]*Life for Life's Sake* (New York: Viking, 1941), p. 151.

have never employed for expression the permanancies of paper, canvas, stone or cat gut, reed and brass."[7] Further, "wherever there were creative thinkers was my country. A country without artists in words, in colours, in stone, in instrumental sounds—such a country would be forever an Enemy Nation. On the other hand every artist of whatever race was my fellow countryman—and the compatriot of every other artist."[8] In writing of the Pre-Raphaelite Brotherhood, he used the image of the Round Table for the same thing. Subtract everything annoying about Ford—his vanity, his self-delusions, his pomposity, his mythomania, his impracticality, his sometimes disastrous affairs with women—and what remains is a loyal citizen of the Kingdom of the Arts, not least in the literary journals he edited. His worth may be indicated by MacShane's remark that the *English Review* was "one of the most extraordinary literary magazines ever to be published in England."[9] The *Transatlantic* may be somewhat less, but it is in the same company.

The *English Review* was founded by Ford (then Hueffer) and Arthur Marwood who initially put up £500 apiece and lost in the end £2800 and £2200, respectively. The first issue was in December 1908; Ford's last editorial in February 1910. Goldring said the thirteenth issue was the last one over which Ford had full control; the January and February 1910 issues are relatively weak. Money ran out, and the review was sold twice in efforts to save it. The second buyer, financier and munitions maker Sir Alfred Mond, did save it, but not for Ford, who was replaced as editor by Austin Harrison. The literary quality, being of no interest to the new proprietors, declined rapidly. Legend and Ford upon occasion have it that the magazine commenced because Thomas Hardy was unable to publish "A Sunday Morning Tragedy" in any of the established journals. Ford's devotion to literature was such that the story is possible, though he and Wells had discussed the idea of a jointly edited journal as early as January 1908, and Wells had withdrawn. When actually issued, it was a monthly of approximately two hundred pages. Duckworth, Edward Garnett's company, distributed it. Editorial offices were upstairs at 84 Holland Park Avenue, which was also the editor's residence; downstairs was a fishmonger's and poulterer's shop. Soon the address became a literary center for the leading writers of the day. Violet Hunt gives the most vivid description of the establishment in *I Have This to Say,* but like Ford her fidelity is to impression rather than fact. Goldring was Ford's editorial assistant, who came in at night after he finished another editorial job. No more than a thousand copies a month were ever distributed. The editor's name never appeared as such in the magazine.

The first issue opened with Hardy's sexually frank poem, followed by

[7]*It Was the Nightingale* (Philadelphia: Lippincott, 1933), p. 5.
[8]Ibid., p. 74.
[9]"The *English Review,*" *South Atlantic Quarterly* 60 (1961): 311.

Henry James's "The Jolly Corner," Joseph Conrad's "Some Reminiscences," John Galsworthy's "A Fisher of Men," W. H. Hudson's "Stonehenge," and a translation by Constance Garnett of Tolstoi's "The Raid." The next seventy-four pages consisted of the first three chapters of Wells's *Tono-Bungay,* and the last forty pages included Ford's unsigned editorial, pieces by R. B. Cunninghame Graham and W. H. Davies, and also the first part of Arthur Marwood's "A Complete Actuarial Scheme for Insuring John Doe against All the Vicissitudes of Life." Last came two book reviews, one of them a review of Anatole France's *L'Ile des Pingouins* by Conrad. (Pound responded to the Marwood piece; insofar as it took him to the economics of Major Douglas, it may have been the first step down the trail that ended in Saint Elizabeth's.)

The editor kept up the quality in subsequent issues, which contained Arnold Bennett's "The Matador of the Five Towns" and his own novel *A Call,* subtitled "A Tale of Passion." Other contributors were Walter de la Mare, H. M. Tomlinson, E. M. Forster, William Butler Yeats, and Pound. When it came to recognizing new talent, Ford was very nearly infallible. Examples, about which cluster a number of anecdotes and reminiscences, are Lawrence, Wyndham Lewis, and Norman Douglas. Also, there were articles and poems in German and French, by Gerhart Hauptmann, Anatole France, and Emile Verhaeren, as well as translations from the Russian of Dostoevsky and Tchekhov. Older writers were nicely balanced with new, the respectable with the as yet undetermined. American President Taft answered critics of the Panama Canal in Ford's pages. Although featuring literature, the review is more nearly comparable to Rémy de Gourmont's *Mercure de France* than to any English journal. The *Athenaeum, Cornhill, Blackwood's,* the *Contemporary Review*—these are from another era, whereas Ford's is very much of our time. What Poli said of the *Transatlantic* also fits the *English Review*—it may still be read with pleasure.

In after years, Ford expressed satisfaction at what he had achieved: "It had got together, at any rate between its covers, a great number—the majority of the distinguished writers of imaginative literature in England of that day and a great many foreign writers of distinction."[10] At the time, however, his last editorial was bitter, and in it he acknowledged a major failure. "On the Objection to the Critical Attitude" spoke of "several purposes, chief among these being the furthering of a certain school of Literature and a certain tone of Thought." Furthering the school of literature was a brilliant success, the source of his later satisfaction. The "certain tone of Thought" was "the critical attitude," and that was another matter. Goldring remembered how Ford and Conrad talked far into the night about "just what the *Review* was intended to accomplish for English letters. It was going to set up

[10]*Return to Yesterday* (New York: Liveright, 1932), p. 394.

and maintain a standard of literary values, of *real* writing." With the perspective of twenty years, Goldring insisted that "no one can now say that it failed in its purpose."[11] At the time, however, Ford did say it: "no sane man would set out to make the ass play upon a musical instrument, the respectable journal to take broad views, or the hyena distil eau-de-cologne. For these things upon the face of them would be insane enterprises. So with the *English Review,* which set out to enjoin upon the Englishman a critical attitude." He added, "nothing will make the Englishman adopt a critical attitude."[12]

Ford's editorials were collected in the 1911 book *The Critical Attitude* with a few other pieces from the same time. The major aim of promoting "the critical attitude"—lifelong with Ford—had no doubt many strands. One of them was probably Henry James, whom Ford admired only a little short of adulation and who was something of a mentor to the writers the editor sought to promote. Using the example of the French stage (and possibly the emotions of his own unsuccessful efforts on the English stage), James regretted the absence of a critical attitude in English-speaking audiences. He noticed a tendency to *ad hominem* criticism, "for confounding the object . . . with the subject, for losing sight of the idea in the vehicle, of the intention in the fable," which amounted to judging art on improper terms, for example morally rather than aesthetically.[13]

MacShane makes the point that the germ of Ford's idea for the review was stated in a letter to Edward Garnett in which he proposed a series of critical monographs, similar to those on painters in the Duckworth Library of Art, "conceived on the broad general idea of making manifest, to the most unintelligent, how great writers *get their effects,*" as opposed to the moralistic approach then current or equally bad mechanical descriptions of poems. (The art series contained by 1906 Garnett's study of Hogarth and Ford's studies of Rossetti, Holbein, and the Pre-Raphaelite Brotherhood.) Although Garnett was unsympathetic to this rallying cry from the Kingdom of the Arts, Ford saw him as a potential center around which a small group could form and become the start of a new approach to literature, a movement. He vowed to "make a desperate attempt in other quarters."[14] A letter to Galsworthy in 1900 shows Ford very much aware of how writers get their effects when he analyzed his friend's novel *Villa Rubein.*[15]

Other likely influences were the collaboration with Conrad, those long and excited discussions of the purposes and ways of art still green in the

---

[11]In *Ford Madox Ford: The Critical Heritage,* p. 207.

[12]*English Review* 4 (1910): 531–32.

[13]*The Scenic Art,* ed. Allan Wade (New Brunswick: Rutgers University Press, 1948), p. 269.

[14]*Letters of Ford Madox Ford,* ed. Richard M. Ludwig (Princeton: Princeton University Press, 1965), pp. 15–16. The letter is dated by the editor a questionable 1901; owner David Garnett had earlier dated it for MacShane 1901–4.

[15]Ibid., pp. 10–14.

younger man's memory. Also, Ford had recently become involved in literary discussion groups. One, anonymous, included Edward Thomas, Edward Garnett, Hudson, Galsworthy, and Conrad, while The Square Club had G. K. Chesterton, Hilaire Belloc, John Masefield, Galsworthy, de la Mare, Maurice Baring, and Pound. For a much wider audience, Ford wrote a series of fourteen weekly newspaper articles in 1907 for the *Daily Mail,* and a second series of twenty-seven in 1907–8 for the *Tribune.*

Probably a stronger strand and a different kind from all of these came from his family heritage, notably his father, Francis Hueffer, and his grandfather, Ford Madox Brown—both examples of failed brilliance. Surrounding them were the Pre-Raphaelite connections by marriage, sympathies, and long-time association. (The details are sufficiently well known not to need repeating.) The father had founded two journals in England, one to promote Schopenhauer and the other Wagner; both had failed. (He had written a successful music column for the *Times.*) Even Ford's Rossetti cousins in their childhood had put out a small anarchist paper from a press in their basement. All were examples of idealistic but ineffectual journals.

Ford was even closer to his grandfather and had been his official biographer. In *The Pre-Raphaelite Brotherhood* he saw the painter as "a singularly luckless man, whether as an artist or an individual," who "never did justice to the remarkable powers that were his; it is certain that he never received any material reward at all commensurate with his diligence, his sincerity, or his very considerable achievements."[16] The actual Brotherhood in the middle of the century he had supported but not joined. The group owed its power to their union, whereas possibly greater artists working alone had done "nothing to change the public mode of approach" to art. They supported each other unselfishly with patrons and purchasers in a "fine record of generosity."[17] Their significance was that they "attacked an accepted idea, and to do that has always been to show oneself an enemy of the people."[18] Finally, the group came "as near to being a union for the furtherance of the technical qualities of any art—as near to such a union as seems to be possible in this country where social conditions make it almost impossible for any man to take a whole-hearted interest in the practices of his art and in nothing else."[19] With this knowledge and for all his role-playing, I do not see how Ford could have entered the lists blindly, astride the *English Review,* wearing the colors of Art.

Another one of Ford's ideas for the review—one that caused him much trouble and misunderstanding with some of his contributors—was surely

[16](London: Duckworth, 1906), pp. 12–15.
[17]Ibid., p. 75.
[18]Ibid., p. 110.
[19]Ibid., p. 173.

influenced by this source. A letter to Garnett of 17 October 1908 shows that he anticipated trouble from his "profit-sharing idea." Garnett had advised against it. On the grounds that only his intimate friends were involved, Ford said he had offered "£2 a thousand words" or "a sporting risk which might be estimated as a two to one chance against you, as a shareholder." He guaranteed privately but not legally to pay, if they insisted, any of their claims so that they would bear no liability. He admitted that "inevitably there will be quarrels and recriminations, but in some things I am an idealist and my ideal is to run the 'English Review' as far as possible as a socialistic undertaking. The kicks I shall get will be the price I shall pay for indulging my idealism and these I trust to bear with equanimity."[20] Evidently, he expected his contributors to be citizens of the Kingdom, and not all were. This scheme, plus the problems with Wells and Bennett, may have been the source of rumors that some contributors were never paid. Edgar Jepson recalled, however, that he and every other contributor he knew had been paid.[21] Today, what Garnett regarded as foolish and Arthur Mizener as one more instance of Ford's ineptitude in practical matters remains ambiguous. One is confident, however, that Madox Brown would have approved.

When Ford founded the *Transatlantic Review* in Paris in 1923, after consultation with Pound, James Joyce, and John Quinn, it was with money put up by himself and Quinn. The American lawyer gave one thousand dollars in the fall of 1923 and promised that much more—only that much more. On 11 January 1924 he sent another five hundred dollars from New York and cabled his last pledge of five hundred dollars on 27 January. After his meeting with Ford he noted, "He is an honest man and an able man and I hope he will succeed."[22] If Quinn had not been in ill health from which he died in July, the fortunes of the review might have gone otherwise. Ford put up the same amount of money, though his and all other versions are somewhat speculative, as no records have survived, perhaps were not kept in any formal way.

The world of postwar Paris was considerably different from prewar London. Ford was in a different country, with a different audience in mind, and a different set of potential contributors. By now literary magazines abounded, especially noncommercial "little" ones. These often were willfully limited in their appeal. It is hard not to think, however, that the *English Review* had pointed a general direction for them to go. As several had connections with Pound, many of Ford's ideas were no doubt alive. Missing

[20]*Letters,* pp. 27–28.

[21]*Memories of an Edwardian* (London: Martin Secker, 1937), p. 149.

[22]B. L. Reid, *The Man from New York: John Quinn and His Friends* (New York: Oxford University Press, 1968), p. 615.

were his unerring eye for quality and the allegiance to the Kingdom of the Arts and its civilities. If temporal conditions were different in the brave new postwar world, that ideal was not, at least to Ford. Certainly absent from the journals were his humor, geniality, and broad tolerance.

The *Dial* in America was in its best years. In seeking the best among international contributions, in seeking a critical standard (perhaps more narrowly urging a critical method), in what it sought, combatted, and published, the *Dial* was very much in the spirit of Ford's *English Review*—except that it was not much interested in new and unknown writers. For the literary part of it, *Dial* and *Transatlantic* had some of the same contributors—for example, William Carlos Williams, Glenway Wescott, Paul Morand—but most of Ford's came from the amorphous international group in Paris, the noisiest of which were Americans. Harriet Monroe's *Poetry*, Margaret Anderson's *Little Review*, and T. S. Eliot's *Criterion*, all journals Ford had contributed to directly, were doing valuable service for the cause Ford believed in; they were helping to create and carry on different aspects of modern literature. The *Transatlantic Review* could hardly seem as good as the *English* because it functioned in a context of values Ford had pioneered.

Although the war had impelled the new onto the scene, with its various confusions, including for many a blanket repudiation of the old, Ford was too wise, too loyal to repudiate the old uncritically. It may have seemed to him, as Poli put it, that "the time had come for a review that would be neither too sedate nor too defiantly iconoclastic, which allied the combined virtues of the original and the genuine, in other words, a new *English Review*."[23] Pound's version is different in emphasis. It was very much at his urging that Ford became an editor one more time. Could he resist an appeal "to preserve the vestiges [of civilization] or start a new one anywhere that one could"? And so, "against the non-experimental caution of *Dial* and *Criterion*, the *transatlantic review* was founded."[24] For the rest of it, the course of Ford's second review went very much like the first.

The first issue was dated January 1924; the last, December of the same year. Arrangements had been made for simultaneous distribution in Paris, London, and New York. Basil Bunting and Ernest Hemingway were to become Ford's assistants. Poli estimates that five thousand copies of each issue were printed. Poli's *Ford Madox Ford and the "Transatlantic Review"* gives a detailed account of its founding, difficult course, and unhappy demise. One disagrees with his interpretations only here and there—and at one's peril. Ford's own accounts are as usual fascinating, though not for their fidelity to fact. Poli sees a kind of war that went on most of the time between Ford, his values and judgments, and the young American expatriates with

[23]Poli, *Ford*, p. 10.
[24]Quoted in ibid., p. 10.

their brash rebelliousness, the most notable being Hemingway. Ford supported them in a way they never supported him. A letter to Gertrude Stein, dated 18 September 1924, says, with Fordian irony, "I really exist as a sort of half-way house between nonpublishable youth and real money—a sort of green baize swing door that every one kicks both on entering and on leaving."[25] Poli concludes that "the *Transatlantic Review* was not a new *English Review* after all, and, at any rate, it was not the review Ford had wanted to edit. Had Thomas Hardy, Joseph Conrad, and H. G. Wells agreed to become regular contributors, and had T. S. Eliot given Ford more than a patronizing blessing. . . . the review might have been a financial success. . . ."[26] None of these things happened.

Evidently, the review was never legally established under French law. The *gérant,* or financially responsible person, was required by law to be a French citizen. This one was listed as E. Séménoff, supposedly a White Russian. Poli is uncertain whether he ever existed or not. Ford's secretary, who like most of the personnel was suggested by Pound, remembered "discussing with a couple of French lawyers the ways in which we might be breaking corporation laws. . . ."[27]

The first issue followed the format of the *English Review,* for which Ford had claimed, in MacShane's words, "a carefully worked-out plan, whose purpose was to introduce a slight shock to the reader's interest so that he would approach each piece in a fresh frame of mind."[28] Poems from E. E. Cummings, A. E. Coppard, and Pound led off. What came next remains somewhat ambiguous, at least in intent. *The Nature of a Crime* was one of the lesser collaborations between Ford and Conrad when it had first been printed in the *English Review* under the pseudonym of Baron Ignatz von Aschendrof. Then came the first of a series of the memories of Luke Ionides, a Greek octogenarian who had known the friends of Ford's grandfather. (Pound liked the pieces, but Hemingway dropped them when he got the chance, as he also dropped the serial installment of *Some Do Not. . . .* Ford restored both, the latter to be resumed if there was sufficient demand. There was, he said—two requests.) Daniel Chaucer, a pseudonym Ford had used to publish two novels in 1911 and 1912, followed with the first of a series called "Stock Taking: Towards a Re-Valuation of English Literature." On the old theme, "Working Out a Standard," he asked, "Why has Anglo-Saxondom no literary standards?" and immediately added, "For we have none!" From the servant of the Kingdom, the familiar question, the familiar plaint.

If there is anything new, it is the passing shot at the modern business/technological barbarians that were already figuring in his Tietjens story and

[25]*Letters,* p. 162.
[26]Poli, *Ford,* p. 164.
[27]Ibid., p. 29.
[28]"The *English Review,*" p. 314.

would become rampant in the last decade of his life in *Provence* and *Great Trade Route,* as well as in the world: "And who of us is not the poorer by the crass ignorance or the direct dishonesty of Men of Business whom we have trusted in our negotiations and who, again have all their lives been too busy to acquire from works of the imagination either an ordinary knowledge of life or the commonest standards of morality and civilization?"[29]

"Chroniques" had London, Paris, and New York letters, one by the editor. "Communications" had letters from Hardy (actually Mrs. Hardy in her husband's name), Wells, Eliot, and Conrad. Ford had wanted contributions and got letters. The first issue was 120 pages. Subsequent issues added music, art, and literary supplements. In the last category was "Fragments from Work in Progress or to Appear," in which did appear an episode of what became in time *Finnegans Wake.* Joyce liked Ford's phrase "Work in Progress" so well he adopted it until his book was named upon completion. Several notes came out over pseudonyms the editor had used in the earlier journal.

Among the contributors to the twelve issues were Lincoln Steffens, Djuna Barnes, Mary Butts, F. S. Flint, H. D., Selma Lagerlof, Dorothy Richardson, John Dos Passos, Glenway Wescott, Hemingway, William Carlos Williams, Tristan Tzara, Paul Valéry, Philippe Soupault, Jean Rhys, Robert McAlmon, George Antheil, and others old and new, French, English, and American. Ford also serialized Gertrude Stein's *The Making of Americans,* written nearly twenty years earlier. His own contributions, *Some Do Not . . .* and his reminiscences of Conrad, were at least as good as any of the others.

There are tales attached to nearly every contribution, certainly to each issue, and Poli tells most of them. The usual financial difficulties came about and the sale to new proprietors. Ford lost his own (and Stella Bowen's) money, but his last editorial spoke of resuming publication as soon as finances could be worked out.

Why did the *Transatlantic Review* fail? For that matter, why did the *English Review* fail? By now, Ford's editorial brilliance is acknowledged without a cavil. Poli and Mizener tend to take the practical viewpoint that Ford's efforts were futile because they did not succeed. Mizener does, however, also say: "Apart from the unfortunate effects of Ford's loyalty to the great tradition and his evident pleasure in advertising his own share in creating it, his selection is critically admirable. Its fatal defect is its superiority to the power politics of publishing, its confident disregard of the prejudices of both writers and readers."[30]

Why did the reviews fail? In both, Ford placated no one, offended many,

[29] *Transatlantic Review* 1 (January 1924): 75.
[30] *The Saddest Story: A Biography of Ford Madox Ford* (New York: World Publishing Co., 1971), p. 332.

especially by keeping his standards high, his loyalties true. In both, he had, in his way, attacked established ideas (morality in the one and rebellion in the other as aesthetic and cultural standards). How far can Aldington's explanation be extended? The failure of the *English Review,* he said, must be blamed on "the stupidity and genuine hatred of culture displayed by our countrymen."[31]

All the evidence against Ford as a poor businessman makes him not any less true to the cause he served, the Kingdom of the Arts, which was also the cause of civilization. It does not show his ideal unworthy of his devotion, nor in any degree disprove his belief that the modern world needs literature and the arts to civilize it. The lack of business sense—if that is what it amounted to—may have been unfortunate, first of all to Ford himself, but look at what the world lost. Poli observes, "His disappointment was bitter and his financial loss heavy, but he bore his misfortune with equanimity as part of his responsibility in the defense of art and literature."[32] He cannot have been as surprised as he may have been in 1909 to discover how few people would buy an education for half a crown a month.[33] Three months before he died in 1939, he was trying to start the *Transatlantic Review* up again. Like his grandfather Brown, Ford came under the iron law of the world's wages for his services to the Kingdom. Robert Lowell put it precisely: Ford was "a kind man," and he "died in want."[34]

[31]Quoted by MacShane, "The *English Review,*" p. 319.
[32]Poli, *Ford,* p. 163.
[33]Ibid., p. 6.
[34]See "Ford Madox Ford," in *Life Studies* (New York: Farrar, Straus and Giroux, 1959), pp. 49–50.

C. H. SISSON
The Critical Attitude

It is very hard to gauge the weight of Ford's contribution to the critical mind of the twentieth century. There is a sense in which this cannot be done by looking at his critical books; it can certainly not be done by looking at those alone. For readers who, over the years, have browsed over any considerable number of his seventy or eighty volumes—novels, reminiscences, even the verse, read in the light of the prose—there remains an atmosphere, an uncertainty in the air, which is really the critical benefit received. An uncertainty, because about Ford's most swashbuckling assertions there is something tentative. He claims no more than that unprovable verity, "absolute truth as to the impression." And to hell with the facts! It is the stance of a man who knows he cannot rely on his memory and yet is aware of a level of apprehension which takes account of past experience as it were tacitly and gives him an assurance among his uncertainties. The surface of Ford's writing is wavering, offering sometimes sharp, definite sketches and assertions which are inconsistent with one another; yet one carries away from his work the impression of a truthfulness hidden somewhere in this unstable mass. At the center, wherever it is, there is a passionate and painful care for good writing. In a sense the seriousness of Ford is in his technical interests, which a few times in his life met a subject worthy of them, but often did not. The absorption in technical matters gives even his lesser work a solid point of reference against which the uncertainties show up. To his explicitly critical writing it gives an interest which might easily be missed by anyone who does not suspect the recesses behind his casual and often throw-away tone.

One cannot point to a single, decisive critical work which will at once put the reader in a position to see what benefits are to be had from this author —as one might, for example, at once give someone a notion of the technical wisdom of Pound by directing him to *How to Read* or the *ABC of Reading.* There are explicit critical remarks here and there even in the novels—as for example that clear piece of self-reflection in *Some Do Not . . .* to the effect that "abstractions of failing attention to the outside world are not necessarily in a writer signs of failing, as a writer." In the volumes of reminiscences critical preoccupations are never far away, and when Ford talks about Conrad or Christina Rossetti it is with an eye to their idiosyncrasies as writers. When he conjures up some incident in the brief history of the *English Review,* as it concerned him—say his worries about how much a thousand H. G. Wells thought he should get—it is not merely to replay a scene he might have managed better but to insist on the essential function he saw for that periodical during his brilliant editorship. The huge survey called *The March of Literature, From Confucius to Modern Times* (1939)[1] is tendentious and partial even beyond the necessities of the impossible task set by the publisher. "It is the book of an old man mad about writing," he says, dating his "dedication which is also an introduction" from Olivet College, Michigan. It is "an attempt to introduce a larger and always larger number of my fellows to taste the pleasure that comes from always more and more reading"; and Ford is very near the things for which he cared most in the world when he adds: "I must write only about the books I have found attractive; because if I lead my reader up to unreadable books I risk giving him a distaste for all literature." That Ford never did. Where he exaggerates, even where he denounces, it is in the course of making some enthusiastic recommendation which will assuredly not disappoint the reader, if he follows it up. Ford has no critical theory which will not give way before the work itself, to which he brings you, and where he leaves you. So in *The English Novel* (1930): "I may be perfectly wrong in almost everything I say. If I am, that is the end of me." He really does concede that possibility, in the face of his own assertions. "But the great use of technical discussion," he goes on, "is that it arouses interest in the subject discussed." That is Ford's object as a critical writer.

If there is one book in which, more directly than in another, Ford attempted to indicate his radical concerns, it is *The Critical Attitude* (1911), which consists of articles contributed originally to the *English Review.* Even here it would be wrong to look for anything like an unimpugnable statement, for it is of the very nature of Ford's method that what is offered is provisional —"suggestions not dictates," as he says in *The English Novel.* Ford does not want to be taken too literally, but he does want to be taken seriously; "in perusing this sort of book the reader must be prepared to do a great deal of the work himself—within his own mind." There is no place for the goggle-eyed student with a notebook, who expects to be told all. The most that can happen, Ford knows, is that the reader is put on the way to seeing for himself —much or little according to the acuteness of his vision. In *The Critical Attitude* the chapters, the pages within a single chapter, are of very unequal value, but they all help to cajole the reader to take up the desiderated attitude

[1]All quotations are from the British edition (London: George Allen and Unwin, Ltd., 1939).

and, with his mind thus primed, to go into the world of literature and look for himself.

The object of the *English Review*, Ford says in his introductory chapter, was "to make the Englishman think"—a state of affairs so unusual, he thought, that the very name of the magazine was "a contradiction in terms." "No sane man would set out to make the ass play a musical instrument, the respectable journal take broad views, or the hyena distil eau-de-cologne." No less hopeless was it "to enjoin upon the Englishman a critical attitude." With these characteristic flourishes Ford set out to do just that, and it may be said that in England at least—let us not venture any opinions about *elsewhere*—the task always remains to be done afresh, for no sooner has a critical mind persuaded a number of people that some widely diffused view does not contain the whole truth about a problem than most of the number settle down to be as smugly convinced that the new aspect of the subject just brought to light is all there is to be said about it—lethargy being the condition to which most of us long most of the time to return. Ford pursues his subject with characteristic enthusiasm, for the moment looking neither to right nor to left. "But for his own particular islands, where Luther and Darwin like consecutive steam-rollers extinguished by force of criticism all possibility of simple faith, the Englishman has founded three hundred and forty-seven religions. And each of these religions is founded upon a compromise. That is what the Englishman does to, that is how he floors—the critical attitude." The point is that, rather than make a clean break, the Englishman will move to an intermediate position. To arrive at this conclusion, which is itself merely a stage in the formulation on which Ford is bent in the introductory chapter, "The Objection to the Critical Attitude," he flounders through several assertions more or less approximate and misleading, so that the reader who is unwary may imbibe as he goes half-suggestions that Luther was particularly influential in England—which is not true—and that in the rest of the western world "revealed religion" survived with less damage—which is hardly true either.

The next stage of the formulation is to maintain that "logic is inhuman and that criticism, though it need not be actively inhumane, must, as far as possible, put aside sympathy with human weaknesses." The illustration Ford gives is again one-eyed, boisterous and could not for a moment withstand the force of the sort of criticism he himself proposes. He takes his stand on logic but uses it sparingly himself. "If it be granted . . . that a Poor Law system based on kindness will be a drag upon a State whose necessity is economic strength, it would become the duty of the critic of that state to put forward some such theories" as, for example, that "the consumptive or the sufferer from any permanent infectious disease, or the man or woman who is temperamentally unlucky" should "be either executed or relegated to pest colonies."

The reader of Ford will never for a moment suspect Ford of recommending such measures—what he says is part of the pattern of hyperbole and other misrepresentation which will leave the reader convinced at least of the instability of opinion. It is boisterous—and tender-hearted rather than otherwise, even sentimental. Ford is too lazy to work out the practical complications of any social action; it is not his function. He is—again misleadingly—merely using his half-baked illustrations to make the point that the critic who acts as devil's advocate, and explains "remorselessly" the logical consequences of current muddles, in the face of widespread sentiment and prejudice, is performing a valuable function "in the republic." There is little enough that is remorseless, logical, or even tolerably coherent about the process by which he gets there.

What Ford is recommending is not so much criticism as a lack of dogmatism, and not so much lack of dogmatism as a humane recognition of variety, the endless qualification of one view by another. And beyond that, what he is contending for is the variety of impressions, and the validity of such variety in the arts. Of a critical statement of his own he will say: "That is perhaps an exaggerated statement of the case, but it is for a moment worth setting down." That is his provisional way of proceeding, setting things down not as a final truth, but as an interpretation that may help in the formation of a final picture, which however never quite becomes clear. It is with the lighting up of the *reader's* picture that he is concerned, so that he always hangs back a little doubtfully from the final effect of what he has said. It can be argued that such reticence is pusillanimous, that the "serious" critic stakes his reputation on the truth of what he propounds. There is, however, a good deal of civilized wisdom in Ford's hesitations. The justification is in the closeness of the method to that of the artist himself: "the province of the imaginative writer is by exaggeration due to his particular character—by characteristic exaggeration, in fact—precisely to awaken thought." The sort of "thought" Ford stands for is the recognition of differences, and there is a humane basis for this inasmuch as the differences rest on differences of impression, which turn on the variety of character in the observers. Ford adopts without question the romantic and post-romantic language of art as "self-expression." One may regard that phrase with scepticism, but one can hardly dissent from the critical distinction he thus introduces: the artist's "expression of himself exactly as he is, not as he would like other people to think him, the expression of his view of life as it is, not as he would like it to be."

The theme is developed, as always with Ford, in a manner which does not win our assent as being entirely true—which is evidently untrue, at some points—but which assists our discrimination if we understand it with reservations. He is speaking of the value "to the Republic"—by which he means the *res publica* of wherever it may be—of "a really fine renderer of the life of his day." He has in mind the writer in general and the novelist in particular. "Whatever his private views may be," he says, "we have no means of knowing them. He himself will never appear, he will never button-hole us, he will never moralize. He may be a Republican, he may be an Anglican; he may be a believer in autocracy. But he will never, by the fifth of an inch, drag round his pictures of life so as to make it appear that, if the social state were what he desires it to be, all would be well with the world." We do in fact gather a good deal of Ford's "private views" from the manner in which he presents his fictions, as we do with other writers. The point nonetheless is critically valid. It must be taken to mean that the writer's impressions, however superficially disjointed, must be presented as they are, and that this material, which has not been rounded into a theory, is the fundamental matter of art, to which all considered opinions are secondary if not irrelevant. So much for what is sometimes referred to as "commitment" in the artist. "In England, the country of Accepted Ideas, the novelist who is intent merely to register—to *constater*—is almost unknown. Yet it is England probably that most needs him, for England, less than any of the nations, knows where it stands, or to what it tends." Looking back seventy years to the time when those words were written, and in the light of the intervening history, they can hardly be faulted. It is moreover still true that England is a place of Accepted Ideas. What is accepted has changed, but the sloth is the same. It is for other countries to determine whether they enjoy a great superiority in these matters.

Ford believed that the artist who recorded the life of his day was adding to knowledge, and if he denounced the accumulation of facts it was merely because the knowledge he was interested in was—he thought—of a refinement which made it dependent on the observer who could set down his own impressions as only the artist can. Truthfulness to the impression was overridden by a "flaccid and self-satisfied commercialism"—and if that was true in 1908-11 it is overwhelmingly so now. Against this Goliath he saw as the only defense a possible "sober, sincere, conscientious and scientific body of artists, crystallizing, as it were, modern life in its several aspects." That such a body "would be commercially unsuccessful is to be premised and to be neglected." That it would be out of favor with the various political groups is also to be premised, for it would claim a political importance of its own. "Indeed," he says,

> the appearance of any great body of imaginative effort, the work of authors single-minded in the effort to express, and felicitous and successful in expressing, in imaginative terms, all that is most real, most permanent or most fugitive in the life around us—the appearance of such a great body of imaginative effort would have to be regarded as an event

at least as important in the history of a civilisation as the recording of the will of a sovereign people with regard to some policy of exclusion, of admission, of humanitarianism, of pugnacity. For the record of events, assimilated by the human mind today, moulds the event of tomorrow, and the nearer the record comes to registering the truth, and to so rendering it as to make it assimilable by the human apprehension, the more near it comes to being an historic event itself.

WILLIAM H. PRITCHARD
Fabulous Monster: Ford as Literary Critic

The first half of my title is taken from *Some Do Not . . .* at a moment when, in exasperated wonder, Sylvia Tietjens so characterizes her husband. But the epithet has general application to Ford and serves as a suitably outrageous label for his critical audacities and heresies. Only when we respond to these pronouncements about other books, writers, and literary forms, with a blend of annoyed disbelief and fascinated attention akin to Sylvia's toward Christopher Tietjens, are we seeing Ford for the truly interesting critic he seems to me to be. More than forty years ago, in reviewing his late book of literary portraits, *Mightier than the Sword* (published in this country and hereafter referred to as *Portraits from Life*), V. S. Pritchett caught exactly the right note when he described the reader of Ford as "stunned by a volubility in which every word strikes and starts a dozen echoes which distract him to further effects like a boy shouting under an archway." "One sways giddily but enlivened," declared Pritchett, insisting that Ford was "before everything else a personality."

Yet not everyone has been charmed by this personality, at least as it showed itself in the reminiscences *(Memories and Impressions, Thus to Revisit, Return to Yesterday, It Was the Nightingale),* the appreciations of Henry James and Joseph Conrad or the ones in *Portraits from Life*—to say nothing of the more ostensibly critical works *(The Critical Attitude, The English Novel, The March of Literature).* Early along, the unsigned *Times Literary Supplement* (22 January 1914) reviewer called Ford's "critical study" of James a "farrago of irrelevancies" and "a piece of trifling" and declared that the author "has a knowing and jaunty style of humour, very freely indulged, which suggests the essay of the schoolboy who discovers, as he approaches his subject, that he has nothing to say." Twenty-five years later, at the time of Ford's death, Edward Sackville-West was appalled by the just-published *The March of Literature* (1938),[1] an "intimidating tome" which would join the books that "lie

---

[1] All quotations are from the American edition, *The March of Literature, From Confucius' Day to Our Own* (New York: The Dial Press, 1938).

about the centuries like so many puddings gone cold and uneatable," and which was filled with "the promulgation of enormous and parodoxical views" Sackville-West found absurd. In more friendly and understanding terms, Ford's admirers have apologized for his famous inaccuracies (those tall stories which, repeated, grew ever taller) or warned us not to expect the sort of reasonable behavior one gets from other modern critics of literature. Frank MacShane, to whose labors on Ford's behalf we are all in debt, distinguishes Ford's achievement in criticism from that of a John Crowe Ransom or F. R. Leavis by saying about Ford that, "as an enthusiastic pioneer, he was incapable of the balanced and scholarly assessment that characterizes their criticism."[2] The "old man mad about writing" label which Ford hung around his own neck in prefacing *The March of Literature* could in these terms be a gloss on his whole career as a critic: young or old, he was in more than one sense mad about writing, an enthusiast whose opinions evidently need to be taken with a grain of salt, a bit of discounting.

This way lies patronizing, and although MacShane does not indulge in it, his distinguishing of Ford from presumably more responsible critics like Ransom and Leavis seems to me a step in the wrong direction. We need not argue the ways in which "balanced and scholarly assessment" will not quite do as a description of either the moral fierceness or the homely elegance with which Leavis and Ransom, respectively, conducted their critical operations. But it may be suggested that as the major nonacademic modern critics of literature recede into historical distance, their interest for us (in a phrase Leavis hated) becomes increasingly a purely literary one. No longer reading them for news about their responses to a particular writer, or for their theoretical or ideational content (which we are already familiar with, having read them more than once), they appear and appeal to us in ways which more closely resemble those of a good poem or piece of fiction: it is their powers of imaginative creation, rather than the demonstrated truth of their judgments, which engage us.

Already it may sound suspiciously as if I am setting up a special plea for Ford by converting his critical irresponsibilities and excesses into exactly the things to be delighted in. This may be true, but if so, I am convinced that other significant modern artist-critics must be similarly apologized for: I am thinking, for example, of such names as Ezra Pound, T. S. Eliot, D. H. Lawrence, Wyndham Lewis; or on a lesser scale, of William Carlos Williams, Robert Graves, or Ransom. (Even though he wrote no literature himself, Leavis belongs with this group.) Not all artist-critics fall inevitably into this category of "strong" practitioners: one might adduce E. M. Forster, or

[2]Frank MacShane, Introduction to *Critical Writings of Ford Madox Ford* (Lincoln, Neb.: University of Nebraska Press, 1964).

Virginia Woolf, or W. H. Auden, or (perhaps) George Orwell, or Edwin Muir, as appreciators with more catholic tastes, reviewers who give at least the illusion of seeing the object as in itself it really is, rather than pressing the claims of some special vision. Strictly on the basis of Ford's last book, the immensely long *The March of Literature* with its patient surveying of the whole of literature "from Confucius' day to our own," Ford himself bids to be included in the second, "catholic" category. But for more compelling reasons I propose to assign him a place in the first one, in the ranks of Pound, Eliot, Lawrence, and Lewis.

Of this intimidating foursome, the only one really to speak well of Ford was Pound, who prefaced his 1914 review of Ford's *Collected Poems* by calling him the lonely possessor of a "vision of perfection."[3] "Mr. Hueffer" had committed the crime of insisting on the importance of "good writing as opposed to the opalescent word, the rhetorical tradition." He, like Pound, admired Stendhal, Flaubert, Maupassant, and Turgenev; therefore it was inevitable that he be disliked or ignored in London—"a capital where everybody's Aunt Lucy or Uncle George has written something or other, and where the victory of any standard save that of mediocrity would at once banish so many nice people from the temple of immortality." Pound has only to say these words to establish, as it were, Hueffer as the best critic in England, "one might say the only critic of any importance."

It may be observed that one sure way to make yourself more disliked was to be extravagantly praised by Pound: at the same moment Pound was booming Ford, Robert Frost was successfully detaching himself from the ministrations of his "discoverer"; Lewis was to do the same during the 1920s. Ford never did so; indeed the connection with Pound was used explicitly, in Sackville-West's attack on *The March of Literature,* as indicative of Ford's unsoundness as a critic. But it is important to insist that, while we recognize the strong affiliations between Pound and Ford, particularly in their dislike for the "rhetorical tradition" as it showed itself most egregiously in the Victorian novel, and in their compensatory adulation of Continental practitioners of "the prose tradition"—that we not rest content with Pound's way of praising Ford. There is no more inert idea to be discovered in 1980 than that Stendhal's sentences or *Trois Contes* are healthy prose, whereas the periods of Thackeray, Dickens, or George Eliot are diseased, at least "opalescent." If we are to appreciate Ford rightly, in other words, it will not do to abstract the doctrine and pin it on the wall for daily contemplation and agreement.

[3]"Mr. Hueffer and the Prose Tradition in Verse," *Poetry* (June 1914). Both Lawrence and Lewis were interested in Ford while he was publishing them in the *English Review,* but became markedly less so after he ceased to edit the magazine. Eliot never appears to have taken an interest in Ford.

Another way of putting this caveat is to say that however much we respect Pound for his perspicuity about Ford's intelligence as a critic, there was some sentimentality about the portrait, since Pound presumed to make the fabulous monster nothing more or less than a lonely, sane, accurate perceiver of "good writing." Pound says winningly that if a man insists on talking about perfection he is going to get himself "disliked." What in retrospect we see about Ford is the extent of his alienation from what, in words from *Hugh Selwyn Mauberley,* "the age demanded." In the tenth section of *Mauberley* we are introduced to what is usually understood as a Ford-like artist who has, as Pound is about to do, forsaken the "march of events" and what passes for culture in postwar London:

> Beneath the sagging roof
> The stylist has taken shelter
> Unpaid, uncelebrated,
> At last from the world's welter
>
> Nature receives him. . . .

And we are told that "the soil meets his distress." Of course one should not hold Ford responsible for Pound's heroic or mock-heroic portrait of him. But in setting himself off from what the age demanded, Ford accentuated and cultivated certain human tendencies that had been there all along, were there in his *English Review* essays and in his book on James. The remainder of this essay will direct attention to some ways and instances in which those human tendencies expressed themselves in his literary criticism.

It may help to compare Ford's critical personality with those of two other English writers whose procedures seem to me interestingly related to his. The first is Coleridge, a writer whom he barely mentions ever and then only to be named (in *The March of Literature*) as one more English Romantic. Yet is it not possible to think of Ford's critical writings as constituting one book, a biographia literaria which must be perused with excitement, exasperation, and disbelief; a book in which marvelous bits of humor and irony alternate with self-defensive exculpations, boastings, "digressions" which set out to undermine the notion of a digression; in which lists of bad names and good ones are called up for catcalls or admiration; in which the general sense is that there are no limits to what may be expressed? As Randall Jarrell once said of William Carlos Williams, "Why he'd say anything, so long as he believed it was true." With both Coleridge and Ford, the reader often gasps at something he cannot quite believe they believe to be true; yet they have said it. And in both men there is a feckless quality, something in the voice, in their stance toward "the world's welter" which makes us want to sympathize with their "distress," be indignant that their visions of perfection are so little appreciated and valued by all those other successful authors and worldlings.

One thinks of chapter 10, the long, thirty-six page ramble from the *Biographia* in which Coleridge sets forth "a chapter of digression and anecdotes" as an "interlude" preceding his tackling the question of The Imagination. Yet even as he postpones explicit dealings with his subject, his style demonstrates the very "poetic power" in question. Ford's indirections similarly work to coax a reader into acceptance of his truth about the only way to write a novel; as when, in *It Was the Nightingale* (part 2, chapter 2), we hear successively about (among other things) classical scholarship, Harold Monro's villa in the south of France in 1922, memories of World War I and Ford's loss of memory, the death of Proust, the death of Marie Lloyd, Joyce and the Parisian literary scene, a Pen Club lunch in Paris, the possibility that Ford might have become a French writer, Pound, memories of Arthur Marwood (the prototype of Christopher Tietjens), how Ford found the "Sylvia" of *Some Do Not . . .*—and then at last the following "truth":

> The first thing that you have to consider when writing a novel is your story, and then your story—and then your story! If you wish to feel more dignified you may call it your "subject." Once started it must go on and on to its appointed end. . . .
>
> Of course you must appear to digress. That is the art which conceals your Art. The reader, you should premise, will always dislike you and your book. He thinks it an insult that you should dare to claim his attention, and if lunch is announced or there is a ring at the bell he will welcome the digression. So you will provide him with what he thinks are digressions—with occasions on which he thinks he may let his attention relax. . . . But really not one single thread must ever escape your purpose.

What is promised or recommended here has already been performed in the previous pages of the chapter.

Ford may also be usefully compared with his contemporary Wyndham Lewis, whose earliest story he published in the *English Review* but from whom he seems thereafter to have kept his distance. And no wonder, if Lewis acted at all as Ford says he did. In "There Were Strong Men," the final chapter in *Portraits from Life,* Lewis catches Ford "mysteriously by the elbow" (a nice way to catch anybody) and delivers, inaudibly, the message that the elder novelist is a has-been: "You and Mr. Conrad and Mr. James and all those old fellows are done. . . . Exploded! . . . *"Fichus!* . . . Vieux jeu! . . . No good! . . . Finished!" These old fellows take infinite pains to convince their readers that they are undergoing a character's experience; they are after something called "verisimilitude," but, Lewis continues, that is not what people want any more:

They want to be amused. . . . By brilliant fellows like me. Letting off brilliant fireworks. Performing like dogs on tight ropes. Something to give them the idea they're at a performance. You fellows try to efface yourselves; to make people think that there isn't any author and that they're living in the affairs you . . . adumbrate, isn't that your word? . . . What balls! What rot! . . . What's the good of being an author if you don't get any fun out of it?

There may be some truth in the distinction this amusingly rendered scene makes between Ford's careful novelistic composition and Lewis's breezier efforts, although *Tarr* and Lewis's other early fictions look to have been carefully enough composed. But Ford's critical procedures do not provide analogous examples of self-effacement and can be assimilated more naturally to the performance-showman aspect Lewis speaks up for here. The brilliance, the fireworks, the amusement—indeed the self-justifications, the boastings, the "digressions"—are at least as much to be found in Ford's pages as in those of his ill-mannered younger contemporary. Neither of them puts much stock in disinterested, rational, "objective" critical demonstration.

It should also be noted that, in a most important sense, neither Ford nor Lewis was English. Lewis, born on his mysterious American father's yacht anchored off the coast of Nova Scotia, then brought up by his mother and sent to Rugby as if he belonged there, left England at the beginning of this century and, in Paris and in Germany, formed a self that was to dedicate much of its future energies to castigating English humor and the English inability ever to know what Art was really about. Ford, born in Surrey and brought up in Hammersmith, liked to think of himself as not to the English manner born. Decades later in *It Was the Nightingale,* he delightedly spun out a moment when, lying on a grassy knoll in Kent and talking to E. V. Lucas, the editor of Charles Lamb, he abuses Lucas for admiring that "buttered-toast-clean-fire-clear-hearth-spirit-of-the-game-beery-gin-sodden sentimentalism." The invective continues for the next two pages, while Lucas takes long puffs at his pipe and eventually, when challenged to say why Ford *cannot* appreciate Charles Lamb, gently tells Ford that he is "not really English." Ford protests, producing his credentials as a cricketeer and golfer, a public schoolboy who takes cold baths in the morning, knows about sheep and flower-gardening, has a tailor in Sackville Street and a barber in Bond Street. Why then is he not English?

Mr. Lucas said with dejection:
"Because you do not appreciate. . . ." He paused; I supplied: "Charles Lamb?"
He said:
"No, I am thinking." He added *"Punch."*

That did it, and Ford admits defeat; indeed, the reader feels, Ford is quite pleased by the whole exchange and wouldn't have missed giving us the full benefit of it.

Thus it was that in *The Critical Attitude* (1911), made up of pieces published in the *English Review,* he insisted that the title of the magazine was a contradiction in terms. Nothing on earth will make an Englishman adopt the critical attitude, since nothing can make him review his thoughts: "The ass draws his cart; the respectable journal preaches respectability; the hyena disinters and crunches his bones; but the Englishman—he is just God's Englishman." This complaint picks up where Matthew Arnold had left off, but in an airier, more disillusioned way. Englishmen go around grunting that they "like" something or do not like something; whereas the critic, Ford says, exists to point out defects, the defects of a writer's qualities, or to point out the difference between "commercial books" and works of art. To behave in this way is supposedly to make unpopular, un-English discriminations against, in Pound's colorful words, "everybody's Aunt Lucy and Uncle George."

Ten years later in *Thus to Revisit* (1921), when Ford considered the contemporary prose writers ("Prosateurs" is his chapter title) who wrote not commercial books but authentic works of art, he confronted the English reader, not surprisingly, with somebody more pure, more purely The Writer, than they had imagined could exist. Conrad and James are supreme novelists, but their effects can be studied, their books admiringly understood for the craftsmanship with which "life" is rendered. But "the unapproached master of the English tongue," the writer whose gift is "immense, tranquil or consummate," is . . . W. H. Hudson! Not only, like Conrad and James, has Hudson escaped the perils of being English, and thus of having been influenced by such monuments as the Authorized Version, or Shakespeare, or Sir Thomas Browne, but—unlike Conrad and James—his effects are unaccountable. " 'You can't tell how this fellow gets his effects!' " Ford quotes Conrad, who said as he looked up one day from reading *Green Mansions:* " 'he writes as the grass grows. The Good God makes it be there. And that is all there is to it!' " This state of affairs Ford finds irresistible. In Hudson he can admire a writer who, like Ford's beloved Turgenev (the "beautiful genius" as he too often refers to him), is quite beyond critical categories of description. After devoting a full-length chapter in *Portraits from Life* to Turgenev, he finally admits that he has said nothing about the "technique" employed by this writer, because it cannot be done: "No one can say anything valid about the technique of Turgenev. It consisted probably in nothing but politeness . . . in consideration for his readers." Remarks like these would of course put out of business all those aspiring to write books on Turgenev's art, since its technique is really all politeness and thus all really inexpressible. And it is exactly the sort of remark for which one reads Ford and which when encountered makes the reading worth the effort.

Hudson's effects are not in fact inexpressible; at least Ford is able to write vividly about them in *Thus to Revisit* by comparing him to Turgenev, who watched humanity as raptly, with as much engrossment as Hudson gave to nature. It is "that note—of the enamoured, of the rapt, watcher" which Ford rightly finds consummately there in Turgenev's "Byelshin Prairie" ("Bezhin Lea" or "Bezhin Meadow" as it is also called), and to express his impression of this note in Hudson's writing Ford has to write hard himself. He comments that in Hudson "the watcher disappears, becoming merely part of the surrounding atmosphere amidst which, with no self-consciousness, the men, the forests or the birds act and interact"; and he continues to render this "selflessness" in the following paragraph:

> It is no doubt this faculty that gives to Mr. Hudson's work the power to suggest vast, very tranquil space and a man absolutely at home in it, or motionless vegetation, a huge forest and a traveller who wishes to go nowhere, nor ever to reach the forest bounds. For you can suggest immensity in your rendering of the smallest of British birds if you know an immense deal about the bird itself; if you have watched innumerable similar birds, travelling over shires, countries, duchies, kingdoms, hemispheres—and always selflessly. So the rendering of one individual bird will connote to the mind of your reader—if you happen to be Mr. Hudson!—the great distances of country in which you have travelled in order that, having seen so many such birds, you may so perfectly describe this one. Great plains will rise up before your reader's mind: immensely high skies; distant blue ranges, woodlands a long way off. . . .[Pp. 71.]

The style here sounds as if Christopher Tietjens had added another feather to his cap, revealing himself to be a fine naturalist and splendid writer, along with his abilities as analyst of government financial figures and computer of the trajectory of golf balls. The paragraph breaks off perfectly with the expressive ellipsis (though often in Ford's writing the ellipsis feels merely habitual), inviting us now to contemplate for ourselves, and raptly, the "distant blue ranges, woodlands a long way off. . . ." What Ford does here, and at other good moments in his writing about another writer, is to imagine a richly responsive reader—more responsive perhaps than we are able to be when we put down Ford and pick up Hudson—as large and capacious in his sympathies as is presumably the writer who evokes them. This reader would be able fully to appreciate the immense consideration, the politeness being shown him by Turgenev; would be fully in tune with Hudson's expressive effects, though like Conrad he cannot describe how they come about. Ford is most irresistible as a critic when, rather than pointing out a writer's defects (as *The Critical Attitude* said the critic must do) he devotes his own verbal resources to imagining the virtues of those whom most he admires.[4]

One of the best recent critics of Ford's art, Samuel Hynes, has usefully noted the centrality of Romance to his subject's behavior in both his novels and his other prose works. Hynes suggests that we should read books like *Thus to Revisit* or the memoir of Conrad—and we can add *Portraits from Life,* even by extension *The English Novel* and *The March of Literature*—as "experience transformed by memory, idealized versions of people, books, places, conversations which never occurred but somehow should have." This is the method of Impressionism: in Hynes's formulation, "the method by which experience, transformed by romancing memory, may be rendered."[5] It was in part his possession of such a memory that must have caused Sylvia Tietjens to throw up her hands in dismay at the fabulous character she had married.

But Romance was also a habit of imagination Ford looked for, and often found, in the contemporaries he cared most about. In *Henry James* he calls *The Spoils of Poynton,* surprisingly, James's best novel, "a romance of English grab." *What Maisie Knew* and *The Turn of the Screw* are also romances: the former, "a romance of the English habit of trying to shift responsibility"; the latter, "a romance of the English habit of leaving young children to the care of improper maids and salacious ostlers" (a quite good description, that). In *Portraits from Life,* Hudson's *The Purple Land* is the "supreme—is the only— rendering of Romance in the English language." As for Conrad: *"The Secret Agent* is the romance of international communism . . . *The Arrow of Gold* is the romance of royalist machinations . . . *Under Western Eyes* is the romance of Russian-Swiss nihilism." Even when he does not use the term, one sees the concept behind his preference for certain books over other ones. He is much taken with Galsworthy's character and with that writer's admiration for Turgenev, but the only book of Galsworthy's Ford seems to admire is the early *Villa Rubein,* "a work of sunlit genius." After it, however, Galsworthy's humanitarianism got the better of him, and he wrote satirically pointed novels with Ideas in them. From Romance to Reform, one might put it. H. G. Wells is called a "lost leader" because he deserted the "glories" of works like *The Invisible Man* (and how right Ford is to admire that piece of fiction), "The Country of the Blind," and "The Time Machine," for novels with political and social purpose. He is eloquent in lamenting such desertion when he says at the end of the Wells portrait that "every real artist in words who deserts the occupation of pure imaginative writing to immerse himself

---

[4]A more recent instance of this encomiastic performance can be found impressively in Randall Jarrell's appreciations of Frost, Whitman, Ransom and many others.

[5]"Ford and the Spirit of Romance," in *Edwardian Occasions* (New York: Oxford University Press, 1972), p. 78.

in the Public Affairs that have ruined our world, takes away a little of our chance of coming alive through these lugubrious times." We remember that these words are uttered by the writer who spent much time in collaborating with Conrad on a novel eventually called *Romance,* a piece of "pure imaginative writing" if ever there was one. That book, at least to my eyes, is virtually unreadable; yet I never tire of listening to Ford talk about its composition. It is the romance of *Romance* that has remained.

Until the end of his life, Ford liked to pretend to himself and his readers that criticism was a calmly judicious activity—"not the warm expression of sentiment but the cool exposition of a man standing back and viewing with relatively cold eyes the object on which he is to descant." There was a part of him that remained Arnoldian and "objective" in his aims. Yet, as has been evident from my emphasis thus far, I do not think Ford succeeded very often in being this sort of critic; his descanting, whether in praise or in blame of the writer, is usually a good deal warmer in expression than his above definition of it leads one to expect. Take for example the following comparison of Donne with Herbert, from *The March of Literature.* The page is titled "Unhappy Donne," and Ford describes him as "a man who has seen into Hell and conceived of Heaven otherwise than on the smooth paths about the country vicarage's hedge"—which brings him to Herbert:

> Heaven forbid that one should seem to despise Bremerton and its parsonage. Herbert's vision of a perfected High Church Earth, near Salisbury Plain with its high elms and smooth pastures, and Love's table set is of a beauty and confidence that we could ill, indeed, do without.
>
> "You must sit down," says Love, "and taste my meat."
> So I did sit and eat.
>
> may well mark the final height to which devotional poetry may attain. But one has, if one lets oneself be fanciful, the image that round the vicarage hedge, mumbling a mildewed crust, stands hunched a great, hobo figure, the fruit of whose despairing meditations strike in English poetry a note that, lacking which, English poetry would have been something narrower, something merely regional with a tang at once of lavender and of the unimportant provincial. [P. 488.]

If one is Ford, one does indeed let oneself be fanciful, and the result is a memorable, fabulous construction: Donne the "great, hobo figure" standing outside the table where Herbert so shyly and successfully dines. As is often true in Ford's portraits, it verges on the sentimental but is saved from that by the vigorous originality of its language. It is typical of much that one encounters in *The March of Literature.*

When we come to a writer or book Ford really dislikes, he can be equally invigorating. "God forbid that I should say anything really condemnatory of any book by any brother-novelist alive or dead," he solemnly swears in *The*

English Novel before launching into a full-scale disparagement of Fielding, especially of *Tom Jones,* than which there are few books he more cordially dislikes:

> But as regards *Tom Jones* my personal dislike goes along with a certain cold-blooded critical condemnation. I dislike Tom Jones, the character, because he is a lewd, stupid, and treacherous phenomenon; I dislike Fielding, his chronicler, because he is a bad sort of hypocrite. Had Fielding been in the least genuine in his moral aspirations it is Blifil that he would have painted attractively and Jones who would have come to the electric chair as would have been the case had Jones lived today. [Pp. 98–99.]

Ford dislikes this "papier mâché figure" on which a morality "of the most leering and disastrous kind" is exercised; and "fellows like Fielding who pretend that if you are a gay drunkard, lecher, squanderer of your goods and fumbler in placket-holes you will eventually find a benevolent uncle . . . who will shower on you bags of tens of thousands of guineas . . . these fellows are danger to the body-politic and horribly bad constructors of plots" (pp. 99–100).

I think it undeniable that Fielding is made here to bear the brunt of Ford's personal experience that squandering and sexual imprudence lead to worldly success only in bad novels, bad because they are idealized versions of the world. When it came time, in *The March of Literature,* to take up Fielding again Ford accuses him of "smart-Aleckery," of engaging in verbal juggling or any trick which will delight a reader. At which point he introduces, this time anonymously, the Wyndham Lewis figure who presumably lectured Ford on how modern readers do not care about verisimilitude but want to be amused by showman-performers. This, Ford insists, is what Fielding himself might have said to Defoe, or Richardson, or even to Smollett. An interesting connection is thus made, not for the first time in his writing, between the desire to perform in a "brilliant" manner and a disregard for Jamesian-Conradian form. Fielding was, at least partly because of his self-indulgent penchant for display, a "horribly bad constructor of plots." (One would like, incidentally, to have had Ford's opinion of R. S. Crane's lengthy essay, "The Plot of Tom Jones.")

Ford's long-standing quarrel with English literature was that its most famous writers had too much personality and expressed that personality by imposing richly idealized versions of existence on the overwhelmed reader (he himself practiced, in his criticism, what he preached against). So "the novels of Dickens, Fielding, and Shakespeare are in form (leaving aside the question of texture) fairy tales for adults," and—snorts Ford, pulling himself up—"there are other occupations for grown men." Of significance here is the parenthetical "leaving aside" of something called "texture"; one may suppose that Ford was responsive enough to the poetry in Shakespeare, or the great feats of verbal play in Dickens's novels (if not in Fielding's) but that, or perhaps for that very reason, he insisted upon leaving them aside, speaking as if "form"—the telling of a story, the rendering of an affair—were what counted and what had been horribly mishandled in English novels written between Richardson and Conrad. One may also suppose that the reason (for all Pound's tributes to Ford as the man who *knew* about poetry, the "best critic in England," and so forth) his criticisms of poets remain less in the mind than do those he made of novelists is that modern poems do not render affairs but get their effects through "texture." When in *Thus to Revisit* he turns his attention to recent poets he has admired, we hear praise of Robert Bridges, Walter de la Mare, Christina Rossetti, and Robert Browning for "the simplicity of the wording; the beauty of the image evoked by the contact of simple words one beside the other." As criticism this appears to be itself rather simple, not to say simplistic; one has the sense that Ford is being protective of the species, and certainly he was shockingly easy on some of his own poetic compositions he allowed into print.

Ford's attitude toward novels was fully formed by the time he came to edit the *English Review,* and its most essential opposition was between the writer who merely renders, or presents, or records, and the one who shows off or writes fairy tales for adults. In *The Critical Attitude* he uses Trollope and George Eliot to show why "we can take up with interest 'Barchester Towers' in a hand from which nervelessly 'Adam Bede' drops." It is not that Trollope cares about "form," but that

> never taking himself with any attempt at solemnity [he] was content to observe and to record, whereas George Eliot, as if she had converted herself into another Frankenstein, went on evolving obedient monsters who had no particular relation to the life of her time—monsters who seduced or admitted themselves to be seduced, who murdered their infants or quoted the Scriptures just as it suited the creator of their ordered world. [Pp. 56–57.]

Did Ford ever read *Middlemarch?* He certainly never modified his opinion of George Eliot, and she appears in *The March of Literature* only as one of the writers he is forced to skip over. But Trollope returns, indeed plays a rather large role in Ford's discussion of nineteenth-century English fiction, since he belongs to a select group, including Jane Austen and Stendhal, of "realist" or "psychological" writers from whom almost all the rest of the century's novels fall away.

The marvelous thing about Jane Austen, Ford says, is that she is "free from the moral preoccupation that troubles the waters of that greatest of her predecessors, Richardson himself." She does not "denounce or scarify the vices of her age" (nor did the author of *The Good Soldier*) but freely indulges her "continually lambent humor that plays around the weaknesses" of her characters. You have to go back to Chaucer, Ford declares, to find her spiritual counterpart; and even Henry James is heavy-handed in comparison. Jane Austen then is admired for what she managed to avoid; for the way, in T. S. Eliot's phrase about James, her mind was fine enough to be unviolated by the "ideas," the idealizations which, say, George Eliot was prey to. Here one wants to interrupt again and ask whether Ford had read *Mansfield Park*. The answer is yes, since he cites as evidence of Jane Austen's "vividness" her rendering of the theatrical rehearsal at the moment when, unannounced, Sir Thomas Bertram returns. But Ford was a good deal less interested in the moral judgments about people and society that *Mansfield Park* and Jane Austen endorse than in the purer activity of listening to the "gossip," or watching Mrs. Norris prepare conserves, or hearing about the troubles of a neighbor.

It takes a pure imagination to be interested in gossip. Trollope then is admired as "The Master Snooper," the writer who heard more gossip than anybody else, and—having the advantage over Jane Austen of being male—more varied gossip. "Trollope, in short, was an English gentleman" (unlike Thackeray, who sympathized with rogues, and Balzac, who was French) who was somehow, always, just *there*—not "sympathizing," not idealizing, not denouncing:

> When he entered a club smoking-room no one interrupted his conversation; when he shot no one noticed his bag. Synge said that, occasionally, when Trollope was the last member in the lounge of the old club, St. George's Hanover Square, the waiters would put out the lights, not noticing Trollope, although he was under their eyes. [P. 788.]

Here, spectacularly compressed, are the essential elements of Ford's criticism: the honoring of the recorder, the man who was there just to render an affair; the romancing memory that delights in impossible moments when life is no different from art; and the appeal to the charm of that rendered moment as substantiating the judgment, rather than making an argued case from a careful inspection of the novels themselves. (Ford admits that *Framley Parsonage* is his special favorite among English novels—and that is about the limit of his reference to Trollope's books.)

But the fine thing about *The March of Literature,* and the reason it seems to me far and away the best book of criticism Ford ever wrote (although *Portraits from Life,* the series of memoir-essays, is also fine) is that it shows him not wholly at the mercy of the system of judgments and preferences on which his own creative and critical work was based. In other words, there are surprises, moments when, as in Matthew Arnold's phrase about Edmund Burke, "the return of the mind upon itself" is suddenly and gratifyingly evident. For example, when Dickens is brought on stage in the long last chapter of *March,* it will only be, we expect, to be pilloried once more as an exaggerator, a writer of fairy tales for adults. Ford begins that way, complaining that, like Thackeray and Fielding, he "overdraws" characters, especially his hypocrites, who may be roared over but not believed in. Whereas Jane Austen, Stendhal, and Trollope were masters of getting into their books "that element of queer surprise" which only the impressionist rendering of life can achieve, in Dickens there is no surprise—"you always know beforehand what Dickens will do with the fraudulent lawyer on whose machinations hang the fate of a score of his characters."

So it is surprising that a couple of pages on we learn that, at least on the basis of one book, Dickens can be called "the founder of the realistic school." That book is *Great Expectations,* which Ford dares to compare with the *Divine Comedy. Great Expectations,* and Thackeray's *Vanity Fair* as well, "are infused with the views of life of two writers who have lived intensely, who have known real griefs, and who have attained to wealth and celebrity at the expense of disillusionment." Dickens's novel qualifies for those reasons as an authentic realist product, unconcerned with propounding a moral solution to some evil; it (and *Vanity Fair,* though less convincingly it seems to me) "are simply records, that from time to time attain to the height of renderings, of life transfused by the light of their writers' temperaments as modified by their vicissitudes." Ford continues to reflect upon *Great Expectations* as "a product of world-weariness . . . of a passionate world-weariness with humanity and humanity's contrivance." He imagines Dickens as an early Christian eremite "who should have grown weary with denunciation and was set merely on depicting the failure of his efforts." It is a "muted book," inspired by "deep pessimism"—

> And the hero is no hero and the heroine, no heroine; and their hands are not in the end united; and there is no immense fortune to be chanted over by a triumphant Wilkins Micawber; no conspiracy to be unveiled; no great wrong righted. The book is, in fact, one of those works, rare in the English language, that can be read by a grown man without the feeling that he is condoning childishness and would be better employed over John Stuart Mill. [P. 822.]

It is as if, during this discussion, Ford has truly discovered Dickens, and not just the untypical *Great Expectations.* For there is also expressed a more general admiration, forced out of him as it were against his Pre-Raphaelite upbringing. Dickens overwrites and exaggerates and is full of "literary faults": "on the other hand, like Homer, he gave us a world and his writings were epic because his illustrations of life came from the commonest popular object. And it is impossible not to see that Anglo-Saxondom was a better double world because he had passed through it." A better world, even if the writer was no master of *progression d'effets.* At such a moment it becomes possible, without sentimentality, to speak of the humanity of Ford's imagination. Then he leaves Dickens simply by quoting without further comment what he calls the "masterly opening" of *Great Expectations,* its early paragraphs, the marsh country, the churchyard, the convict. After such writing the only place to go, so it seems, is to Flaubert, James, Conrad; though it is fascinating that *The March of Literature* ends with, of all people, Dostoyevsky —"the greatest single influence on the world of today"—who is too large for any terms the critic can bring to him (Ford must have been a bit tired at this point, having achieved page 850). The concluding bow to Dostoyevsky is another instance of his willingness to honor giants who break the rules of critical systems and snatch whatever is there beyond the reach of art.

With these impressions of Ford's practice as a literary critic I have tried to suggest the kind of reader he was as well as the kind of reader we must be to appreciate him. I am convinced at any rate that his criticism is filled with lovely moments, *mots justes* (but not too juste, as R. L. Stevenson was guilty of) and equally just paragraphs of creative characterization that bring their subject—Donne, Hudson, Charles Lamb, Dickens—to new life. I am convinced also that the familiarity of reencountering these characterizations breeds the opposite of contempt; that Ford's effects gain in subtlety and in the pleasure they provide upon rereading—though in as unsystematic a way as were his own operations conducted. "One of the scamps of literature" as Graham Greene called him in his obituary review, he was also surely a scamp of a literary critic. But perhaps also, as Greene insisted, a great writer; and if not quite that, one whose like we shall not come across again in this century, let alone beyond.

ALISON LURIE
Ford Madox Ford's Fairy Tales for Children

Once upon a time there was a large, pink-faced, yellow-haired man who liked to tell stories: adventure and spy thrillers, historical dramas, romances and fantasies, war stories and personal reminiscence, social comedy and social criticism—and four juveniles, one of which at least deserves a place among the classics of English children's literature.

Ford Madox Ford's books for children were written at the start of his career, before the economic pressure on him had become heavy, when his energy was high and his creative impulse strong. His first two fairy tales appeared when he was only eighteen, and the third before his twenty-first birthday. Although *Christina's Fairy Book* was not published until 1906, most of the stories and verses it contains were probably composed some time earlier.[1]

The Brown Owl, Ford's first published work, which appeared in September 1891, is a remarkable achievement for someone of his age.[2] It began as a story told to his sister, Juliet, who was ten years old that year. Later he wrote it down and showed it to his grandfather, the Pre-Raphaelite painter Ford Madox Brown. Brown "was so delighted that he immediately made two illustrations for it, bullied Edward Garnett into seeing that Fisher Unwin published it, and rushed copies to all his friends."[3] The book was favorably noticed in several London newspapers and had a considerable success.[4]

[1]Arthur Mizener, *The Saddest Story: A Biography of Ford Madox Ford* (New York: World Publishing Co., 1971), p. 68. I am much indebted to this excellent book, without which my article could not have been written.

[2]Ford H. Madox Hueffer, *The Brown Owl: A Fairy Story,* with two illustrations by F. Madox Brown (London: T. Fisher Unwin, 1892). Published as volume 1 of The Children's Library. Ford's original name was Hueffer; he changed it legally in 1919, partly to avoid the current prejudice against Germanic surnames. Although *The Brown Owl* actually appeared in 1891, it was postdated, as was common at that time, especially for children's books.

[3]Mizener, *Saddest Story,* p. 17.

[4]See David Dow Harvey, *Ford Madox Ford 1873–1939: A Bibliography of Works and Criticism* (Princeton: Princeton University Press, 1962), p. 275. *The Brown Owl* was reprinted in 1966 as *The Brown Owl: A Fairy Tale,* illustrated by Grambs Miller (New York: George Braziller).

Late-Victorian England, of course, was the golden age of the literary fairy tale. The translation into English of Grimm and Andersen had inspired not only folklorists but writers. While scholars sought out and recorded native British folktales, well-known authors composed their own and sometimes used stories heard in childhood as models. Criticism of such tales as unscientific nonsense and a waste of time for children was met by the assertion that, on the contrary, fairy tales are the best way to teach moral and spiritual truths. Efforts along these lines ranged from the ridiculous to the sublime: in many now-forgotten stories the improving message bulges out of its conventional fairy-tale wrapping like a cow in a silk ballgown. Yet the same period produced George MacDonald's poetic fairy tales and Lewis Carroll's Alice books, as well as many other works of real wit and imagination.

The line between adult and juvenile fiction was less strict then than it is today; for one thing, contemporary standards of reticence in matters of sex and bad language meant that most novels "would not bring a blush to the cheek of a Young Person," as Mr. Podsnap put it. They could be, and were, read aloud to the whole family, which thus shared the monthly installment of the latest Dickens novel just as families today share the episodes of Masterpiece Theatre or some other favorite television show. And, just as we may watch the Muppets or a cartoon version of Tolkien with our children, so Victorian families read together what we would now think of as juvenile literature, often by the best authors of the time. Not only Dickens himself, but William Thackeray, Charles Kingsley, John Ruskin, Oscar Wilde, and Christina Rossetti (who was Ford's aunt by marriage) all wrote fairy stories. That Ford himself should decide to do so is therefore not surprising.

The plot of *The Brown Owl* follows the standard structural model of the fairy tale as outlined by Claude Bremond.[5]

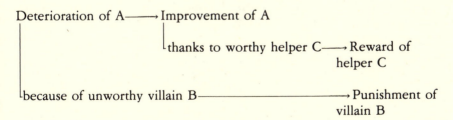

Its heroine, the Princess Ismara, suffers "deterioration" at the start of the story when her father the king dies and leaves in charge a Chancellor who turns out to be an evil magician. The Princess is protected from his various

[5]"The Morphology of the French Fairy Tale: The Ethical Model" in *Patterns in Oral Literature,* ed. Heda Jason and Dimitri Segal (The Hague: Mouton, 1977), p. 50.

schemes by a large owl, the classical Animal Guardian, who also helps to unite her with a prince. The pattern is repeated in several episodes, as the magician is routed and returns again in different disguises and with different helpers.

The style of *The Brown Owl,* like that of many contemporary fairy tales, varies between flowery-elaborate and comic-realistic. Ford's descriptions tend to be conventionally pretty:

> A beautiful day was dawning after the last night's rain, and the sun was rising brightly over the edge of the blue sea . . . everything was quiet except the shrill chirp of a solitary sparrow.[6]

There is a good deal of rather heavy-handed farce involving the court doctor and his umbrella, a little dwarf and a large giant, and so on. *The Brown Owl* also contains the customary ironic asides and references to contemporary events for the amusement of the adult reader. For example, the wicked Chancellor is said to be "inciting the people of far-off lands such as Mesopotamia and Ireland to rebel,"[7] and in his last and most dangerous transformation he is called "The Knight of London" and aided by a giant named Magog.[8]

Other aspects of the tale seem to be more personal to Ford—even prophetic. The Knight of London, who destroys all his opponents, can only be defeated by a paper sword and paper armor—the same weapons that Ford himself was to employ all his life. Princess Ismara is described as looking very much like Ford's sister, Juliet, who also had blue eyes and long rippling golden hair; and she is extremely active, courageous, and enterprising for a Victorian heroine. She does not wait at home when the enemy attacks, but leads her soldiers into battle; she is also so skilled in diplomacy that she wins most of her opponents over to her own side. Like latter-day feminists she refuses to be addressed as a child:

> "Now I won't be called a girl, for I'm nineteen, you know. His Majesty the Emperor of India there insulted me by calling me a girl, and I have not forgiven him yet."[9]

Although his tone here is gently mocking, Ford appears to have admired independent, outspoken women. All the women he later formed serious

[6]*Brown Owl,* p. 18.

[7]*Brown Owl,* p. 50.

[8]Gog and Magog are traditional giants whose statues stand in the Guildhall, London.

[9]*Brown Owl,* p. 66. Later Ford did some writing for Mrs. Pankhurst, came out in various essays in favor of the vote for women, and made Valentine Wannop, the heroine of *Parade's End,* a militant suffragette. I am indebted to Sondra J. Stang of Washington University for this information.

attachments to were strong-minded, and three of them were also self-support-ing. The first, Violet Hunt, was a popular novelist; her successors, Stella Bowen and Janice Biala, were both successful painters.

It is also interesting to look at the story of *The Brown Owl* in terms of family history. Ford, Juliet, and their brother, Oliver, spent their earliest years in Hammersmith—then a separate, almost rural suburb of London. But early in 1889, when Ford was barely sixteen, his father, Dr. Hueffer, died and the family was separated. Mrs. Hueffer and the two boys went to live with her parents (Ford Madox Brown and his wife) near Regent's Park in London. Juliet, then only eight, was boarded two houses away with Mrs. Hueffer's sister, Lucy Rossetti, and her husband and four children.

The Brown Owl opens with the death of a beloved father, King In-tafernes. The grieving heroine is protected by an old owl that is brown—(Ford Madox) Brown perhaps. At first it seems difficult and ill-tempered, like Ford's and Juliet's grandfather. As Ford wrote later, his grandfather

> had his irascibilities, his fits of passion when, tossing his white head, his mane of hair would fly all over his face, and when he would blaspheme impressively. . . .[10]

Yet after you got to know him he was much less frightening; Ford spoke of him as "the finest man I ever knew,"[11] and Juliet remembered him as "one of the kindest, gentlest, handsomest old gentlemen that ever lived."[12]

In Ford's story it is gradually revealed that the brown owl is a wise and noble being; finally we learn that he is the spirit of the Princess's dead father. It is as if, through his fairy tale, the young Ford is consciously or uncon-sciously urging his little sister to let their grandfather take the place of their lost father. Ford Madox Brown's enthusiasm for *The Brown Owl* may also have been partly due to his conscious or unconscious recognition of its hidden message. In the two illustrations he did for the book, the Princess looks very much like a grown-up Juliet, and the Owl's eyes resemble his own spectacles.

Whether the wicked Chancellor who tries and fails to take King In-tafernes's place is to be taken as a version of Ford's uncle William Rossetti (in whose house Juliet was living) is not clear. Rossetti, the most practical and conventional member of a very bohemian family, was Secretary of the Inland Revenue (the British tax office) and thus also a high government official in

---

[10]Ford Madox Ford, *Memories and Impressions* (New York and London: Harper & Brothers Publishers, 1911), p. 246.

[11]*Memories and Impressions*, p. 246.

[12]Juliet M. Soskice, *Chapters from Childhood* (London: Selwyn and Blount, 1921), p. 30.

an economic post; it is possible that his cautious attitude toward money had displeased the already extravagant Ford.

After *The Brown Owl, The Feather,* published a year later, comes as a considerable disappointment.[13] It is rambling and disorganized; probably nobody who did not have to write a scholarly article would read it through. (The pages of the Cornell copy had not been cut in over eighty-six years.) Again we have an independent-minded Princess, a kingdom ruled by a wicked usurper, a giant, a dragon, and a Prince. The principal magic device is an eagle's feather which gives invisibility and makes it possible for the Princess to go on a supernatural voyage to the Moon, save the Prince's life, and play many tiresome practical jokes on friends and enemies alike. The conventions of the fairy tale are violated by the inclusion of episodes involving the goddess Diana, the Three Fates, and the Man in the Moon.

There are some nice touches: Diana lives on the Moon in a Greek temple made entirely of green cheese and is militantly chaste ("I hate men —nasty, vulgar things!" she remarks).[14] But there is also a lot of meaningless horseplay and many conversations full of bad puns which have the air of having been included only to pad out the story. The tone of the book is more skeptical and detached than that of *The Brown Owl.* When the Prince brings the Princess home and is congratulated by the populace, Ford remarks,

> This is a habit of populaces, they are all fond of congratulating anyone who is successful—but they never assist anyone to success if they can help it.[15]

Although *The Feather* is dedicated "To Juliet," the description of Princess Ernalie—who has brown hair and hazel eyes—sounds more like Elsie Martindale, the fifteen-year-old girl who was in two years to become Ford's wife. (Possibly the dedication has a double meaning: Shakespeare's Juliet, like Elsie, was a very young girl.) In the summer of 1892 Ford was already writing to her and calling on her regularly—and beginning to annoy her parents, who thought that Elsie was much too young to have a serious suitor. In the story when Princess Ernalie tells her father of her feelings for the Prince, the King exclaims "You don't mean to say that you're in love with one another? Now I call that too bad."[16] But as befits a fairy tale his opposition is fleeting. The Princess starts to cry,

[13]Ford H. Madox Hueffer, *The Feather,* with frontispiece by F. Madox Brown (London: T. Fisher Unwin, 1892). Published as volume 10 of The Children's Library. According to Ford's bibliographer it appeared on 8 October 1892, to a less than enthusiastic critical reception.

[14]Ibid., p. 141.

[15]Ibid., pp. 84–85.

[16]Ibid., p. 181.

and that of course softened the heart of her father. "There, there," he said, as if he were soothing a baby. "Don't cry, you shall marry the Prince."[17]

In real life things did not go so smoothly for Ford and Elsie. By the summer of 1893, Dr. and Mrs. Martindale's annoyance at the romance had hardened into serious opposition. The Martindales were rich, respectable Victorian parents with no particular reverence for the arts. Although Ford had already published two books, they thought of him as "an irresponsible young man unlikely ever to earn a decent living" and "suspected him of wanting to marry Elsie for her money."[18] The more they saw of his influence over their daughter, the less they liked him; and in March 1894 Dr. Martindale forbade him to come to the house again. Soon afterward he arranged to send Elsie away to the country, where he hoped she would be inaccessible to Ford.

On March 16 Elsie was put on a train to Winchelsea to visit an aunt. But she never arrived there; at a way-station she eluded the older sister who was her chaperone, returned to London, and took another train to Bath, where Ford had arranged for her to stay with relatives sympathetic to his suit. Dr. Martindale responded by trying to get Elsie made a ward in Chancery in order to force her to return home. But before the law could act, on May 17, she and Ford were married; she was seventeen and he twenty.

The Queen Who Flew, Ford's best book for children, was written during his courtship of Elsie Martindale and appeared about a week before their wedding.[19] It is a first-rate story, lively, imaginative, and well written; stylistically it represents a great advance over the two earlier books. It compares favorably with contemporary fairy tales by such writers as Andrew Lang and Oscar Wilde and should be far better known today than it is.

Ford was aware of the romantic parallel between the story of *The Queen Who Flew* and his own; indeed, soon after he and Elsie had returned to London he arranged with a journalist friend to place an article connecting fact and fairy tale in a daily newspaper, *The Star.* "A Poet's Love Affair: A Chancery Court Chapter of 'The Queen Who Flew'" appeared on 6 June 1894. Three other newspapers later picked up the story, creating considerable publicity for the book.[20]

[17]Ibid., p. 182.

[18]Mizener, *Saddest Story,* p. 24.

[19]Ford Huffer [*sic*], *The Queen Who Flew: A Fairy Tale,* with a frontispiece by Sir E. Burne Jones (London: Bliss, Sands, and Foster, 1894). It was probably published on 8 May 1894. In 1965 it was reprinted by George Braziller, New York, with illustrations by Grambs Miller.

[20]Mizener, *Saddest Story,* p. 33. Ford's first book of poems, *The Questions at the Well,* had appeared in 1893.

The Queen Who Flew not only is an allegory of Ford's love affair with Elsie Martindale but predicts its outcome. Young Queen Elrida, the heroine, is lonely, bored, and overprotected; her kingdom is ruled by a sour, heavily bearded regent named Lord Blackjowl.[21] The Queen's only companion is a talking bat who shows her a flower which gives the power of flight. She makes herself a wreath of the flowers and flies away over the castle wall into a series of adventures. At one point in the story another large disagreeable black-bearded man called King Mark (*Mar*-tindale?) tries to kill Queen Elrida because she has refused to marry him. He throws her off a tall tower, but she merely flies away, while he is imprisoned by his oppressed subjects and starves to death. (This fantasy revenge on Dr. Martindale may appear rather extreme; but the situation before Elsie's elopement was extreme: at one point Mrs. Martindale told her daughter that she would rather see her dead than married to Ford.)

One interesting feature of *The Queen Who Flew* is its antiaristocratic, antimilitary bias, otherwise rare in Ford's work. The unpleasant Lord Black-jowl has strong reactionary opinions: when it is proposed that Queen Elrida give her wornout stockings to the poor, and she (having lived a very sheltered life) asks, "What *are* the poor?" Lord Blackjowl replies, "The poor are wicked, idle people—too wicked to work and earn the money, and too dirty to wear stockings."[22] The Queen, on the other hand, risks her life to get food for a beggar and is shocked by the wanton destructiveness of the soldiers.

The Queen Who Flew has an antiaristocratic and also an antitraditional conclusion. This annoyed the reviewer for the *Academy,* who was otherwise well disposed toward the book; he remarked:

> The story is well, but not too well written, and will probably please a large class of readers. The ending however . . . will, it is to be hoped, displease the lovers of old fairy lore.[23]

Contrary to the traditions of "old fairy lore," the Queen does not marry a king, nor is she restored to her own kingdom; instead she retires to the country. In the course of her adventures she has been taken in by a blind ploughman and his mother. Acting on the advice of her friend the bat, she makes tea out of her wreath of magic flowers and gives it to the blind man, whose sight is thus restored. She appoints the bat as King in her place and goes off to marry the ploughman and live happily ever after in his cottage.

Ford thus expresses the hope that Elsie will choose love in a cottage with

---

[21]Dr. Martindale was a tall man with a full beard; in the photograph reproduced in Mizener's biography the beard is white, but his mustache remains dark; he may have been a Lord Blackjowl earlier in life.

[22]*Queen Who Flew,* p. 15.

[23]Harvey, *Ford,* p. 277.

him over London luxury and loneliness. He also echoes his recurring dream of a self-sufficient rural life as what he called a Small Producer. This was not just a fantasy; Ford did spend much of his life in the country, though he was too restless to stay in one place for long. As he wrote much later:

> I have dug, hoed, pruned, and sometimes even harvested twenty-six kitchen gardens that I can remember. . . . If I had not so constantly travelled, I should have reaped better harvests and written more and better books.[24]

The outcome of *The Queen Who Flew* also suggests that Elsie will sacrifice her freedom (Queen Elrida's ability to fly) for the sake of the man she loves. Not only is this conventionally Victorian, it fits in well with Ford's idea of the artist's overwhelming need for an ideal, truly sympathetic woman who will care for him in an almost maternal way.

Apart from its ending, *The Queen Who Flew,* unlike its predecessor, follows the traditional fairy-story pattern. The central episode, in which Queen Elrida flies over the countryside with the wild geese (who later turn out to be enchanted mortals) is very well done. Although it may have been inspired by such old folk tales as "The Six Swans" (Grimm) it also looks ahead to one of the classics of children's literature, published thirteen years later: Selma Lagerlof's *The Wonderful Adventures of Nils.* It would be interesting to know whether Lagerlof had read or heard of Ford's story, some passages of which recall her own account of Nils' flight with the wild geese over Sweden.

> And then, towards sunset, they all rose in the air, and the Queen with them, and went whirling round in great clouds of rustling pinions, dyed red in the sunset, geese and peewits, and snipe and herons, all wheeling about in sheer delight of life; until, when the sun was almost down, the geese, with a great cry of farewell, flew off through the gloaming with the Queen towards the hut.[25]

It will be noticed that Ford's first three children's books all feature heroines who fly with or by the agency of large birds. Four of the nine stories in his fourth juvenile, *Christina's Fairy Book,* also contain flying females, and in two of them fairies are carried over long distances by birds—in one a gull, in the other a crow. It is impossible to say what this may have meant to Ford, though both Freudians and Jungians might have suggestions.

The illustrations for Ford's first two books featured the owl and the eagle. Wild geese appear on every page of *The Queen Who Flew* as part of

---

[24]Georges Schreiber, *Portraits and Self-Portraits* (Boston: Houghton Mifflin, 1936), pp. 39–40; quoted in Mizener, *Saddest Story,* p. xiv.

[25]*Queen Who Flew,* p. 59.

the elegant border design by C. R. B. Barnett that is also reproduced on the cover of the trade edition. (Ford Madox Brown was unable to illustrate this book; he had died in October 1893, after giving his blessing to his grandson's courtship of Elsie Martindale. But Ford Madox Brown's friend Edward Burne-Jones contributed a frontispiece: a red-crayon drawing of a girl in Pre-Raphaelite costume pouring water from a vase; though attractive and typical of his work, it bears no relation to the story.)

After the wedding, Ford and Elsie went to live in a country village in Kent where Ford started the first of his many gardens. In spite of recurring worries about money, they were happy during these early years. Ford was working steadily, and Elsie's parents gradually came to accept the marriage. In July 1897 their daughter Christina was born, and in April 1900 her sister Katharine. Ford began to write the poems and tell the stories which were later to be collected in *Christina's Fairy Book,* published in 1906.[26]

This final children's book, though it has moments of wit and charm, is weaker and slighter than *The Brown Owl* and *The Queen Who Flew;* and it does not have the energy and invention of *The Feather.* In writing for his own daughters, Ford was handicapped by a sentimental and fearful view of childhood. He saw Christina as very small and vulnerable, in need of constant protection, as he described her in the dedicatory poem, "To Christina at Nightfall," first published in 1901 when she was four:

> Little thing, ah, little mouse,
> Creeping through the twilit house, . . .

> Good night! The fire is burning low;
>   Put out the lamp;
> Lay down the weary little head
>   Upon the small white bed.
> Up from the sea the night winds blow,
>   Across the hill, across the marsh;
>   Chill and harsh, harsh and damp,
>   The night winds blow.

> But, while the slow hours go,
> I, who must fall before you, late shall wait
>   and keep

[26]Ford Madox Hueffer, *Christina's Fairy Book* (London: Alston Rivers, Ltd., 1906); it appeared in December of that year. I have not seen a copy of this edition. The references that follow are to a later edition: Ford Madox Ford, *Christina's Fairy Book,* illustrated by Jennetta Vise (London: Latimer House, Ltd., [1949]). An additional story, "The Other," was not included in *Christina's Fairy Book* and seems never to have been published; it appears following this article.

> Watch and ward,
> Vigil and guard,
> Where you sleep.[27]

As a boy Ford had been frightened by the stories told by his nurse, who had a predilection for tales of violence and disaster; he was determined to shelter his daughters from the sort of night-terrors he had known. In the prefatory note to *Christina's Fairy Book* he writes:

> As a child I used to see wolves and demons: I can feel still some of the agonies I felt then. I wished to spare my children some of these fears by peopling their shadows with little friendly beings.[28]

Unfortunately, this wish led him to produce in *Christina's Fairy Book* shallow and whimsical brief tales of a type all too common at the time, in which the fairies are tiny, silly, helpless creatures who wear cowslip caps and whisper in seashells. Ford's fairies are so small that one gets caught in the fur of the family dog, Cromwell, when he is out for a walk and is expelled with flea powder; only then is he noticed:

> When I came in in the evening, after you had gone to bed I heard a little clitter-clittering noise against the pictures, as if it were a moth beating against the glasses; and then I saw a fairy, not so large as a moth, in blue scale armour and with blue wings all dusted with insect powder. . . . this fairy was quite blinded with what Mother had sprinkled into Cromwell's fur, and there it was, battering against everything in the room, trying to find a way out.[29]

Six of the nine stories in *Christina's Fairy Book* are of this sort. Two others, "Mary and Matty and Lob" and "Bingel and Bengel" are conventionally told tales of the well-known Kind and Unkind type, in which a good child who helps a brownie or dwarf is rewarded and a bad one mildly punished. Internal evidence suggests that the stories were made up over a period of some years. In the early ones, only Christina is addressed. In "The Fairy Who Lived in a Steeple," however, we hear that the poor child who has been given a two-shilling piece can now buy "some almonds and some raisins and some chocolates and some figs, and some cotton to sew up the hole in her pocket, and a beautiful doll for her baby sister,"[30] suggesting that it must have been written in 1902 or later, when Christina would have been old enough to sew and Katharine, though still a baby, old enough to appreciate a doll.

[27]*Christina's Fairy Book,* pp. 7–8. The poem originally appeared in the *Athenaeum* on 26 October 1901.

[28]Ibid., p. 9.

[29]Ibid., p. 13.

[30]Ibid., p. 30.

The seven poems that appear between the tales are a mixed lot. Most are slight and conventional, weak imitations of Robert Louis Stevenson or of old nursery rhymes. But "The Unwritten Song" has real Edwardian charm, as it proposes

A song of greeny glow-worm lights,
In the long grass of summer nights,
Or flitting showers of firefly flights,
    Where summer woods hang deep:

Of wavering, noiseless owls that find
Their way by dusk, and of a kind
And drowsy, drowsy ocean wind
    That lulls the sea to sleep.[31]

This was the period of Ford's close association with the novelist Joseph Conrad, with whom he collaborated on *The Inheritors* (1901) and *Romance* (1903). The Ford (then Hueffer) and Conrad families were often together and sometimes shared a house. Christina and Katharine played with Conrad's son Borys. "The Three Friends," which appears in *Christina's Fairy Book,* has a verse for each of the children. "Pumpums" was their nickname for Ford, "Mummums" is Elsie, and "Blank-dash" is Conrad. Pumpums, Mummums, and Blank-dash are "old" only by courtesy; at the time Ford was probably about twenty-nine, Elsie twenty-six, and Conrad forty-five.

There was an old Pumpums who said,
"It is time little kids were in bed,"
    So they took up Christina
    And washed her much cleaner,
And carried her quickly to bed.

There was an old Mummums who said,
"It is time little girls were in bed,"
    So they caught up Miss Katharine
    And made a great lather in
Her bath and then popped her in bed.

There was an old Blank-dash who said,
"It is time little scamps were in bed,"
    So they bore Master Borys
    Upstairs where the door is,
And bathed him and put him to bed,

>   And they said
> "Oh it's peaceful now they are in bed!"[32]

The years just before the publication of *Christina's Fairy Book* were difficult ones. Elsie was often ill, there was never enough money, and Ford had completed two books for which he could not find a publisher.[33] Gradually he fell into a state of severe depression complicated by bouts of anxiety and agoraphobia.

His state of mind is reflected in the last story of *Christina's Fairy Book*, which begins "There was once an old Pumpums who was tired and ill and sick and sorry. And he lay on the big bed beside his little kiddies; and his little kiddies said: 'Tell us a tale, Pumpums.' "[34] Ford then becomes the bough of a tree outside the window and proceeds to tell a tale involving the theft of a king's jewels by a magpie, a false accusation against the page the Princess loves, and a trial and hanging which is only saved from being fatal when the bough breaks, revealing the true culprit and uniting the Princess and the page. Ford seems to be saying that justice can only be done and happiness achieved if he himself is destroyed. The meaning he suggests in the text is vaguer, but no less sad:

> So the tired Pumpums told them the story. And when he had finished telling it, he added: "I suppose that the moral is that there is no avoiding troubles, even if one turns into tree boughs. All the same, I hope my little kiddies will find, somewhere in the world, the good place where no troubles are. Who knows?"[35]

Arthur Mizener has suggested that much of Ford's depression and anxiety at this period "was . . . a product of the destructive clash between his dreams of glory and the actualities of his existence."[36] Better times were soon to come for Ford, but he was to suffer all his life from this clash between fact and fantasy, between hard everyday reality and the romantic world of the imagination in which he preferred to live.

Ford knew that most grown men and women do not choose to live in the world of the imagination, or even believe in its existence. To children, however, it was as real as it was to him; and while his daughters were young, they could share it with him. But, all too soon, they outgrew it. And so at the end of *Christina's Fairy Book* he writes, with a pathos not entirely destroyed by self-pity:

[32]Ibid., p. 46.
[33]Both of these books, *The Benefactor* and *The Soul of London,* were later published.
[34]*Christina's Fairy Book*, p. 54.
[35]Ibid., p. 60.
[36]Mizener, *Saddest Story,* p. 97.

I think that this is the last fairy tale that this Pumpums will tell his kiddies. For now when at nightfall he goes to them they say no longer: "Tell us a fairy tale," but: "Tell us some history." For, you see, they have grown out of believing in the untruths that are most real of all, and they are beginning to believe in these truths that are so false. And I do not know that that does not make this Pumpums a little sad. Still, it is the way of all flesh.[37]

[37]*Christina's Fairy Book,* p. 60.

FORD MADOX FORD
The Other

"'Tis said & by discrete persons credited that very yonge children of certeine lands have still speech with the soulis of other yonge children yet uncreate, until such time as, their ears being clogged up by our wordis, & their eyen gaining a different &, as it were, grosser, strength, they neither hear nor see the Others any mow . . . How this be I will not stay to devise".
Sir. T. Urquhart.

The
Other:
"Do you not remember?"; the Other pleaded.
Christina had crawled undetected out of the open front door, down the steps cautiously, & triumphantly to the foot of the pole on which the dovecot is. She shook her head & dabbled her hands in the fascinating dirt.
"Oh; but you must; you must"; the Other went on.
"I can't even see you"; Christina answered.—There were so many things that one could see. There were stones & grains of Indian corn blades of grass & an infinity of little things down near the Earth. The Other had come from the World Before where there are neither little things near the Earth nor big things afar off—nor even anything at all. It was so very lonely for the Other without Christina.
"Come back oh come back"; she besought her.
"Not till I have seen all round & all through all the little things". Christina said.

This story by Ford Madox Ford, which appears never to have been published, is preserved as a typed manuscript in the Rare Book Room of Cornell University and is undated. It is published here by permission of Janice Biala and is unedited. It takes off from the report of Sir Thomas Urquhart (1611–60) that "very yonge children . . . have still speech with the soulis of other yonge children yet uncreate." Ford describes a conversation between one of these uncreate souls and Christina, who in this sketch is still too young to talk. When the baby speaks her first word, she loses the ability to see and hear her heavenly playmate.

The theme of the infant's loss of divine vision, most familiar from Wordsworth's *Ode: On the Intimations of Immortality,* recurs throughout nineteenth- and twentieth-century literature. A scene very like that in Ford's story, for instance, occurs twice in P. L. Travers's Mary Poppins stories.—Alison Lurie

"There is no pain with us" the Other urged.

"But there are no little stones & no pink toes to play with".

"One day they will ache & ache & ache".

"One day they will hold me up & I shall walk for miles & miles: right up to where the chickens live & to Cromwell's kennel by the gate".

"You will fall down & the little stones will cut you".

"I shall get up & go on again" Christina said proudly.

"It will be so long before you do—hours & hours & days & days. Oh dear my dear come back to us".

"I shall never come back." Christina answered; "There is the World that Shall Be to go to. Besides—".

Christina frowned; an ant had come creeping close to her feet; & an ant is a thing that demands undivided attention.

The Other sighed.

"Don't you remember" she said again.

"There is nothing to remember"; Christina answered.

"But there is so much"; the Other said "Oh cruel to forget. Think how we lay for ever on the tides of the winds; just lay & did nothing & waited & waited for nothing".

"I shall never come back".

"And the great stars &—Oh; when you are weary & weary you will—"

"I shall never come back"; Christina said again. She was forgetting so swiftly that now she had forgotten everything but that—every word but those five. The Other felt her last hope die within her.

"Oh; you will stay in this weary world"; she said; "among the cruel eyes & the cruel lips & the cruel hearts & hands".

"I shall never—" Christina began. But she had forgotten what it was that she would never do. The whole World that Is swept on around her & for her. The rose bushes nodded for her; the blue sky hung over her & the pink clouds passed overhead just for her to see. On the red roof the white pigeons fluttered & cooed for her. She had come into her inheritance.

The Other said over again all that she had said before & Christina answered with the one word that one never forgets:

"I—I. ["] And just then, swaying his broad white breast above his orangefeet & snapping his tawny bill, round the corner came the old drake with the beady black eyes.

"Da—da—duck"; Christina said. It was the first that she had uttered of all the words that are.

Then the Other passed away. For she knew that never again would Christina have speech with her & never again know her presence—never—never—never.

Ford Madox Hueffer.

L. L. FARRAR, JR.
The Artist as Propagandist

Ford's place as a writer rests today on a relatively small portion of his oeuvre. Among his many volumes of cultural commentary are two little-known books of wartime propaganda (1915) which he wrote rapidly within six months of each other—*When Blood Is Their Argument,* subtitled "An Analysis of Prussian Culture," and *Between St. Dennis and St. George,* subtitled "A Sketch of Three Civilizations." Generally unknown to historians, they reveal a good deal about the wartime attitudes of the English ruling class. Reading critically, as a historian, one is struck by both Ford's grasp of the issues and the limitations of his approach. Indeed the books illustrate very interestingly some of the distinctions that can be made between historical and literary approaches to reality. And to the student of Ford, these works provide some understanding of the characteristic ways his mind worked—his preoccupation with how truth is perceived, the way he looked at his own experience, the processes by which he generalized, and how he thought about and used language. In other words, these books, read carefully, take us to the origins of his fiction and seem to support the contention that the artist reveals himself as much in his lesser as in his greater works.

In September 1914 Ford began his propaganda activities at the request of his old friend, C. F. G. Masterman, who was in charge of the Ministry of Information. Masterman recruited many publicists and authors in a secret operation designed to counter German propaganda in the United States[1] and, as Frank MacShane put it, "to encourage close feelings with England's traditional enemy, France, and antagonism towards Germany, with whom England had racial ties and even the same royal family."[2] Ford was provided with two secretary-research assistants, Richard Aldington and Alec Randall:

[1] The books "were sent to influential Americans accompanied by tastefully printed cards announcing them to be the gifts of this or that distinguished British professor" (Arthur Mizener, *The Saddest Story: A Biography of Ford Madox Ford* [New York: World Publishing Co., 1971], p. 251).

[2] Frank MacShane (ed.), *Ford Madox Ford: The Critical Heritage* (London and Boston: Routledge & Kegan Paul, 1972), p. 51.

We worked every morning. I took down from his dictation in long hand. . . . He was a great worker. He did a long literary article every week and at the same time he was engaged on a novel, *The Good Soldier,* and his propaganda book, *Between St. Dennis and St. George.* During the months I worked with him I believe he turned out 6000 to 8000 words a week.[3]

Aldington's details of this account were inaccurate, but Ford did seem to have been producing a great deal of work at this time, the result of which was the two books that are the subject of this essay. Both were written "without pay, for H. M. Government."[4]

One can only speculate about Ford's motives for undertaking the assignment. In addition to his friendship for Masterman, the most likely explanation is that he shared the general desire—"We [presumably writers] were all writing propaganda"[5]—to contribute in the best way he could as a forty-one-year-old writer, until his commission was granted (July 1915).[6] But Ford may have had the more specifically personal desire to prove himself a good English patriot. He was astonished and greatly disturbed when his loyalty as an Englishman was questioned—as it had been after he published an article in *Outlook* (September 1914) on "the gallant enemy" and a story in *The Bystander* (November 1914) about scaremongering. In fact Ford had to turn to Masterman to countermand an order from the chief constable of West Sussex to leave the county.[7] Of German descent, Ford was keenly aware of his ambiguous national status; as he commented after his enlistment in August 1915, his German "uncles, cousins and aunts" would "suspend [him] on high" as a traitor if he were captured.[8] By the time he wrote the books, he felt thoroughly betrayed by Germany. In *Between St. Dennis,* he asserts: "I am ashamed to think that less than a year ago I had, for the German peoples, if not for the Prussian State, a considerable affection and some esteem." He had "been deceived and [had] willingly let himself be deceived. I feel as if the whole German nation had played upon me, personally, the shabbiest form of confidence-trick."

Another equally personal consideration may have been the temptation to take a slap at his English literary and academic critics by linking them with Prussian educational and scholarly practices. He declares in *When Blood Is*

[3]Mizener, *Saddest Story,* p. 251.

[4]David Dow Harvey, *Ford Madox Ford: A Bibliography of Works and Criticism* (Princeton: Princeton University Press, 1962), p. 214.

[5]Ford Madox Ford, *A Mirror to France* (New York: A. & C. Boni, 1926), p. 9.

[6]Ford to Lucy Masterman, 31 July 1915, *Letters of Ford Madox Ford,* ed. Richard M. Ludwig (Princeton: Princeton University Press, 1965), p. 60.

[7]Mizener, *Saddest Story,* pp. 250–51.

[8]Ford to John Lane, 12 August 1915, *Letters,* p. 61.

Their Argument that "all my life a large part of my miseries" were caused by the baleful influences of Prussia on British intellectual life, influences that explain both "the stupidities of the ordinary English reviewer" who "really wishes not to be troubled with the consideration of new metrical forms" and also the fact that "prominent chairs of learning throughout the world are occupied by non-gifted individuals whose claim to occupy those chairs is solely that of an uninspired capacity to aggregate facts."

Ford does not seem to have been troubled by the notion of producing propaganda. While condemning German propagandists and seeking to present his work as less biased than it was, he acknowledges in *Between St. Dennis* that it was "polemical" toward Germany and "a labour of love" regarding France; and he came perilously close to blowing his cover when he hinted in *When Blood Is Their Argument:* "If I were a propagandist and tried to preach to the United States. . . ."!

The two books form a general whole in being unembarrassedly pro-Anglo-French and anti-German, but there are differences between them in approach. *When Blood Is Their Argument,* the earlier book, is, as the subtitle indicates, the more scholarly of the two. It is a severely critical "analysis of Prussian culture," which cannot "charitably dispose of anything, when blood is their argument"; the phrase is from Shakespeare's *Henry V* (IV, 1, 142). The first third of the book is a "civil and financial history" of Germany to 1880, followed by studies of notable Germans (including Bismarck, Nietzsche, and Wagner), a condemnation of German materialism and Prussian education, and an exposure of the Prussian government's perversion of the Goethe myth. The title of the second book is also drawn from *Henry V* (V, 2, 207): "Shall not thou and I, between St. Dennis and St. George compound a boy, half-French, half-English, that shall go to Constantinople [read Berlin?], and take the Turk [read Prussian?] by the beard?"—and reflects Ford's advocacy of an Anglo-French political and cultural union against Prussian Germanism. The book, more polemical than its predecessor, begins as an answer to "Anglo-Prussian apologists" (particularly G. B. Shaw, Bertrand Russell, Norman Angell, and Henry Noel Brailsford), contrasts English and German culture, argues that Germany is more bellicose than England or France, defends British naval predominance, offers a paean to British behavior and French culture, and ends with a lengthy appendix condemning "Anglo-Prussian apologists" and quoting German militarist statements. The general purpose of both books was the same, namely, to counter defeatism and increase the self-confidence of the British and French people: "all I have been trying to do is . . . to put some heart into unnecessarily depressed populations."

Much interested in hearing how the books were received, Ford asked Masterman for reviews and offered his own opinion that *Between St. Dennis* was the "more valuable" of the two books.[9] The works were in fact favorably received by the London press, which recommended *When Blood Is Their Argument* to all Englishmen and Americans as a persuasive indictment of Germany. Rebecca West's review of *Between St. Dennis* in the *Daily News* was particularly favorable.

> It is really not quite fair that a man who spends his whole existence in the consideration of beauty, the values of life, and the niceties of language, should be able to stroll out of his garden, look on for a minute at the fight of the controversialists in the highway, and say the right, the illuminating, the decisive thing that settles the whole affair, and leaves them sitting, hot and silly, in the dust.[10]

Nor was it surprising that the French translation of *Between St. Dennis* was welcomed by the French government; in fact, the French minister of instruction formally congratulated Ford. The French themselves could hardly have presented France in a more favorable light.[11]

In *When Blood Is Their Argument,* Ford is candid, in fact, unabashed about his method and his intention in writing as a special pleader. Impartiality is, as he sees it, a sort of hypocritical subterfuge used for propagandistic purposes by German professors who are as much special pleaders as he. "For impersonalism is a professorial product, the refuge of an empty and non-constructive mind that is afraid of setting down its own conclusions as its own conclusions." Instead of impartiality, Ford proclaims his partiality:

> While maintaining that I have certainly not falsified any sources or employed any forms of argument that seem to me to be unfair, I do not lay claim to any aspirations after fairness of mind. Let me say frankly that I consider myself to be a special pleader . . . on behalf of French learning, French art-methods, habits of mind, and lucidity. . . . I am bringing forward and putting as incisively as possible everything that I can select to make these things appear lovely and desirable. . . . That being so, I determined to adopt as far as possible the personal tone in this work.

[9]Ford to Masterman, 28 August 1915, ibid., p. 62.

[10]MacShane, *Ford,* p. 51. West goes on: "One is surprised when one reads this masterly appendix that an artist can make so fine a controversialist; but as one reads the book of which that is only the sting in the tail one wonders how any but an artist can ever be a controversialist."

[11]Ford to Lucy Masterman, 25 August 1916, *Letters,* p. 70; Mizener, *Saddest Story,* p. 290; Douglas Goldring, *The Last Pre-Raphaelite: A Record of the Life and Writings of Ford Madox Ford* (London: Macdonald, 1948), p. 178. Evaluation of the two books by Ford scholars is, on the whole, uncritical.

Editor's note: See p. 172 of this volume for an expression of Ford's pleasure at being commended by the French.

And he tells us, in the Preface, that his attitudes have their origins in the profound feelings attached to his German father, who had put his German heritage behind him, and his English grandfather:

> From my father as from my grandfather, Madox Brown, I imbibed in my very earliest years a deep hatred of Prussianism. . . . At the same time I was by those same men, inspired with a deep love and veneration for French learning. . . . I may be said to have passed the whole of my life reflecting upon these propagandist lines.

Although he very well knew to what extent he was a prejudiced and partial observer, these are *his* experiences, his prejudices, his way of seeing that he offers the reader. He cannot offer anyone else's with the same degree of accuracy. We are here very close to Ford the novelist and, indeed, to Ford the impressionist novelist, whose distinction between impressions and facts has been a problem for readers out of sympathy with this particular sensibility. Four years before, he had written to his daughters in the dedicatory letter to *Ancient Lights:* "This book is full of inaccuracies as to facts, but its accuracy as to impressions is absolute. . . . I don't deal in facts, I have for facts a most profound contempt."

Between St. Dennis was launched on what at first seems to be the reverse premises. "What happened," he writes in the Preface, "was that I set out to confront various pacifist writers or other writers who were opposed to the Government of this country entering upon a war side by side with France—to confront them with various facts and with various figures." But facts and figures seem to have gone against the grain:

> I dislike denouncing my fellow-beings, even though they be pacifists, and it seemed to me to be only fair to present these gentlemen with my own constructive view of the state of Europe before the outbreak of the present war.

Thus the "constructive portion" of the book—by which Ford meant his general impression of the realities before him—"has overshadowed the controversial"—by which he meant the various facts and various figures, which nevertheless have their function:

> A time like the present calls for different methods. . . . We must get down to the facts; we must not listen to *ex parte* statements; we must insist upon documentation. . . . In compiling rather than writing this present work I am attempting to put before the reader a large body of what I may call "ground facts" or what the Germans call *Quellen*.

That the press was "dead," that "gossip sits upon a throne," that "literature seems to have died out of [the] world" made it time for "the historian and the historian's methods." The need for this approach arises from Ford's annoyance with the "Anglo-Prussian apologists" and "pro-German propagandists" like Shaw, Russell, Brailsford, and Angell, who, "in dealing with matters of real history," use what seemed to Ford to be the "methods of the intellectual fictionists."

> They invent and clothe dummy figures with attributes which have some faint resemblance to the attributes of the persons or of the ideals that they pretend to portray, and then, getting these characters into circumstances of their own devising, they proceed to foil, confute, and hopelessly confuse their puppets according to the traditions of Adelphic melodrama.

The distinction Ford makes here is a familiar one to readers of theoretical pronouncements on the art of fiction in the second half of the nineteenth century.[12] The tendentious "fictionist," as Ford calls him, "will make all landowners appear to be oppressive and unimaginative . . . or all socialists appear in the guise of wife-beaters or usurers." The true novelist, on the other hand, with no axe to grind, will not treat his characters like puppets; he will endow them with all the life of which he is capable. In the same way, the true historian will not simply amass documentation; he will "re-create past times." Ford sees the work of the historian and the work of the novelist as inseparable.

Paradoxically, *When Blood Is Their Argument* is in many ways closer to the historical approach advocated in the later book; in fact, each book is closer in spirit to the approach advocated in the other. But on the whole, detachment is seldom found in either work and documentation is notable by its absence, except in the appendixes. In *Between St. Dennis,* Ford's criticism of British pacifism, his claims about German bellicosity, and his assessment of German prewar economic trends are buttressed with extensive appendixes. But there is on Ford's part so strong an antiacademic bias that he would have made it a point of honor to conceal rather than exhibit his sources in the course of his discussion—the facts, figures, and documents that are "normal" practice for historians to present. Documentation then is confined to the appendixes because art must conceal art; and Ford relied on the popularizer's gift, the use of metaphor, symbol, anecdote, and interpolations from fiction, to appeal to readers brought up on the novel and make the books accessible to the general reader. His use of historical sources is limited and at times eccentric, though always interesting. For example, he relies upon Wagner's memoirs as the basis for an account of the revolutions of 1848. And some of his causal connections are so tenuous as to approach the bizarre, for example, his attribution of the German navy's founding to the establishment

---

[12]See Richard Stang, *The Theory of the Novel in England, 1850 to 1870* (New York: Columbia University Press, 1959).

of the Jesuit order. The books are strongly novelistic: he writes in *Between St. Dennis* that he is

> attempting to reconstruct from my own consciousness the psychologies of the three Western Powers . . . I am about to give very exactly phrased first-hand evidence, not of the Englishman as he is or was, not of the Englishman as I have found him to be, but of that individual as I have found myself to be. And I am about to give exactly phrased first-hand evidence of the German as I have found him to be, and of the Frenchman.

What he cares most about rendering is a frame of mind. "I am attempting," he tells us, to provide as "exact an historical document as if I were reporting the *procès verbal* of the trial of Joan of Arc or the speeches and votes during a sitting of Parliament." That a frame of mind rendered with scrupulous accuracy can be a historical document is Ford's premise in both works. "I claim in short to be the *Quellen*": in reconstructing from his own consciousness the "psychologies" of the three Western powers, he is a novelist creating three characters.

But to explain how he does in fact arrive at the "psychology" of the individual country—Germany, France, or England—he speaks in *Between St. Dennis* of his own "individual mental camera" and elaborates an analogy with photography:

> Supposing that the photographer desired to get at a rendering of A Poet rather than of any one poet, he took upon the same plate photographs of profile portraits of Dante, Shakespeare, Milton, Burns, Goethe, Wordsworth, and Tennyson. The result was a queer, blurred image, but the result was none the less striking, and the individual arrived at by this composite process had an odd but quite strong individuality.

His generalizing then is analogous to the composite process in photography:

> In exposing, then, his more or less sensitised mind to life in this or that country the observer is subjecting his mind to precisely the same process as that to which the photographer in the 1890's used to subject his plates when he was making a composite photograph.

Yet another metaphor—which Ford used often in his writing—suggests to us something of what he had in mind in the organization of his material in these books of propaganda. It is the game of cat's cradle, and a number of critics use the image to suggest Ford's approach in other books as well:

> Roughly speaking, he used this method in all his books—those he frankly called fiction and those he called memoirs, biography, sociological impressions, etc. The idea of reworking the same material from different angles lent itself to his special genius for the psychological

novel, and in some way, he conceived every book he wrote as a psychological novel.[13]

In both books topics are picked up, dropped, and picked up again, as Ford himself acknowledges. In *When Blood Is Their Argument,* he crosses and recrosses chapter divisions which themselves overlap. He takes the reader on excursions without stating their purposes. Conscious of these tendencies, Ford suggests elsewhere that his digressions may make the reader wonder "what the devil is the fellow driving at?" But it is the same method he used in *The Good Soldier,* published the same year, and Ford implies that our minds work the same way in confronting historical and fictional realities.

As an artist, Ford has a good deal to say in the two war books about language and the uses of language in our century. "The relative values of civilisations come down always to being matters of scrupulosity of language . . . for language . . . is the very soul of man. . . . If a man or a race do not exercise themselves as carefully in the use of phrases as in the use of their limbs, that man and that nation will go to the devil in a greater or a lesser degree." This indeed is what was happening in the modern world. "By the madness of phrase-making, by the madness of the inexact and aspiring phrase-making . . . Europe, if it be lost, will have been lost . . . very largely on account of German inexactitude." George Orwell might have read this passage with satisfaction. For Ford, perhaps more than anything else, language distinguishes French from German civilization: "France is always exactly right according to her aspirations as she is true in her phraseology. It is always only Germany that is absolutely wrong . . . [and] accepts with inevitable voracity every phrase that is bombastic and imbecile."

It is consequently all the more striking when Ford himself makes extensive use of hyperbole, as in the passage just quoted from *When Blood Is Their Argument.* He is particularly inclined toward positive superlatives when he discusses France and negative superlatives when he discusses Germany. But this is hardly unconscious, because his avowed intention was—and he is here very much the novelist—"most immediately to strike the imagination of the reader and the better to awaken his attention," or as he put it, "by hook or by crook, employing now colloquialism, now rhetoric, to unmask the face of this barbarism [Prussia]." Rebecca West, in her review, implies that his tone is "casually right": "we see him, with no abandonment of his languor, and his preoccupation with style, picking up that good creature, Mr. George Bernard Shaw, by the scruff of the neck, and shaking him to rights." One can, in fact, see his style as a good deal more heated than West says and given

---

[13]Sondra J. Stang, *Ford Madox Ford* (New York: Frederick Ungar Publishing Co., 1977), p. 7; see also John A. Meixner, *Ford Madox Ford's Novels: A Critical Study* (Minneapolis: University of Minnesota Press, 1962), pp. 6–10, 72.

to overstatement, perhaps as much a sign of the times and of his own frame of mind as a matter of rhetorical strategy.

Most of his attention and all his antipathy are directed at Germany. Although he grants both the difficulty of ascertaining national character and his own distaste at indicting a whole people, he does both, but occasionally demonstrates some sympathy for Germany, especially southern Germany. As Ford reads German history, the turning point was the period from 1848 to 1870 when Prussia established its hegemony over the rest of Germany. Despite Bismarck's critical role in this process and his attack on Roman Catholicism *(Kulturkampf)*, Ford treats him sympathetically and places the blame for subsequent perversions first on the selfish princes and political parties and later on Bismarck's successors, William II and Admiral Tirpitz, who manipulated the German people into building a navy against their will. After their failure to establish democracy in 1848, the German middle class renounced politics and poured its energies into the pursuit of wealth in the spreading industrial revolution. Simultaneously German culture ceased: "the main thesis of this book, then, is that there is no such thing as 'modern German culture.' . . . Every German who has contributed anything noteworthy towards German culture" was born southwest of the line from Dresden to the mouth of the Elbe, before 1848, and for the most part before 1815. The Germany of post-1870 was "a purely commercial affair." Despite Prussian efforts to remake the rest of Germany, the distinction between the north and the southwest remained: "Germany divides itself sharply into two sections so diverse in point of view, in characteristics, and in the relative values each attaches to life, that it may almost be said that they are absolutely differing races . . . the South German, Catholic type . . . upon the whole cultivated, spendthrift, and gay, good-humoured and quite as much concerned with the workings of the next world [as with commerce] . . . and the North German, non-religious and purely materialistic species."

Ford is sharply critical of Prussian education, whose great prestige in the West he deplores and seeks to deflate by charging that it produces only "intellectual laziness and constructive cowardice . . . having destroyed in the world the spirit of scholarship, and of having substituted for it 'philological' pedantry." This tendency was fostered "consciously and of set purpose" by the Prussian government, which used education as propaganda "machinery" and "influenced the character of the whole German people." Thus the Prussian state, "cool-headed, remorseless, and utterly practical, has taken the culture of the Germanic nations in hand" and transformed it into "a device for giving into the hands of the State powers more disastrous than those ever held by any body of men since the world began." Part of this campaign was the creation of "Goethe as superman" to encourage the notion of German cultural superiority.

Ford sees as the ultimate objective of these policies the subordination of the individual to the Prussian state, whose goal was war. Since the Prussian government demanded that the educational system "provide a population tenacious in acts of war, infinitely courageous in the contemplation of death," it is not surprising that the Germans are, Ford observes, more warlike than the French or British in domestic and international politics, and more brutal both in their treatment of subject peoples (e.g., the Poles and Alsace-Lorrainers) and in their conduct of the war (e.g., the sinking of the *Lusitania*). Thus the war is a conflict between German (above all, Prussian) *Kultur* and western culture; between "materialist and altruist" societies; between "monomania and graceful all-roundedness"; between "professionalism and amateurism"; between the German doctrine "that the object of the State is to wage war"—that "Might is Right"—and the Anglo-French view that "the object of the State is the good of the State's individual constituents."

Ford has little doubt that Germany caused the war but is not precise on where the responsibility lies; he usually places it on the government but occasionally it is shared by the people who, he suggests, may have opted for war to escape national bankruptcy. What he sees as the aims of war follow from this analysis: complete German military defeat, an imposed change of political system, the removal of Prussian dominion over the rest of Germany, a Rhenish confederation of France and south Germany under French leadership and guaranteed by the rest of the world, and national self-determination for the peoples under German and Austro-Hungarian rule.

Many historians share Ford's general conception of German history but would shrink from his exaggerated formulations and explanations which rely on deficiencies in national character. Ford's contention that German culture before 1870 was more impressive than after is difficult to deny, but the argument that none existed between 1870 and 1914 is justifiable only as a war cry; and his explanation of creeping Prussianism is simplistic. Ford himself admits that he had read little German literature written after 1870 and is offhand with what he knows (e.g., the Mann brothers). Cultural undulations are a fact of history and a fascinating problem for cultural historians: "materialistic" prewar Germany was to prove a seedbed for European culture in the 1920s. Ford's idealization of preunification Germany is understandable, and most of us creatures of industrialized society tend to romanticize preindustrial culture. But the fact was that many Germans—not only Prussians—responded to the seductions of nationalism and applauded unification. After all, why should they not have, since the French and British had been glorying in their national grandeur for centuries! The major feature of German history during the nineteenth century, however, was not Prussian influence but industrialization, which was neither exclusively nor indeed primarily Prussian. Ford seeks to link Prussianism with materialism and in turn with Protestantism, which he implies somehow either became secularized or sold out; but in fact the major industrial area—the Rhineland—was

Roman Catholic. In any case the primary ingredient of industrialism was not the predisposing culture but the presence of natural resources.

Ford's argument that German policy was aggressive after 1870 and especially on the eve of war is well taken and generally accepted by historians. But many historians today see Germany as only the first among many powers to pursue their interests as aggressively as they could. Perceiving German aggression, the other powers sought to contain it, an effort which the Germans took as encirclement. Thus German policy—like that of other powers—is probably best understood as an oscillating mixture of arrogance and anxiety. Most historians would accept Ford's assertion of German bellicosity but not his assertion of British and French pacifism, because it is generally agreed that militarism and jingoism increased universally as war approached. Ford's implication that Germany was solely responsible for the war (the Versailles verdict) is rejected by most historians—although, interestingly, not by all German historians. The most generally held view is that responsibility—to the extent that it is an acceptable notion at all—should be shared; in fact, many regard the 1914 crisis as a diplomatic impasse that defied solution and thus rendered culpability an elusive and perhaps misleading explanation. It was indeed perceptive of Ford to spot German economic difficulties on the eve of war, but his argument that these difficulties induced Germans, particularly industrialists, to advocate war is not widely accepted.

Ford's interpretation of the war as a crusade of good against bad certainly reflected the prevailing opinion in Britain and France, and in the United States after—and only after—we entered the war. As for opinion in Germany, studies of German war aims reveal without much doubt that government and ruling classes—there is less clarity about the masses—favored what amounted to German domination of Europe, a domination not very different in extent from what Hitler imposed; and so in this sense the Germans were, as Ford said, indeed bad. But the war aims of the Allies (Britain, France, and Russia) were not all idealistic and selfless, and Ford surely makes this point about England in *Parade's End,* written, to be sure, after the war. Allied resistance to Germany was accompanied by expansion —it was believed at the time, and still is, that states are supposed to enlarge themselves. The war should therefore more realistically be seen as a conflict of bad against less bad, or at least less-than-perfect good. Ford's prediction in 1915 that an undefeated Germany would threaten the future peace of Europe was eerily correct, but his solution of dividing Germany, while hypothetically useful, was probably unrealistic. In fact this was precisely the German problem until 1945: Germany was too weak to dominate Europe but too strong to be pacified and prevented from trying. Only a Hitler could solve it by producing total German defeat and bringing Russia and the United States irrevocably into Europe.

Ford's view of the role of the state in Prussian-German education is largely accepted by historians, certainly Anglo-Saxon historians. The system buttressed the social order by being exclusive and resistant to mobility. After 1870 and increasingly in the first decade of the twentieth century, the state —by applying the lever of financial dependence—imposed conformity (exclusion of political dissidents, Social Democrats, Jews, and sometimes Roman Catholics from faculties) and control upon faculties and students, both of whom were made "victims of the corrosive influence of materialism, feudalism, and nationalism."[14] Ford's picture, however, neglects and in fact denies the achievements of German education. Primary education was the best in Europe in its virtual elimination of illiteracy by the mid-nineteenth century (at which point half of the English, French, and Belgian populations and three-quarters of the Italian and Spanish people were illiterate). And German universities made outstanding contributions to the humanities and social sciences during the latter half of the nineteenth century. But it is surely true that the traditional university ideals of self-government, *Lehrfreiheit* (freedom in the choice of teaching subject-matter) and *Lernfreiheit* (freedom of movement for students among universities) were jeopardized, though not destroyed. Perhaps most important, the deficiencies Ford found were not exclusively German: all contemporary European university systems were socially exclusive, rigid in their curricula, pedagogically authoritarian, and—with the exceptions of Oxford and Cambridge—state-controlled.[15] Although mitigated by subsequent reforms, these features still obtain in Europe and may strike American observers as far less likely to produce a favorable climate for fostering independent and critical thinking than our own universities.

England and France were, in Ford's discussion, all that Germany was not. The English state "appears to me to be an almost perfect organ"; the Prussian state is "the deleterious converse of this perfection." It is a difference "not of degree, but of species . . . as great as that which separates men from angels": "Amongst Anglo-Saxon races in fact the State is almost universally regarded as a necessary evil [whereas] in the German Empire the State is the be-all and end-all of human existence." As for class, "in Germany the ruling classes really rule and really are a class. This is one of the main facts which differentiates between Great Britain and Germany." German and British personal behavior are poles apart: "English life, as I knew it then, was a matter of keying things down, German, of tightening things up." English society required "concealing as far as possible one's own qualities," whereas German society demanded the trumpeting of accomplishments. The distinction applies in international behavior as well, England's being characterized by "correctness of attitude," while Germany "has broken loose from all rules." It follows that "the Englishman ignored war . . . the German desired

---

[14]Gordon A. Craig, *Germany 1866–1945* (Oxford: Oxford University Press, 1978), p. 206.
[15]Ibid., pp. 186–206.

war . . . the Frenchman dreaded and detested war." German militarism is "branded with the mark of Cain and it is original sin . . . purely destructive and accursed"; British navalism, peaceful, efficient and honorable, "remains one of the most beautiful things in the world." That the German navy challenged the British navy's supremacy and thus contributed to the outbreak of war Ford calls, in *Between St. Dennis,* "the saddest story in the chronicles of the world."

His admiration for England seems largely untempered by the critical attitude (a term he liked to use and in fact used as the title for a book of essays in 1911) which he applied to England elsewhere in his many books. But his "immense Francophile tendencies," as he calls them, were to be a constant and characteristic cultural attitude that came to fruition in *Provence* and *Great Trade Route.* In *When Blood Is Their Argument* and *Between St. Dennis* his method of treating France is virtually unhistorical. He deals little with politics and relies almost entirely on his own experience and reading of French literature. In short, he is more candidly impressionistic than he is in his treatment of Germany or even England. He presents the French people idyllically—as "patient, efficient, industrious" and as evidencing "honour . . . self-sacrifice . . . probity." But he does distinguish between the people and their government, the "bad" and "unsatisfactory" Third Republic, which he condemns for attacking the army and the Roman Catholic Church, and which he compares unfavorably with "the First Empire, which was peculiarly adapted to letting the great men of France have some influence upon public actions." It is "these wonderful people" who will save Europe "if Europe is to be saved" and the French language which will rescue modern civilization—by "the mental processes to which the French subject all phenomena"—from the "phrase-making of the industrial system . . . of materialism . . . of false Napoleonism and the rest of the paraphernalia of life as we live it today." For these reasons "in the whole world it is only France that incontestably matters," and "that England should be at last the ally of France is the greatest privilege ever afforded by destiny." In compliance with Masterman's intentions, Ford therefore recommends an Anglo-French union (expressed in the title of his book *Between St. Dennis and St. George*), since for him "the British nation and the French nation are, and always have been, one and indivisible—one by race, by tradition, by civilisation, and even, strained as the proposition may sound, by construction of language." To encourage this "double civilisation," Ford advocated compulsory study of the other's language in the schools of each country. He also urged a larger role for France after the war by the division of Germany and the formation of a French-dominated Rhenish confederation. Since he saw the French and the south Germans as "racially and historically" similar, as he did the British and the French, he implied by this confederation a cultural union of "the races affected by that Romance culture" from Provence to Scotland.

Read as documents of their time, *When Blood Is Their Argument* and *Between St. Dennis* can be taken as period pieces reflecting views prevailing in upper-class England and probably in the country-at-large. Perhaps unwittingly Ford achieved the goal proclaimed in *A Mirror to France* and elsewhere: "It has always been my humble ambition to be a mirror to my time."[16] Prewar pacifism had indeed given way to aggressiveness: "Because the necessities of the day are so essentially martial we are ashamed to think that we were ever pacifist." The shrill tone of the books was widely shared, and Ford's attacks on the government's critics were applauded, in fact, supported by a government that imprisoned Russell for obstructing recruitment. Yet to the credit of English society, Ford had to respond to these critics who were permitted to express their views freely, views that attacked the old diplomacy which had, they contended, caused the war. What particularly antagonized Ford and others was the assertion that the two sides were equally responsible and morally indistinguishable.[17] Thus Ford's books accorded precisely with the official view put by government spokesmen such as Grey, Asquith, and Lloyd George that the allied war effort was a crusade against evil. Paradoxically, in the process, the government adopted some of the principles of its critics—including the formation of a League of Nations, open diplomacy, and the principle Ford supported, national self-determination. Ford's efforts to counter defeatism and German cultural imperialism were very real concerns in early 1915, when the war had stalemated, with Germany in control of considerable conquered territory. His praise of France was doubtless heartfelt, but it was also a response to a not inconsiderable suspicion toward France in some English quarters. Ford's ambivalence toward the war was characteristic. The widespread initial glorification of it, to be seen, for example, in the work of the early war poets, was followed almost universally by bitter disenchantment and acceptance of the war as at best a necessary evil.[18] Ford's criticism of modern urban, materialistic society and his hankering after a better, simpler, but vanished society was widely shared, especially by young intellectuals, and

[16]*A Mirror to France* (London: Duckworth, 1926), p. 7.

[17]For accounts of the views of the government's critics, see A. J. P. Taylor, *The Trouble Makers: Dissent over Foreign Policy, 1792–1939* (Bloomington, Ind.: Indiana University Press, 1958), pp. 132–66; and Laurence W. Martin, *Peace without Victory: Woodrow Wilson and the British Liberals* (New Haven: Yale University Press, 1958).

[18]For Ford's romanticizing of war, see *Between St. Dennis,* pp. 74–75, 78, 92, 95, 97, 101, 161–62, 183. For his criticism of war see ibid., pp. 11–12, 151–52. When he received a commission, Ford wrote to Lucy Masterman: "it is as if the peace of God had descended on me —that sounds absurd—but there it is! Man is a curious animal" (12 July 1915, *Letters,* p. 61). For one account among many of the war poets, see Paul Fussell, *The Great War and Modern Memory* (New York: Oxford University Press, 1975).

was reinforced by the horrors of mechanized war on the western front.[19] Ford's belief in "national psychologies" and races was also widely shared, and so, too, was his belief in the determinist theory that national differences are the products of "environment and circumstances."

The books seem to have marked a turning point in Ford's ambivalent attitude toward his German heritage, a kind of declaration of independence from Germany, and one wonders not that he dropped his German middle names at the beginning of the war but that he waited until 1919 to renounce his family name. *Parade's End* was to be another turning point for Ford—in his criticism of England's conduct of the war. In these two books of 1915 Ford repeatedly anticipates the Tietjens novels: he asserts, like Christopher Tietjens, that he has "no heroics" in his makeup, his own merit being "in concealing as far as possible [his] own qualities." The English suffer, he observes, from "general obtuseness" and "an appearance of slackness," but their great virtue is "correctness of attitude" which, however, "can be stigmatised as implying frigidity"; moreover, the Englishman finds it "disagreeable to write praise of one's own side." Ford's demands for a prosecution of the war until Germany was defeated and for a Rhenish confederation under France would be put by Mark Tietjens in *Last Post.* One even catches a whiff of the title of *No More Parades* (and later *Parade's End*) when Ford condemns "the whole military parade of the world which was a monstrous nonsense and a monstrous nuisance."

The books *contra* Germany beg to be appreciated from more than a single perspective. They suggest what occurs when the author of impressionist, psychological novels assumes the mantle of historian and writes what may be called impressionist history. Impressionism, as Ford understood it, is the expression of a particular personality, the recording of the almost involuntary perceptions of an individual observer, with his own complex personality, who takes in some aspect of reality that might elude another observer, with his individual and complex personality. The books are pervaded by Ford's personality, and we come away with a strong sense of how he looked and saw, how his particular temperament responded to the phenomena in question. For the role of historian, his powers of understanding and interpreting the scene before him were considerable, though his avowed prejudices, unorthodox methods and ambivalence toward what constituted fact (sometimes honoring what others call fact, sometimes not) leave his "analysis" and his "sketch"—these are his designations in the subtitles of these works—very much in need of correction and supplementation. Yet as a propagandist, Ford

---

[19]For analyses of the criticism of modernity and the mechanization of the war, see Eric J. Leed, *No Man's Land: Combat and Identity in World War I* (Cambridge: At the University Press, 1979).

did more than give the impressionist's rendering or the historian's interpretation of the past; he sought to change the course of events by arousing men to action. The books were in effect calls to arms in a holy war, and often reason is asked to yield to belief. The circumstances—those of England in World War I—determined not only the spirit in which the books were written but also the spirit in which they were read: the books insist on their context.

H. G. Wells's poignant and startlingly perceptive novel *Mr. Britling Sees It Through,* published in September 1916,[20] grows out of the same climate and in fact incorporates many of Ford's themes—the contrast between British and German character, the implications of German *Kultur,* "Teutonic" militarism and German responsibility for the war, the war as a contest between good and evil, the notion of race, the sense of betrayal by Germany, the British fetish of fitness but lack of military preparedness, the pitch for American support. Only Ford's strong French bias is lacking.[21] The essential difference is that, while Wells seeks—and wins—our hearts rather than our minds in the novel, Ford ostensibly tries in these books to win our minds; but in fact he must assume that our hearts are already his if he is to succeed. It is tempting to imagine this material as the basis for a section omitted from *Parade's End.* Had Ford put his views in the mouths of fictional characters, had he conceived the issues as inherent in a dramatic situation, the reader—at least this one—would have applied a different standard and would have looked, not for what the historian considers truth, but for the life imparted to the subject and the possibilities for imaginative sympathy. But perhaps Ford, who as a novelist was so fair and unbiased in imagining other possible points of view, turned away from treating the matter of Germany in a novel—precisely because it would have been impossible for him to sustain the single point of view of adversary to those who made blood their argument.

---

[20]H. G. Wells, *Mr. Britling Sees it Through* (New York: Macmillan, 1916).

[21]In an unsigned "Avant-propos" in the French edition of *Entre St. Denis et St. Georges* (Paris: 1916), the unidentified writer quotes in translation a review of H. G. Wells, *When Blood Is Their Argument* (*Cassell's,* May 1916)!

> Ce qui a perdu les Allemands, c'est avant tout leur respect pour l'instruction, qui a fait d'eux l'instrument de la folie des Hohenzollern. M. F. M. Hueffer l'a prouve de façon absolument concluante dans son admirable livre.
> (What the Germans have lost is first of all their respect for learning, a loss which has made of them the instrument of the Hohenzollerns' madness. Mr. F. M. Hueffer has proved it in absolutely conclusive fashion in his admirable book.)

See Harvey, *Ford,* p. 49.

EDWARD NAUMBURG, JR.
A Collector Looks at Ford Again

In the late 1920s, with my first rather limited earnings, I began to fulfill a long postponed desire to collect first editions of my favorite author, Joseph Conrad. I was lucky in coming upon a bookseller who offered me a number of books from Conrad's library. Among them, with affectionate presentation inscriptions, were several early volumes of Ford Madox Hueffer. In this way was my interest awakened in Ford Madox Ford and in the circumstances of his friendship and collaboration with Conrad—and, of course, in the search for *both* authors' works. Some of my reasons for collecting, my admiration for Ford's genius, and any contribution my collection has made to the serious study of his work—these matters are all touched upon in "A Collector Looks at Ford Madox Ford," an article I wrote for the *Princeton University Library Chronicle,* April 1948. That issue also included articles by Herbert Gorman, R. P. Blackmur, and Mark Schorer, as well as my own checklist of Ford's works (possibly the first detailed one ever compiled). Of this issue, J. A. Bryant, Jr., wrote: "After that, things began to happen."[1]

And they did! There followed the Knopf publication of the Tietjens tetralogy, *Parade's End* (1950) and *The Bodley Head Ford Madox Ford,* edited by Graham Greene in England (1962–63). In the last three decades, a comprehensive bibliography, a volume of letters, biographies, essays, full-length critical studies, dissertations, and reminiscences have appeared; and so too has my collection grown. Yet Ford's proper place in twentieth-century literature is still to be determined. In the *Times Literary Supplement* of 2 January 1977, under the title "Reputations Revisited," Anthony Burgess wrote:

> The most underrated British writer continues to be Ford Madox Ford, despite the Bodley Head's keeping his major work alive (though Graham Greene's truncation of *Parade's End* is indefensible).

[1] "Ford with a Cane," *Sewanee Review* 72 (1964): 495.

And later that year, in the August *Esquire* Wilfrid Sheed wrote:

> When it comes to underrated, Ford Madox Ford still reigns alone. Every few years someone tries to raise his majestic hulk, but he sinks back with a satisfying squush. Ford was born to be underrated and as such is something of an immortal.

These are not optimistic observations, and Robert Lowell's condescending lines—

> But master, mammoth mumbler, tell me why
> the bales of your left-over novels buy
> less than a bandage for your gouty foot.

need to be countered by Emerson's statement, which I quoted over thirty years ago as an epigraph to my essay: "The fame of a great man is not rigid and stony like his bust. It changes with time. It needs time to give it due perspective."

In honor of the "due perspective" implicit in the occasion of the publication of this volume, I offer to readers of Ford a second look at my collection and present here some examples of what I have added to it since 1948 and some pieces collected before that date but absent from my first essay.

I have in my copy of *Ford Madox Brown,* Ford's splendid life of his grandfather (published when he was twenty-three), the following letter, the earliest by Ford in my collection and written in 1893, when he was nineteen. "Mr. Rowley," Charles Rowley, was a good friend of Madox Brown's and a Manchester socialist.

1, St. Edmund's Terrace
Regent's Park. N. W.

Dear Mr Rowley
I write to you, since the news may come less roughly than from another quarter—to say that my poor Grandfather is very near his last—You know he has been ailing much of late & on Sunday he had a choleraic seizure—which so prostrated him—turning to apoplexy—that Mr Gill gives him but six hours of life.—Pray excuse my briefness but I have much to do—only I thought you would feel hurt at not being warned.

Most faithfully yrs
Ford Hueffer

Of Ford's friendship with W. H. Hudson I have several reminders. The first is a presentation copy of *The Face of the Night* (1904), a book so rare that Ford himself said of it "It did not sell more than seventeen copies when the firm of publishers failed." The second is the following letter, undated.

10 Airlie Gardens
Campden Hill Road W.

My Dear Hudson

If you are going to come tomorrow do, pray, stop & have supper with us. It would be so much of a pleasure. I daresay Conrad will be here—but not in all probability anyone of a boring nature.

Always excepted
Yrs most sincerely
Ford M. Hueffer

Nine years after Hudson's death Ford spoke of him in a letter in which he also, quite modestly, justified the writing of *Return to Yesterday*—and by implication his other books of reminiscence.

ford madox ford
32 r. de vaugirard
paris vi
27 Nov 1931
Madame:
Thank you very much for your kind letter of the fifth of this month which has just reached me. If a book of the sort of *Return To Yesterday* can awaken echoes & if those echoes seem true—or even only tru-ish!—to a reader who has seen some of the same scenes it is indeed all that the writer could ask. So I have my reward!
It is very interesting to me to hear from someone who knew Hudson intimately. I don't think I ever knew anyone who did. He had so few intimates except for members of his immediate entourage. I wish I could have the privilege of meeting you—but I am practically never in London. The war damaged my lungs a great deal & I spend the greater part of my time on the Cote d'Azur, making occasional dashes to Paris to breathe, for as long as I can stand it, the atmosphere of a great city. The coal smoke of London undoes me after I have been there a couple of days. . . . But perhaps one day you will come to the French rather than the Cornish Riviera. I think the climate is the sunnier of the two.
If my memory is not playing me a trick, your son[2] married Lord Esher's daughter, Sylvia. In that case she came to me a great many years ago & asked me to give her literary advice as she was think-

[2] H. H. the Rajah of Sarawak (Sir Charles Vyner Brooke).

ing of taking to letters. But marriage put, I imagine, an end to that!

People have changed a good deal since those days. I don't know that they are better or worse. They are certainly different. I, at least, don't seem to make the same sort of friends I made, then, but perhaps other people still do.

In any case I hope Cornish weather will be kind this winter—unless indeed you tried the Riviera in which case I hope you will permit me the honour of paying my respects.

Thanking you again for your letter, I am

Very sincerely yours
Ford Madox Ford

Here is a letter from Thomas Hardy to Ford, and though Hardy does not say which book of Ford's he has just read, I assume it is *A Call,* because the date of the letter coincides with the appearance of the novel, and the newness of the subject matter—psychoanalysis and the subconscious and a telephone call—would make it, as Hardy notes, "modern."

MAX GATE
Dorchester

19 3 1910

Dear Mr Hueffer:

You have given me two or three evenings of much pleasure by sending me your very clever & modern novel. I read so few novels nowadays that I don't pretend to criticize or class it; but I may say that I think the women are admirably distinct in characterization— quite round & real, indeed—oddly enough the men seem less so (to me, at least) till one gets nearly to the end of the book when . . . [torn away] show up their individuality & say good-bye when you are getting to know them. This however may be my own dulness [*sic*] & not their obscurity. With many thanks, I am

Very truly yours
Thomas Hardy

Letters to J. B. Pinker, Ford's and Conrad's literary agent, abound in the collection. Some pertain to financial matters, some to literary. An interesting one, written 13 March 1914 on hotel stationery, Saint-Rémy-de-Provence, encloses the additions and alterations that would convert *The Panel* (1912), published in London by Constable, to *Ring for Nancy* (1913), the American version published by Bobbs-Merrill and Grosset and Dunlap.

Grand Hotel de Provence
Saint-Rémy-de-Provence
March 13, 1913

Dear Pinker

I enclose four sets of alterations for "The Panel"—pages 1—46
—159—and 327 (the end). If you will just ask Messrs Bobbs Mer-
rill to insert them in the copy from which they print that ought to
do the trick. If that isn't enough just let me know & I will do some
more, for I am not expert in this particular kind of devil, or rather
pirate dodging. I have not yet sent you back the agreement for Mr
Fleight as it is impossible to get hold of an English subject to witness
it here, but I shall be going to Paris shortly and will forward it to
you from there.

Yours
F M Hueffer
pp. V. H.

Mr. Fleight was published later that year, in spite of the difficulty of finding
an English witness for the contract. The holograph letter is signed "F M
Hueffer pp. V. H." Not surprisingly, Violet Hunt performed as secretary,
as did Stella Bowen in several later letters in the collection. In one dated 8
October [1922], when Stella and Ford were living in Sussex, she wrote on
his behalf to Edgar Jepson.

Dear Mr. Jepson—

Ford is struggling with a Great Poem, so he asks me to write for
him to say how he'd read straight through your novel as soon as it
came with great delight, and to thank you very much for it. He was
not at all well and had just decided to spend the day in bed when
the post came with your book, so that it couldn't have been more
opportune, it being such a very cheerful work! . . . We are going
abroad about the middle of next month, and are engaged in trying
to squeeze our fares out of the pigs,—which is to say that the whole
eleven are going to market! . . .

Yours sincerely
Stella Ford

Only last year I purchased a rare item—one that has not, to my
knowledge, turned up in any bibliography of Ford and that has particular interest today. It is a pre–World War I pamphlet (1912) entitled
Women's Suffrage and Militancy, with an inscription by the editor, Huntley

Carter.[3] Among the sixty or so contributors—alphabetically arranged—are Hilaire Belloc, Arnold Bennett, G. K. Chesterton, Havelock Ellis, Ford Madox Hueffer, Max Nordau, Upton Sinclair, H. G. Wells, and Israel Zangwill. Here are Ford's pages from that collection.

FORD MADOX HUEFFER.

You asked me what is my chief reason for being the ardent advocate that I am of the cause of Woman's Suffrage. It is like asking a man who is being stung to death by bees which bee most incommodes him. For the reasons for giving women the vote—for encouraging women, that is to say, to take interest in public questions and to regard themselves as members of a State rather than as the scavengers of isolated households—the reasons for this assail me on every side. But I suppose my chief reason for desiring that woman should have the vote—for desiring it rather than for saying that it is right and just that they should have it—for there is no man that denies that it is right and just, every man basing his denial on, and taking refuge behind, expediency!—and you will observe that my emotions upon this subject are so keen that my English has become complicated and incomprehensible;—my chief reason for desiring it is personal. I have, sir, in common with most men, suffered enormously at the hands of women. I have suffered a good deal at the hands of men, but men I have been able to get rid of. But the poor are always with us—and so are women, because they are poor. You will observe that I am taking the ground of the usual opponent of the cause. The usual opponent of the cause says that woman is an inferior, is a mendacious—let us say a generally bothersome animal. Therefore, she should not be allowed to exercise public privileges which are accorded to senile imbeciles and such reprieved murderers as have served twenty years in one of his Majesty's prisons. As a general rule I am accustomed to say and to believe that there is really no essential difference between man as man and woman as woman. I have written a great deal upon this theme, but it is one of some complication, and one which admits of dispute. Let me, then, take up my stand upon the ground that woman *is* the inferior, *is* the bothersome animal. Let that be conceded and we have at once the most powerful reason in the world for giving her a sense of her civic responsibilities. I have been persistently nagged, swindled, worried out of my life, and distracted during the course of my existence by some five or six women. I have been nagged at, betrayed, swindled and worried in one way or another during the course of that existence by perhaps fifty men. The men were intermittent pests, the women were there all the time. I do not mean to claim for myself any special experience in the matter of women. Most middle-class men ap-

---

[3]*Editor's note:* Ford's contribution is an expanded version of his letter to the editor of *New Age,* 9 February 1911. The letter was written in response to a symposium on women's suffrage in the previous issue. See David Dow Harvey, *Ford Madox Ford: A Bibliography of Works and Criticism* (Princeton: Princeton University Press, 1962), p. 166.

proaching middle age support at least five women and are worried by them in one way or another. Most working-men support from two to three women, and are equally worried *pro rata.* I was talking the other day to a prominent Tory gentleman about the Chancellor of the Exchequer. But did this Tory and gentleman abuse that much-abused person? Not a bit of it. He sighed:

"Ah! We ought to have had Lloyd George! We have always had to have someone to do our dirty work. We had Disraeli, we had Chamberlain; we ought to have had Lloyd George."

Sir, man in these islands—man throughout Christendom—is like my Tory friend: is like the Tory party in miniature. No sooner does he set up for himself; no sooner does he determine, with head erect and with courageous eyes, to face the world, than he looks round for someone —to do his dirty work! And that someone is a woman. Sir, I have been through it—moi qui vous parle. Sir, I am a thoroughly manly person. Sir, I am noble and generous; I throw my money about in restaurants, I tip porters with enormous lavishness, I get into splendid troubles through my chivalrous behaviour.

I am talking not, of course, of myself as a person but of myself as a man. All men, as distinguished from all women, are such fine creatures. That is why they have the vote.

I am, in short, a splendid creature, and my shirt-fronts are irreproachable. To look at me you would never think that I had any dirty work to do. But I have, and it is done for me—by from five to seven women. Sir, my irreproachable shirt-fronts are—let me let you into this secret— the products of the labours of my wife's maid. Sir, the fine table that I keep I am only able to afford because my wife goes from one end of town to the other looking for cheap butchers' shops. Sir, the splendour of my tips is due to the fact that my wife never tips at all, and cheats the railway companies whenever she can. Sir, I was only prevented by the persuasions of my female relatives from chivalrously voting six times for the Liberal or Conservative candidate of my division. Had I done it I must have gone to prison, for I observe that a scrutiny is being held in that same division. And finally, sir, I am only enabled to write this improving letter by the devoted assistance of a secretary, who is a female. So here splendid—generosus et filius generosi, homo Europaeus sapiens—I stand with those five all carefully doing my dirty work, and, of course, they are low-minded creatures. Everyone of them is an inferior animal. They bow down before me; they are mendacious; they have no real sense of right and wrong. How should they be fitted to have, equally with myself, the privilege of sending company promoters, stock brokers, brewers, and the like to Parliament? Their business in life is to do my dirty work. It is wonderful that they are not dirty-minded as well as inferior. But, sir, I will not admit that the Daughters of Albion have been trained by me to the latter end. No, sir, I am bound to say that they are inferior animals, but they are not dirty-minded. On the contrary, they are as pure as the skies which hang over the British Islands, as candid as the British cliffs of chalk, as unsullied as their native streams, as original as the first daffodils that are on sale in Covent Garden Market. Sir, splendid creature that I am, I have turned my womenkind into housemaids. They read my postcards, they lie, and their only arguments are woman's arguments. That is why they must not have the vote.

That, of course, is the point of view of the true Briton. But alas, I am not a true Briton. I am a sort of a foreigner, so that I do not arrive at the same conclusions as a gentleman who has been fed on nothing but beef. I am willing to admit that woman is my inferior. It will not worry woman if I do admit it, and it helps my argument. For, whereas I must then admit that I am splendid, I must then admit that I am every day of my life bamboozled, nagged at, and worried to death by from five to seven of these inferior animals; and personally, I want to get hold of a woman that I can trust better than any man. I want to change it. I want to be rid of this monstrous regiment of women. I do not want any longer to have to support from five to seven lying animals of an inferior type, not one of whom can be trusted not to read my postcards. I am sick of women as they are. I want them changed; that is why I want women to have the vote.

Sir, I understand that you have a body of readers who are the most intelligent of the United Kingdom. So that I can trust them to pick out what in this letter is wrong and what is solemn truth. That fact is that I have done so much preaching in this cause that I am tired of uttering solemn truths to excellent persons who cannot understand them. But it would seem to me to be evident to every sane man that if he desires to elevate a class of the populace he will set about educating them. If I want to make my housemaid take an intelligent interest in my household, if I want my workman to take an interest in my factory, I shall begin by giving my housemaid or my workman a share in the household or the family. It is all nonsense for any man who pretends to desire the advancement of the State or the solution of public problems—it is all nonsense of him to make these pretensions if he insists on maintaining the larger half of the population in conditions that make them inferior. If one of these gentlemen says candidly that he likes the present conditions, that he likes to have a harem of from five to seven women, all doing his dirty work and all inferior animals—to such a candid gentleman I have really no answer to make. He is logical and he is sincere. But he won't talk about the good of the nation, for no civilisation can be justified of itself which acknowledges that one half of its population are inferior to its murderers who have done time and to its uncertified imbeciles.

As for the question of militant tactics, I am certainly in favour of them. It is the business of these women to call attention to their wrongs, not to emphasise the fact that they are pure as the skies, candid as the cliffs of chalk, unsullied as the streams, or virginal as spring daffodils. They are, of course, all that—but only in novels. This is politics, and politics is a dirty business. They have to call attention to their wrongs, and they will not do that by being "womanly." Why should we ask them to be? We cannot ourselves make omelettes without breaking eggs. Why should we ask them to? Sir, there is a Chinese proverb which says: "It is hypocrisy to seek for the person of the Sacred Emperor in a low tea-house." Sir, politics is a low tea-house from which, in His mysterious way, God slowly grinds out some good small flour. When they have got that, the women can afford to come out and bake tea-cakes. Of course, if someone can point out a better way than kicking policemen, no one would be better pleased than I, but since Joan the Maid helped the King of France to his sacring at Reims, there was no action which has so called public attention to the capabilities of women as that memorable moment when a journalist invented the helpful lie that Miss Pankhurst spat in a policeman's face. Miss Pankhurst did not do it, but the journalist knew what our public wanted.

In my collection are three of Ford's books, each inscribed affectionately, which he presented to Conrad: *The Benefactor* (1905), *Hans Holbein* (1905), and *The Heart of the Country* (1906). Of even greater rarity is Conrad's *The Rover* (1923), inscribed "FMH from JC"; later, Ford inscribed the same book and gave it as an especially precious gift to "RKDC with love from FMF. 1929."[4]

But perhaps the most remarkable documentation I have of the special nature of the Ford-Conrad relationship is a series of four letters, pencilled scraps, from Ford to Conrad, written from the trenches under enemy fire during World War I. Although these extraordinary letters have been published in part in my earlier essay and included in Richard Ludwig's *Letters of Ford Madox Ford,* they have not, so far as I know, been published as a discrete group. Because of the special effect they produce when read together, I would like to present here all four of the letters, which were written in 1916, together and complete. They bear witness to a communion between the two writers, long after their collaboration was over, one artist sharing the sensory impressions of artillery warfare with another to whom they were equally meaningful. There is no self-pity or self-dramatization, only the interest of the phenomena observed and gotten down, and a good deal of personal warmth and affection. It is all made the more poignant because of the possibility, which Ford was fully aware of, that he might not return; and it seemed all the more important to put those observations in Conrad's safe keeping. The state of the handwriting, suggesting so much stress and physical hardship, required a good deal of deciphering. I was aided by Janice Biala and Wally Tworkov.

---

[4]RKDC was Mrs. René Wright of St. Louis, to whom Ford had dedicated *A Little Less Than Gods* the year before. I am obliged to Sondra J. Stang for this identification.

Letter 1

Attd. 9/Welch
19th Div., B. E. F.
[September, 1916]

My dear Conrad:

I have just had a curious opportunity with regard to sound wh. I hasten to communicate to you—tho' indeed I was anyhow going to write to you today.

This aftn then, we have a *very* big artillery strafe on—not, of course as big as others I have experienced—but still *very* big. I happened to be in the very middle—the centre of a circle—of H. A. and quite close to a converted, naval how[itzer]. The worst had [?] lasted for about an hour—incessant & to all intents & purposes at a level pitch of sound. I was under cover filling up some of the innumerable A. F.'s that one fills up all day long even here—& I did not notice that it was raining and, suddenly & automatically, I got under the table on the way to my tin hat—Out here, you know, you see men going about daily avocations, carrying buckets, being shaved or reading the D'ly Mail &, quite suddenly, they all appear to be pulled sideways off their biscuit boxes or wagon shafts. It means of course shrapnel or minen.

Well I was under the table & frightened out of my life—so indeed was the other man with me. There was shelling just overhead—apparently thousands of shells bursting for miles around & overhead. I was convinced that it was all up with the XIX Div[n]. because the Huns had got note of a new & absolutely devilish shell or gun.

It was of course thunder. It completely extinguished the sound of the heavy art[iller]y, & even the how[itzer] about 50 yds. away was inaudible during the actual peals & sounded like *stage thunder* in the intervals. Of course we were in the very vortex of the storm, the lightning being followed by thunder before one cd. count two —but there we were right among the guns too.

I thought this might interest you as a constatation of some exactness. And, for the matter of that, when the rain did come down the sound of it on the corrugated iron roof of the dugout also extinguished the sound of gun-fire, tho' that is not so remarkable. It probably stopped the guns too, but that I don't know. At any rate they are quiet now, but the rain isn't.

The mud and rain here are pretty bad—after about a fortnight of wet—but they are not really much worse than Stocks Hall—*t'en souviens tu?*—used to be, and I bear them with more equanimity than most of my brothers in arms—I daresay because of that early training. I certainly remember worse weather experiences between

Page two of the manuscript of the first of Ford's four letters to Conrad from the front, September 1916. (Courtesy Edward Naumburg, Jr.)

the Pent & Aldington. But I have lain down wet in the wet for the last three nights & do not seem to have taken any harm except for a touch of toothache. And I am certainly in excellent spirits; tho' of course it is not yet cold & that may prove too much for me. I daresay eulogia of the French Press wh. continues to blaze and coruscate about my gifts has remonté my morale. It *is* gratifying, you know, to feel that, even if one dies among the rats in these drains one won't be—if only for nine days—just like the other rats. Of course these salvos are a little machined by the French Govt— but still, some of them are genuine—& Genl Bridges who kindly commended me on Bn. parade the other day—tho' God knows my fo^n. [formation] was dilapidated enough, with seven smoke helmet buttons & three cap badges missing!!—tells me that he has written to Genl. Plumer to say that I ought to have a staff job. So I may get one—& I don't know that I shd. be sorry. I have been for six weeks —with the exception of only 24 hours—continuously within reach of German missiles &, altho' one gets absolutely to ignore them, consciously, I imagine that subconsciously one is suffering. I know that if one of the cooks suddenly opens, with a hammer, a bacon-chest close at hand, one jumps in a way one doesn't use when the "dirt" is coming over fairly heavily.

An R. F. A. man has just come along & explained that the "rain has put the kybosh on the strafe."—So there, my dear, you have the mot juste. But it is fairly sickening all the same.

I hope you are all right: drop me a line now & then. There are no goats here—but 40,000 mules—mostly from Costaguana!

Yrs. always,
F.M.H.

I have been re-reading *Pierre Nozière* at intervals: it's thin; it's *thin,* my dear. I wonder if the old man won't appear like threadpaper after all this. C'est là son danger, as far as the future is concerned.

Letter 2

9/Welch
19th Div., B. E. F.
6.9.16

My dear,

I will continue, "for yr information & necessary action, please," my notes upon sounds.

In woody country heavy artillery makes *most* noise, because of the echoes—and most prolonged in a *diluted* way.

On marshland—like the Romney Marsh—the *sound* seems alarmingly close: I have seldom heard the *Hun* artillery in the middle of a strafe except on marshy land. The *sound,* not the diluted sound, is also at its longest in the air.[5]

On dry down land the sound is much *sharper;* it hits *you* & shakes *you.* On clay land it shakes the ground & shakes you thro' the ground. A big naval (let us say) gun, fired, unsuspected by us out of what resembled (let us say) a dead mule produced the "e" that I have marked with an arrow.

In hot, dry weather, sounds give me a headache—over the brows & across the skull, inside, like migraine. In wet weather one minds them less, tho' dampness of the air makes them seem nearer.

Shells falling on a church: these make a huge *"corump"* sound, followed by a noise like crockery falling off a tray—as the roof tiles fall off. If the roof is not tiled you can hear the stained glass, sifting metallically until the next shell.[6] (Heard in a church square, on each occasion, about 90 yds away). Screams of women penetrate all these sounds—but I do not find that they agitate me as they have done at home. (Women in cellars round the square. Oneself running thro' fast.)

Emotions again: I saw two men & three mules (the first time I saw a casualty) killed by one shell. A piece the size of a pair of corsets went clear thro' one man, the other just fell—the mules hardly any visible mark. These things gave me no *emotion* at all—they seemed *obvious;* rather as it wd. be. A great *many* patients on stretchers— a thousand or so in a long stream is very depressing—but, I fancy, mostly because one thinks one will be going back into it.

When I was in hospital a man three beds from me died *very* hard, blood pouring thro' bandages & he himself crying perpetually, "Faith! Faith! Faith!" It was very disagreeable as long as he had a chance of life—but one lost all interest and forgot him when one heard he had none.

Fear;

This of course is the devil—& worst because it is so very capricious. Yesterday I was buying—or rather not buying—flypapers in a shop under a heap of rubbish. The woman was laughing & saying that all the flies came from England. A shell landed in the chateau

---

[5]*Editor's note:* The raised "e" of "th^e" was marked by an arrow drawn from the bottom of the page. See facsimile.

[6]*Editor's note:* In the *Letters of Ford Madox Ford* (Princeton: Princeton University Press, 1965), Richard Ludwig reads "sifting mechanically" here. The manuscript seems to read "metallically," and it is probable that Ford, unintentionally omitting an "h," meant "shifting."

Page one of the manuscript of the second of Ford's four letters to Conrad from the front, 6 September 1916. (Courtesy Edward Naumburg, Jr.)

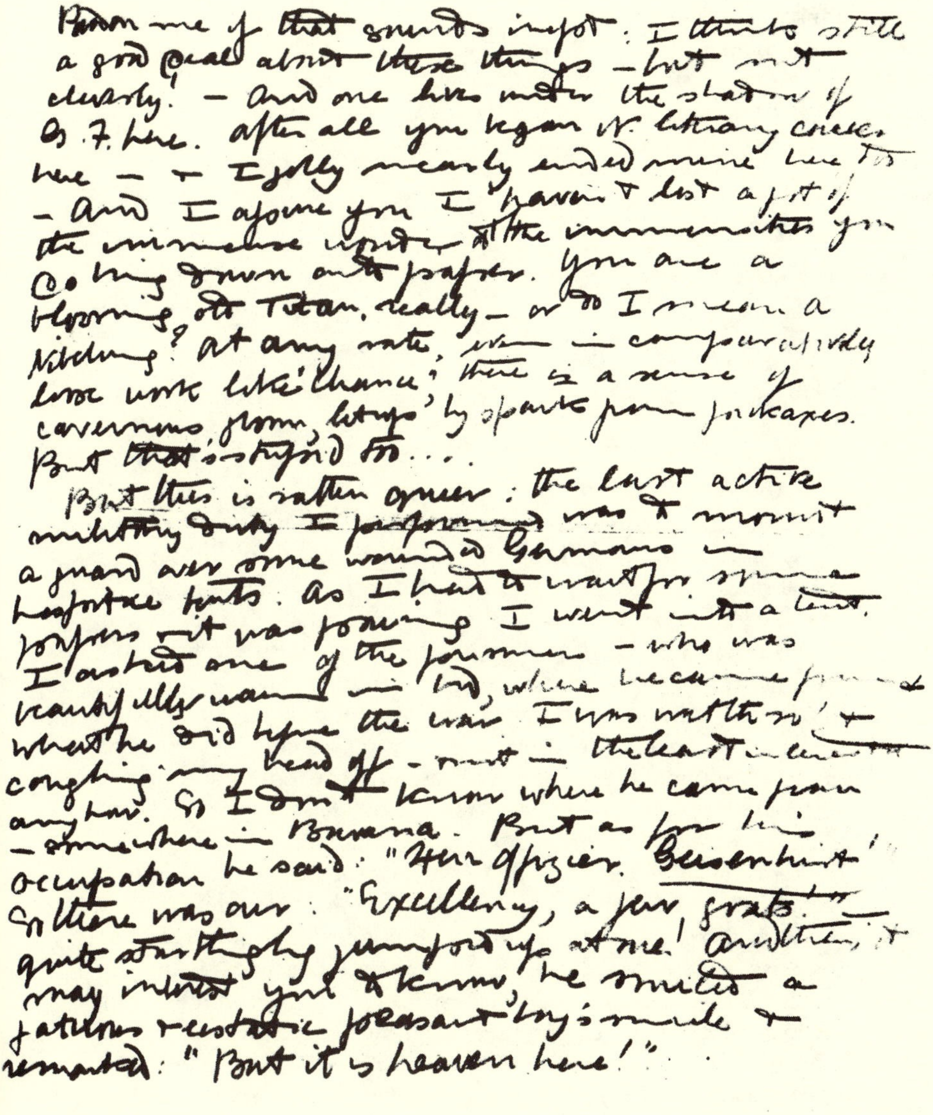
Pardon me if that sounds impert: I think still a good deal about these things — but not clearly! — And one lives under the shadow of G. F. here. After all you began yr literary career here — & I jolly nearly ended mine here too — And I assure you I haven't lost a jot of the immense wonder at the immensities you cooking down onto paper. You are a blooming old Titan, really — or do I mean a Kitchener? At any rate, even in comparatively loose work like 'Chance' there is a sense of cavernous gloom, lit up by sparks from pickaxes. But that's stupid too . . .

But this is rather queer: the last active military duty I performed was to mount a guard over some wounded Germans in hospital tents. As I had to wait for some papers it was going I went into a tent. I asked one of the prisoners — who was beautifully warm in bed, where he came from & what he did before the war. I was rather so! & coughing my head off — not in the least interested. So I don't know where he came from anyway — somewhere in Bavaria. But as for his occupation he said: "Herr Offizier, Besenbinder!" So there was our "Excellency, a few goats." — quite startlingly jumped up at me! And then, it may interest you to know, he smiled a patient & ecstatic peasant boy's smile & remarked: "But it is heaven here!"

Page two of the last of four letters to Conrad from the front, 19 December 1916. (Courtesy Edward Naumburg, Jr.)

into whose wall the shop was built. One Tommie said, "Crump!" Another: "Bugger the flies" & slapped himself. The woman—about thirty, quick & rather jewish—went on laughing. I said, "Mais je vˢ. assure, Madame, qu'il n'y a plus comme ça de mouches chez nous." No interruption, emotion, vexed at getting no flypapers. Subconscious emotion, "thank God the damn thing's burst."

Yet today, passing the place, I wanted to gallop past it & positively trembled on my horse. Of course I cdnt. gallop because there were Tommies in the street.

Post just passing

Yrs
FMH

Letter 3

Attd. 9/Welch
19th Div., B. E. F.
7/9/16

Dear Conrad,

I wrote these rather hurried notes yesterday because we were being shelled to hell & I did not expect to get thro' the night. I wonder if it is just vanity that in these cataclysmic moments makes one desire to *record.* I hope it is, rather, the annalist's wish to help the historian—or, in a humble sort of way, my desire to help you, cher maître!—if you ever wanted to do anything in *"this line."* Of course you wd. not ever want to do anything in this line—but a pocketful of coins of a foreign country may sometimes come in handy. You might want to put a phrase into the mouth of someone in Bangkok who had been, say, to Bécourt. There you wd. be! And I, to that extent, shd. once more have collaborated.

This is a rather more accidenté portion of the world: things in every sense "stick out" more in the September sunlight. The big Push was too overwhelming for one to notice details; it was like an immense wave full of débris. It was France, of course—& this too is France. But this is France of tapestries—immense avenues along the road, all blue in the September twilight—& the pleasant air that gives one feelings of bien aise. It is curious—but, in the evenings here, I always feel myself happier than I have ever felt in my life. —Indeed, except for worries, I am really very happy—but I don't get on with my superior officers here & that means that they can worry me a good deal in details—there are almost endless openings for the polite taquinneries called "strafing" in a regiment—especially if one has had a Regular training & gets attached to R. A. Bn. where all the details are different. However, these things, except in moments of irritation are quite superficial—& it is all matter for observation. One of these days I daresay I shall fly out at someone & get into trouble—tho' not the sort of "trouble" that one minds. But indeed I hope I shan't—because discipline is after all discipline &, [I] begin to believe, the first thing in the world.

God bless you, my dear. Love to Jessie. I hope you have good news of Borys.

Yrs

FMH

Letter 4

3/Attd IX Welch

No ii Red X Hospital

Rouen, 19.12.16

My dear:

It must be all of five months since I heard from you—tho' I heard from you thro' Jessie later than that. I hope you continue the victorious career in various elements that she then spoke of. . . . But it is miserable business, really, wishing anybody who has anybody outhere [*sic*] anything. Only I do hope Borys is all right—& probably back? The trenches are not gay in this weather.

As for me,—c'est fini de moi, I believe, at least as far as fighting is concerned—my lungs are all charred up & gone—they appeared to be quite healed, but exposure day after day has ended in the usual stretchers & ambulance trains—this rather queer Rouen—wh. for its queerness wd. delight you—but I am too stupid to explain. But I saw the trousers[7] of Flaubert & the whole monument of Bouilhet thro' the tail of the ambulance that brought me here, in the Rue Thiers.

I have been reading—rather deliriously—"Chance," since I have been in this nice kind place. The end is odd, you know, old boy. It's like a bit of Maupassant tacked onto a Flaubert facade.

Pardon me if that sounds inept: I think still a good deal about these things—but not cleverly!—And one lives under the shadow of G[ustave] F[laubert] here. After all you began yr. literary career here—& I jolly nearly ended mine here too—And I assure you I haven't lost a jot of the immense wonder at the immensities you do

---

[7]·*Editor's note:* I am obliged to Mary Gallatin, Howard Nemerov, William Karanikolas, and Holly Hall, all of Washington University, for help in deciphering this as well as other illegible words in the manuscripts of these letters.

bring down onto paper. You are a blooming old Titan, really—or
do I mean Nibelung? At any rate even in comparatively loose work
like "Chance," there *is* a sense of cavernous gloom, lit up by sparks
from pickaxes. But that's stupid too. . . .

But this is rather queer: the last active military duty I performed
was to mount a guard over some wounded Germans in hospital
huts. As I had to wait for some papers & it was pouring I went into
a tent. I asked one of the prisoners—who was beautifully warm in
bed, where he came from & what he did before the war. I was wet
thro' & coughing my head off—not in the least interested anyhow.
So I don't know where he came from—somewhere in Bavaria. But
as for his occupation he said, "Herr Offizier, *Geisenhirt!*" So there
was our: "Excellency, a few goats!"—quite startlingly jumped at
me! And then, it may interest you to know, he smiled a fatuous &
ecstatic peasant boy's smile & remarked: "But it is heaven here!"

I suppose he took me to be friendly & benevolent—but as things
drag on & all one's best friends go—(of fourteen who came out
with me in July I am the only one here & of sixty who came from
3/W since, eleven are killed & one gets very fond of these poor
boys!)—one gets a feeling of sombre resentment against the night-
mare population that persists beyond No Man's Land. At any rate
it is *horrible*—it arouses in me a rage, unexpressed & not easily
comprehensible—to see, or even to think about, the dead of one's
own regt., whether it is just the Tommies or the NCO's or one's
fellow officers.

But anyhow: the few goats turned up again!

However, perhaps all this does not interest you: I can't tell. Since
I have been out here this time I have not had one letter from one
living soul. So one's conviction does not get much from wh. to gain
anything!

The M. O. who has just sounded my poor old lungs again says
I am to be sent to Nice as soon as they can move me. God bless
you, my dear. May Xmas be a propitious season to all of you.

Yrs
FMH

It is not much use writing to me because, after Nice, I shall
very likely be transferred to one of the regular Bns. in the East or
some other non-pulmonary district of the war—but wireless me a
kind thought!

Long after Conrad's death, in 1924, Ford wrote what was, on his own
side, a defense of their friendship. (Although the following letter is undated,
the address in Paris suggests 1931.)

F. M. FORD
84, Rue Notre-Dame Des Champs
Paris VIᵉ

TÉL LITTRÉ 90-45

Please address reply
32 rue Vaugirard
Paris VIe

William Jackson Ltd.
16 Tooks Court
Cursitor Street
Chancery Lane E.C.

Dear Sirs,   Yours of the 3d inst

There was never any break between Conrad and myself, which should be apparent to you if you consider that the last work that he completed was a collaboration with myself, nor have I the least intention of writing anything at all about our relationships.

I should however be much obloged [*sic*] if you would let me know the source of this rumour, because, should it have been a newspaper I should like to contradict the statement.

Yours faithfully
F. M. Ford

Much has been written about the Conrad-Ford collaboration and friendship, but a great deal remains to be learned before all the claims and assessments on the subject can be accepted. Ford himself, as the surviving collaborator, was often confronted by ludicrous statements he felt he had to correct. Here is an example of an "inexactitude" Ford challenged.

The City Editor
   The World

Sir:

In his account of yesterday's meeting of the Joseph Conrad Memorial of the Seamen's Church Institute, your representative lamentably misreports my speech.—It was made before *not* after lunch, too!—He makes me say that Sir John Masefield wrote the first chapter of a work called *Romance.*

This is a terminological inexactitude. What I said—it *was* before lunch!—was that that admirable British poet now visiting these shores wrote the first review of *Romance.*

No one—not Sir John, not the Poet Laureate, not Sir Edmund Gosse, not Sir Herbert G. Wells—(The titles are, perhaps only

179

intelligent anticipations: I have been for so long absent from my native country.) no one then of this great galaxy of writers that make England in truth a nest of singing birds: no one of them had any hand in the creation of *Romance*. It was written—where it is splendid—by Joseph Conrad: the rest of it was by, Sir,

Yr. obedient servant
Ford Madox Ford

Many years ago I purchased a grab-bag batch of material from the files of the *Transatlantic Review*. From this came a dummy copy of the magazine, with Ford's notation—"Office Copy"—which was intended to show the format of the forthcoming magazine and which included two Cantos of Ezra Pound, a poem by Mina Loy, a corrected galley of the first page of *Some Do Not . . .* , and twenty-four pages with corrections said to have been made by Ernest Hemingway, who was a subeditor at the *Transatlantic Review*. But the real gem, in three different forms—typescript, galley, and page proof—was an early version of a chapter from *Some Do Not . . .* , with Ford's directions to the printer, presented here from the unedited typescript.

Serial   From SOME do NOT
by F. M. Ford

It was certainly grown lighter. He could see that she had, moving between her breasts, on a little gold chain, a little gold coin that showed the image; certainly of St. Michael. He wondered whom she had at the front. Catholics wear little gold coins with St. Michael on them when they have lovers at the front, the patron saint of soldier men. She said at last:

"Then"—he wondered why she said: "then!"—"you understand that you will in all probability never see me again. I am going into practically permanent retreat with the female Premonstratensians at Slough

He asked:

"You'll be able to look after the boy?" He was glad she was going to Papist nuns.

She said:

"Yes! He'll go to Eton and to Mother's in the holidays. Perhaps your brother will let us have Groby now and again . . ."

He said:

"He probably will!"

She said:

"You understand that, if you ever go near that girl again, ever even into her mother's house, I'll raise such Cain she'll wish she was never born."

He stood up.

"We might as well not quarrel now' " he said.

She exclaimed:

"You oaf!"

He said dully: for he was determined not to quarrel:

"I'd like you to give my really dear love to your mother."

She said:

"She's coming to see you off. She doesn't mind risking meeting your girl . . . That's part of the mischief you've done . . ." He felt a sudden pleasure at the idea of Mrs. Satterthwaite's distracted figure amongst groups of subalterns on a long platform. She said:

"Oh God! How could you be such a skunk! The girl was waiting to drop into your mouth like a grape. Couldn't you bring yourself to seduce a . . . a little kitchen maid? Are they so rare!"

He was wondering by what queer morality a man was a skunk because he wouldn't seduce. Because of the girl's disappointment? That surely was too altruistic.

"Then there'd have been a chance . . . " Sylvia said. She had shaken off her outer garment: the whole of her figure was visible under a film that glistened a little. He felt undoubtedly a desire for her. She, he knew, knew that she could calculate on that. She said, her voice trembling:

"I'm going by the 6.15, if I go. If I go I must go and dress at once . . . No: you won't have to see to the luggage. It has gone: except my dress. If I go you never see me again . . . " The muscles of all her body worked under the thin film that was like the covering of a meringue. He said to himself:

"It must be queer to play Potiphar's wife to your own husband!" The idea of the long hours she had spent crouched in the chair overwhelmed him. She was standing so near him that he could almost feel the warmth. He could quite . . .

He said suddenly:

"I've remembered the words of the song you wanted, my memory's suddenly extraordinarily better."

She recoiled the whole of her body from him, though her bare feet remained where they had been in their red leather mueles.

He said:

> "'Somewhere or other there must surely be
> The face not seen: the voice not ever heard:
> The voice that never yet: that never yet, ah me,
> Made answer to my . . .'"

Whiteness arose before him: there was a peculiar sound: like air escaping from a tyre-valve. He felt great pain on each side of his face. With her fists clenched, downwards, she had struck him with the hams of her hands, using all her strength, on his two cheekbones. There was a tearing sound. She was gone. Her white peignoir lay at his feet as he sank down into his chair again.

"By God!" he said, "I probably am a skunk! . . . I probably am!"

He wondered how he would explain two contused eyes to a trainload of brother officers in three hours time. You couldn't invent an accident fantastic enough. They would certainly say it had been a woman.

The fear of the dreadfulwar dropped down on him and he began to count his chances of escape. What else was there to do? He couldn't in decency, at that moment think of his girl, impregnable. That was to be for tomorrow. Today: it would be like thinking of a new bride over a wife's unfilled grave.

There was no doubt that, by then, it was broad day.

The door just opened itself: a small gold object fell into the room and lay on the carpet, near the door. It was the medallion of St. Michael that had been between his wife's breasts. He wondered if that meant that she cast him off—or that she sent it to him to wear and be safe. It had certainly been blessed by the Pope! He heard down below the great door close. Afterwards he heard, from the street Sylvia's clear, unconcerned voice say:

"Paddington!"

—THE END—

This cache of *Transatlantic Review* material also included corrected type-scripts and galleys of articles by Ford as well as by other contributors, includ-ing, for example, "Stock Taking: Towards a Re-Valuation of English Litera-ture," by Daniel Chaucer (Ford's pseudonym). There are marginal instruc-tions to the printer in Ford's hand, written in French. There is also the original typescript (in its entirety) and several pages of galleys of the Hueffer-Conrad collaboration *The Nature of a Crime.* And of even greater interest, the typescript of chapter 1 of *Romance,* in which Ford provides an "analysis" showing which sentences were his and which were Conrad's. The material on *Romance* was included in the Appendix of *The Nature of a Crime,* when it was published in 1924.

I gave to the Princeton University Library two notes about Ford's *New Poems,* which was published by Rudge in 1927. Along with the original holograph man-uscript was a note written on the stationery of the Hotel Lafayette, New York:

> *New York Poems*
> This is the final ms. that was printed from [*sic*] by Rudge. I changed the title & the order of the poems at the suggestion of Miss Elinor Wylie a note to whom will be found on p.v.

The note to Miss Wylie appears in the lower right-hand corner of a page listing the contents of the volume, with question marks before "Winter Night Song" and "A House":

> Dear Elinor
>   Wd. you look at these? I can't feel certain about the order. Don't you think it might be better to invert A House & Winter Night

Note by Ford accompanying the original holograph manuscript of *New Poems*, dated 11 December 1926. (Courtesy Princeton University Library)

Note from Ford to Elinor Wylie on page listing the contents of *New Poems*. (Courtesy Princeton University Library)

Song? Irita thinks to call it [?] *New Poems* tout court wd. be better than *New York?* as only two we[re] actually written in N. Y.

Of Ford's generosity and help to young writers I have ample evidence in my collection. There has recently been enormous interest in the late Jean Rhys, of whom A. Alvarez in a long critical essay in the 17 March 1974 *New York Times* wrote: "To my mind, she is, quite simply, the best living English novelist." Ford, one might say, discovered her, published a story of hers in the *Transatlantic Review,* and helped to have her books published. Francis Carco's *Perversity,* published in the late twenties, continues to appear in paperbacks with lurid covers and with the attribution of the translation from the French to Ford. But he wrote me in February 1935:

> The translation of *Perversity* was not by me at all but by a lady called Jean Rhys. The publishers fraudently [*sic*] attributed it to me, I suppose, because they thought it would sell better and I had the book suppressed and never heard anything more about it—I mean I don't know whether it was reissued with the proper name of the translator. . . .

Ford himself attempted to help me in bibliographical matters, and in 1935 I received from him a typed letter expressing some amazement at my collection.

> Thank you for the list of my books you sent me. Does this represent your actual possessions? If so, you have the most complete collection of my works in the world.

The letter gives particulars about matters such as publishers, titles, and translations, but it is obvious that he kept no list of what he had written. The letter ends:

> Those are all I can remember at the moment, but there must be a great many more. If they come into my head, I will write to you about them.

And there is a postscript in Ford's hand along the left margin:

> Oh: there is also *The Monstrous Regiment of Women* written about 1913 for the Suffragettes.

It is a great satisfaction to share with readers of Ford the results of a half-century of happy hunting, results that give us glimpses into the life, the work habits, the perceptions, the achievements, and the failures of a great writer. The owner of a great Cremonese instrument knows that he is only the temporary custodian of something that has given and will give delight to many generations. So, too, a collector's achievement, perhaps selfish in nature, becomes later a font of knowledge and enjoyment for future generations. It is a matter of some pride to me that my collection formed the basis for David Dow Harvey's monumental *Bibliography of Works and Criticism.*

Ford playing solitaire, early 1920s, painted by Stella Bowen. (Courtesy Julia M. Loewe)

Ford in Toulon, 1932, painted by Janice Biala. (Courtesy Janice Biala)

With Julie, walking in
Toulon, 1920s. (Courtesy
Julia M. Loewe)

Toulon, between 1924 and
1926. Standing, Juan Gris and
Georges Duthuit; seated,
Josette Gris, Ford, Julie, Stella
Bowen; and Toulouse, the
dog. (Courtesy Georges
Gonzalez-Gris)

Circa 1927. (Courtesy Janice Biala)

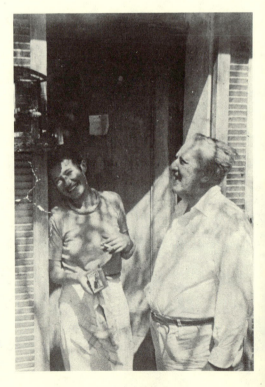

With Janice Biala at the Villa Paul in Toulon, early 1930s. (Courtesy Janice Biala)

With Ezra Pound in Rapallo,
1932. (Courtesy Janice Biala)

With Janice Biala, Nice, 1934.
(Courtesy Janice Biala)

Caroline Gordon, Janice Biala, Ford, and Allen Tate at Benfolly, Clarksville, Tennessee, 1937. (Courtesy Janice Biala)

On the boat with the Walter Lowenfels twins. (Courtesy Janice Biala)

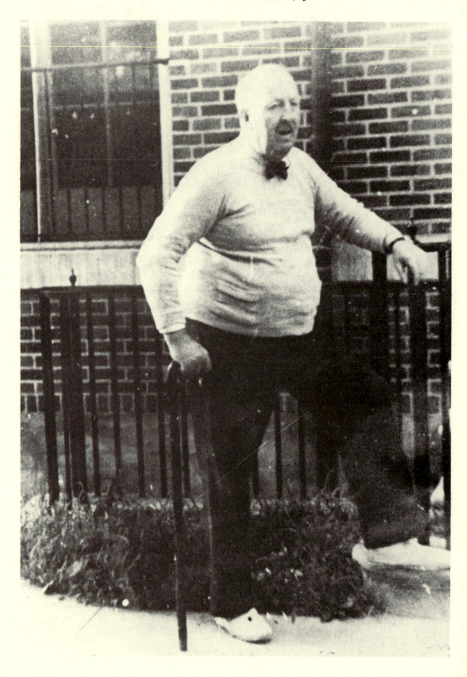

At Olivet College, Michigan, 1938. (Courtesy Janice Biala)

PART TWO
Memories and Impressions

JANICE BIALA

I cannot remember any time when Ford admitted defeat or gave in to despair. As far as he was concerned the artist's life was the only one worth living. You do what you like and take what you get for it and no complaints, and that is how he lived his life. He never defended himself and did very little complaining. He loved to quote Dr. Johnson, who said, "Live merrily and trust to good letters." It was rare when good letters brought him in an income to equal that of a street cleaner—but then he boasted that every member of his family died poorer than he'd been when he was born. The most important thing *about* Ford was that he was an artist. He had infinite indulgence for anything human except cruelty and stupidity. He was himself intensely human in his faults as well as his virtues. I've heard him described as a man and a half. He was also the "happy fishwife who had gotten into a palace," as he called himself in his description of a breakfast at Galsworthy's well-appointed table. He practiced his art and lived by it in the teeth of every disaster. With passion and a wry gaiety he could be happy, and was, at the drop of a hat. The announcement of an unexpected check, no matter how small, would be an immediate occasion for a celebration, generally of a gastronomic nature. In between the announcement and the arrival of the check, there would have been two or three other reasons for celebration. When the check arrived there was of course an absolutely legitimate reason to celebrate—if there was still any money left to celebrate with.

Extravagant things happened to him. The house we lived in on the rue Vaugirard was to be torn down. Everybody was asked to pay their taxes by a certain date—months before they would normally be due—and move out. This was very inconvenient. We were about to leave for Germany. There was no time and no money to do both. A choice had to be made. Germany won. The apartment—with literally everything it contained—was left to the tax collector. Not a saucepan, not a dish, absolutely nothing was taken out, just a four-dollar easel. I might add that the furniture—all Louis XIII or Louis XV—in that apartment would bring fabulous prices today; like Tietjens, Ford

An expanded version of a memoir written for "Memories of Ford Madox Ford," a program taped by Richard Elman for WBAI in New York City, 5 November 1961.

knew furniture. Another time after a long period of financial strain, a lot of money, relatively speaking, arrived. That money was torn from the purse it was in by the mistral and flew into the Rhone at Tarascon. Ford was amused for months at the thought that some astonished housewife cleaning fish might have found a thousand-franc note in its belly.

Once the wolf nearly got us. Ford was writing a series of articles for *The American Mercury* which later came out in book form as *Portraits from Life*. Each month, on receipt of the manuscript, the *Mercury* paid for it and cabled the money to Toulon. All went well for some time, and then for three months running no money turned up. Rather hopeless inquiries were made at the bank, but the answer was always no; no money had come. So many firms were failing that Ford was afraid to confirm his fears that this one too had gone bust and hadn't bothered to explain. Week after week the worry and tension mounted; finally the situation got so bad that Ford blew in the last five dollars on a cable to New York. The answer came back that the money had been paid regularly each month. Restored to life, with the telegram in my hand, I went back to the bank and this time refused to take the usual no. After much running around and looking up of books, it was discovered that the money was there all right. I asked to see the director, to tell him what I thought of his bank, but I was so enraged that I could only open my mouth, but not a word came out. I took the tram home to Cap Brun. It was winter and quite dark by then. There was an accident. Part of the platform I was standing on got ripped off. I didn't even notice it. When I finally got to my stop, I found Ford waiting for me with the announcement that there was to be a total eclipse of the moon in about ten minutes. So we walked up the road, until we got to a comfortable-looking bush. We sat down in the damp grass in front of it and waited for the eclipse of the moon.

Ford used to say that only states of mind counted, not facts. My states of mind about Ford have always been colored by extreme devotion and the desire to praise him. He lived and died in the great tradition of saints and artists.

His life was a battlefield and he died a lonely and terrible death. There were three people at his funeral, a few flowers, and a little bunch of thyme and bay leaves on his coffin. His usual bad luck held even in his burial. When we came back after the war to put the stone on his grave we discovered that thanks to a drunken gravedigger, he was erroneously buried in a plot of ground reserved for temporary graves. They were very apologetic at the Mairie in Deauville, but sooner or later his grave would have to be moved. That was Ford all over. He couldn't rest quietly even in his grave. As he so often said, "The gods to each ascribe a differing lot/Some enter at the portals, some do not."

JENNY BRADLEY

(Mrs. William Aspenwall Bradley)

Ford was known for his "lies." He had a way of writing things as they pleased him. But you must make allowances for an artist. Who deserves them more than he? Those who make statements about Ford's "lies" have only a vague appreciation of a very delicate situation. One goes on things that are so vague and can be so harmful. But there are so many aspects to be considered, and criticism is very easy. It is much more interesting to look for reasons than to make judgments, and far more rewarding. Besides, all novelists are more or less liars—if they are good novelists.

He had a very pleasant presence, but because he had been gassed in the first world war, he didn't have his normal voice, and at times he couldn't be understood at all. After he attended one of my mother's Thursdays, she said about him: "He told the most charming and witty stories, but he was alone to enjoy them." He had, you see, suffered greatly from the war. Afterwards, when my husband saw him at a distance, a fair-haired creature, a little bent, he said: "If that man were not so aged, he would be Ford Madox Ford."

In business he was difficult. He didn't know how to conduct business, and whenever he had money he would spend it, so there were times when he was penniless. He would say to my husband, "I've forgotten my cigarettes," when he hadn't any left.

He was an artist, by God. If only we had some like him now!

CAROLINE GORDON

I was twenty-seven years old when I first met Ford Madox Ford. I had written one novel which landed in the wastebasket—and a good place for it. Ford, at that time, had most of the New York publishers at his feet. I acted as his secretary and handled his mail. One morning I laid a manuscript of poems by Léonie Adams on top of the heap. He read the poems, then pushed a letter from the author of *Oil for the Lamps of China* aside and folded his hands on top of the heap and said, "Tell her that I am completely at her service." I gleefully relayed this message to Miss Adams and they became fast friends.

A few days later Ford heaved a sigh and asked me if I had done any writing. I told him that I had started a novel but that I was going to have to throw it away. He heaved another sigh and said, "You had better let me see it." I brought him the manuscript a few days later. He read the manuscript through, then said: "Why has nobody told me about this? What were you going to say next?" I recited the sentence. He said, "That is a beautiful sentence. I will write it down." This procedure was repeated several times. It ended with Ford taking my dictation for three weeks. The result was a novel called *Penhally.*

I delight to tell of this happening because it shows Ford's almost incredible generosity to younger writers.

I was by no means the only younger writer to whom he showed this generosity. There was one corner of his desk which was never bare. I think that he was the most generous man I have ever known.

He died in Deauville in his late sixties. There were very few people at his funeral. The corner of his desk was still heaped with manuscripts of younger writers whose work he wanted to get published.

JULIA M. LOEWE

I would like to begin by saying that my father was forty-six when I was born and I was eighteen when he died. So my memories of him do not stretch back to any part of his youth, nor do they cover any recollection other than those of a child and adolescent. Any discussion of his work and philosophy I shall leave to others: this is just a child's eye view.

He was very fair, and large, and quiet, his voice soft and his movements gentle and slow. His hair was so fair that when it finally turned white, nobody really noticed, and his eyes were very blue, and he had that white English skin that turns ruddy when exposed to the sun. His voice was somewhat breathless and low (he had been gassed during World War I) and sounded more like Charles Laughton's than anyone else I can think of. I never heard it raised—though it could be, if the occasion called for it, quietly devastatingly cutting and even arrogant.

I first remember him when I was very small, telling me long stories after dinner, a serial that he had invented for me, of a brave sailor and a beautiful Alsatian girl, clockwork creations of an old watchmaker, which came alive at midnight and had the strangest adventures. These he would relate in the somber dining room of a hotel in Toulon, in his beloved Provence, while I sat on his lap and solemnly ate my way through the *corbeille de fruits* which was the inevitable dessert. Even as a small child, I was aware of his magic way with words and the quality of his talk . . .

And what a lot of talk there was. I remember sitting in cafés with Ford and my mother on the waterfront in Toulon or in the Closerie des Lilas in Paris, sedately sipping my grenadine, while for hours the wonderful talk went on, well over my head. In Toulon there might be, among others, H. G. Wells or Juan Gris, in Paris Hemingway, Joyce, Ezra Pound—the Ezra of those days—Katherine Ann Porter, and many other "names," and always the aspiring unknowns, hungry but vital—in those days the young men were hungry rather than angry—with whose work Ford was ever prepared to take endless trouble—an aspect of his character that has always made me specially

An expanded version of a memoir written for "Memories of Ford Madox Ford," a program taped by Richard Elman for KPEK, Los Angeles, 1961.

proud of him. How many times have I heard him called "Cher Maître."

As a child, of course, I knew little about his work—but what an honor it was for me to be allowed sometimes to "help" him when he was working out his ideas preparatory to his daily stint of writing! I had to be absolutely quiet—in Paris, when I was about seven or eight, this usually took the form of sitting beside him while he played game after game of solitaire. This was just an opportunity to keep his hands busy while he thought out his next chapter or article—but I *was* allowed silently to point out possible moves that I thought he had missed! In Provence again, some years later, this phase of his work took the form of early morning irrigation of his vegetable patch—Ford was always a devoted gardener, with a real green thumb—and at the Villa Paul in Cap Brun he would stand at the top end of a furrow and lay the hose there, and I would watch the water trickle down to my end, past the lettuces, cucumbers, and beans, while he did some more thinking and cogitating. Then I would call, he would move the hose, and the process would be repeated again and again. But woe betide me if I started to chatter! The social amenities were for later in the day, when the writing was done —that terrible, all-consuming writing that had to be completed whatever the cost, if the deadline were to be met, the advance earned. We would sit on the terrace under the stars, looking down the hill toward the Mediterranean and watching the twinkling lights of the boats in the water. Then he and I would discuss—oh, philosophy, art, justice—all the things that a teenager grows earnest about. From tolerance of all things but cruelty and dictatorship, to the right amount of garlic and herbs to put in a particular casserole. . . . And what a teacher he was! My rapid improvement in Latin, under his tutelage, positively got me into trouble with my teacher, who could not understand this sudden improvement—and how could I explain to her that it was not that my father did my homework *for* me, but merely that when he taught I could learn—which was more than I could say for her?

To this Villa Paul period too belongs an episode which I have always recalled with great vividness. . . . Ford, Janice Biala, and I were walking down one of the narrow twisted streets of Toulon, where people and vehicles mingled with abandon, when suddenly Ford slipped and fell in such a way that he landed behind the front wheels of a great truck, and in the endless second, while the truckdriver slammed on his brakes, from somewhere beneath the vehicle, came this perfectly calm British voice remarking conversationally, "Now, Saint Christopher, here's your chance!" I guess Saint Christopher heard him, at that, because when truck and father were finally disentangled, though the rear-tire marks were clearly visible on his sleeve, Ford was quite unharmed. We all three put on an extremely nonchalant air and proceeded with the purchase of the pair of espadrilles for me, which was our goal at the time, and I, for one, was extremely glad to sit down . . . Ford, on the other hand, was quite unperturbed and merely amused.

Later yet, when the Depression of the thirties had forced my mother and me back to London—a move which Ford hated but which was economically unavoidable—and when he divided his time between France and America, I frequently visited him in Paris when he was there. There were always people and parties—some of the people well known, some not—and still again the young unknowns, *les jeunes* with holes in their socks, who knew that they could always count on him for advice and encouragement. Some of them later achieved fame, some did not. There was good food, too—in particular a running rivalry with some friends of his, the Le Sons, which took the form of alternating dinners, one week at their apartment, the next week at Ford's, where each side would try to outdo the previous week's efforts. Not very good for the figure, perhaps, but what a marvelous chef Ford was! That was at the rue de Seine, a peacock blue and yellow building owned by Raymond Duncan, brother of Isadora, a gentleman who wore at all times a Roman toga and sandals, his long silver hair bound by a fillet about the brow. The apartment was attractive enough . . . but the building was cold and drafty and not very comfortable, and Ford was getting old . . . and ill. He still had his dream of some day buying a small house in Provence—one of the last letters I had from him, from Olivet College, Michigan, where he was teaching, harped on this again. "We are desperately trying to save up enough to buy a cottage by Lyons where they are cheap and not too far from Paris, and yet still in the Midi. . . . About Valence *où le Midi commence*. We are tired of wandering forever without a home."

But it was not to be. In the spring of 1939, he crossed the Atlantic for the last time, but could continue his journey south no further than Honfleur, in Normandy, where I came to join him, and where, as usual, he had found beautiful but inconvenient rooms. I was just beginning to grow out of my prickly adolescent period and to feel that at last I would really be able to understand and be understood, beyond our various faults and difficulties— and to express the love which I had always had for him. But he was dying, by then. Most of the time he did not really know me, though when he did he was glad of my presence. The French doctor would not give him anything to ease his pain, which was considerable, because of his poor heart, but he was as always quiet and outwardly composed.

He died soon after, at last at rest in the France he so loved, leaving in his room the unfinished manuscript which he was working on to the last— for as he himself said, he was an old man crazy about writing. And that was the important thing about him.

ROBERT LOWELL

I met him in Boston in 1937, two years before he died, and it was a crucial moment in my life. I was having a good deal of trouble, personal trouble with my parents, and it was arranged that I meet Ford at a cocktail party. And I remember him coming in, and I had the fantastic impression that he was very much like the Republican elephant—not that he resembled that elephant, but he was a large man and . . . perhaps that's the key word to him, big in bulk, big in the qualities underneath that bulk. . . . I once asked him the young writer's question, "What does a writer need more than anything else?" and he said, "Memory." And whether that's true or not, it is certainly true of his kind of writing, which was full of a great abundance of things he'd retained.

And after you speak of the largeness of Ford, my second impression would be that he had two qualities almost equally pronounced that are almost contradictory, but were not, and that is the generosity and contempt. No person warmed and was more sensitive to young writers, and he was like a bear more than an elephant. He could hit you with his elbow and knock you down in sort of a blunt way . . . and I think those qualities went together. In my case I will give an illustration. After I met him he told some people that I was—I was nineteen at the time—that I was the most intelligent person he had met in Boston. Now I think that was more his low opinion of Boston than his high opinion of me.

I might say too that Ford is the first Englishman I think I ever met intimately, and he had certain generic qualities of an Englishman—their humor, their rhythm, and so forth, is different from ours—disconcerting and marvelous. And his opinion of Boston . . . I think that was the part of America he perhaps liked least: he saw through Boston. Its English pretensions and its Puritanism were very distasteful, and no man was less puritanical than Ford. Big and easy-going, and I might even say that he knew he was big, and he acted the role, and he could fill the role he chose, . . . ate great amounts.

I remember Colorado when he was lecturing at Boulder at the college. He said he was going to give a dinner with venison, which was illegal at that

This memoir was transcribed by the editor from "Memories of Ford Madox Ford," a program taped by Richard Elman for WBAI in New York City, 5 November 1961.

time, and the dinner was arranged, and I think it's still the best I ever had. The wines were balanced, and every course came as it should, and the venison came, and we ended with syllabub, and you felt in Paradise at the end. You never realized that the venison was mutton that Ford had cooked.

He was writing *The March of Literature* at that time, and I went to Olivet College with him, and his way of writing was to dictate, and I must say that was agony for me. I didn't know shorthand and took down what he said in illegible print, and he mumbled and had a Yorkshire voice, and it was quite difficult to get what his sentences were, and he slurred his words, and I often had to guess, and he would make remarks that I had no sense of prose rhythm when I couldn't hear him. Then in the afternoon—I could hardly type—I would painfully type out what I took down in longhand, which had many gaps, and with my terrible sense of prose rhythm had to improvise phrases here and there which I think still remain in *The March of Literature*—little blemishes that have been undetected.

The Ford I knew was very much like the Ford you find in [*It Was*] *the Nightingale,* one of the later books of autobiography: that is, he dictated his books, and the books went very much as his conversation did. He used that method, and it's quite subtle that good conversationalists don't necessarily write well and good writers are not necessarily good conversationalists. He'd got something that *joined* the two, that being a writer changed his conversation. I've often thought that if you could listen to Ford talk for an hour, say, as he does in *The Nightingale,* . . . you would say this was the most astonishing speaker you'd ever heard, and he gave that impression. He was not quite as consecutive and sustained in presence as on paper, but he was very much that way. Something happened when he had a plot and characters that changed the style, though even there I think he dictated those books—certainly the Tietjens—and they too have something of that quality of someone speaking.

I met my first wife through him. I think she was present when we remet in New York. What I remember is something that didn't happen there. He was so near the end of his life, which I never would have guessed. It must have been six or seven months before he died, so that after I heard about his death, somehow that last meeting stood out in some peculiar way which I have no image of.

MARY MCINTOSH

Ford Madox Ford begins what he said he had always regarded as his best book, "This is the saddest story I have ever heard."

Now, as I begin to write about that spring in Paris when my husband and I lived with Ford I feel that it is a sad story, too—not sad because of events, but sad because at that time I had never read anything that Ford had written—I never knew that I was living with a genius! I was not only young, but also very ignorant—ignorant at least in the literary world that I found myself unprepared to be in. No one who could have informed me or guided me could have conceived of my ignorance.

Then, along with my not having read any of Ford's works, an unfortunate first impression I had of him, that I wrongly kept for too long after, made a barrier as impassable as a guarded wall between the real Ford and my knowing him. I met him first at a party in New York and it was there that the attitude of my host and the other guests shaped and colored my impression—I was oversensitive to other people's opinions and unconfident of my own in those days. So when I felt that the people there were *belittling* this imposing guest from England, I naively supposed there must be a reason for it—that is, some reason within the character of Ford himself. And, strangely, that the attitude of the people in New York was similar to the attitude of those who surrounded him in Paris. I have puzzled about this for years. Why did the people around him belittle him and seem just to tolerate him even as they hovered around him? It is true that his own manner was not a winning one—he had a way of talking and acting superiorly (and even though one is superior it is a peculiarly irritating trait). He was more than a generation older than nearly everyone around him—and I know only one person, the girl he later married, who successfully spanned those years with intelligence and with kindly emotion. He was a mixture of both peer and father to our group, and it seemed it was not a comfortable mixture for him or for any of the rest of us.

The winter before Willard and I went to live with Ford in 1930 we lived at the Hôtel Corneille, across from the Odéon Theatre. A wonderful neighborhood it was—and what wonderful neighbors! Sylvia Beach was just down the rue de l'Odéon in her Shakespeare and Company, Caroline and Allen

Tate, with their little daughter, Nancy, were across the square at the Hôtel de la Place de l'Odéon, and Ford lived only a short walk down the rue de Vaugirard. But it was Ford's large and portly figure that seemed to form a pivot for our lives and that, with our willing submission, dominated them.

Ford was probably the most generous person I have ever known, with the greatest of all generosities, the giving of himself. His memory has become famous for all that he did for other writers, particularly the beginning writers; but this generosity was lavished on everyone, I think. I could weep, now that I understand everything much better, that I was not grateful enough for all his kindness to me and that I, in turn, was not kinder to him, and that I did not do more for him. But I'm sure that he understood youth well and forgave my negligence, my carelessness, and knew that one day my enlightenment would come.

His hospitality was another side of this generosity. What delightful times we had in his apartment at 32 rue de Vaugirard. That winter he had a small apartment at the rear of the fourth floor. Although we often complained about the four long flights of stairs, no one would refuse the climb, knowing that our best of hosts was waiting at the top. The living room was not large and in the late afternoon and evening when Ford had his "at homes," it would be crowded with friends and with friends of friends spending the winter in Paris or passing through on brief visits, for it seemed to everyone that seeing Ford was a very important part of seeing Paris. The feeling there was always lively and sparkling, and if it was tea time the tea was bountiful (I was helping Ford one day and I remember his saying, "Now, put lots of butter on the cinnamon toast—cinnamon toast needs lots of butter") and the fire was so warm (you never really know how good a grate fire can be until you feel one on a Paris winter day).

It was at tea there one day that I met Ernest Hemingway for the first time (I was later to become a good friend of his wife, Pauline). Hemingway was as handsome as I had expected him to be from a description by an enthusiastic admirer of his in America. He had great charm, too, but what I remember most about him was with what complete absorption he regarded you or whatever was the focus of his attention, as though he was extracting everything that could be extracted from each experience. He seemed to be having a very pleasant time that day, and that was long after the period he refers to when he wrote about Ford in his *Moveable Feast*. He didn't act as if his sense of smell was being offended by the presence of Ford in that small, warm room. That chapter about Ford in Hemingway's book is inexcusable. I can't help feeling that Hemingway wrote it from some unworthy, petty motive of personal revenge. . . .

I'm sure Paris was as cold and gray as it always is in the winter, but when I think of those months my first feeling is a glowing one, as though a burnished light suffused it all, and I know that it was Ford's kindness that is responsible in a great measure for this warm memory. . . . He had every week, regularly, on Thursday nights as I recall, what he called "Sonnet Parties." They were great fun—Willard and I never missed one of them. They had the interest of both a steady and a changing group, because there was always a nucleus of those of us who were spending the winter in Paris and there were the transient visitors.

In the nucleus were Polly Boyden, restless and delightful Polly, who was a poet from Chicago and who was then living in Paris with her three children and their German nurse; Allen and Caroline Tate; Lee and Virginia Hirsch (Lee was a painter and Virginia a writer); Walter and Lillian Lowenfels, who always seemed overflowing with youth and good spirits; Howard Baker, a quiet, serious young man from California who was studying at the Sorbonne (a year later Howard married and brought his American wife, Dorothy, back to Paris, but it would be several years before she wrote *Young Man with a Horn*); Alice and Bill Bandy, from one of the southern states in America, newly married and in Paris because Bill was writing a thesis on Baudelaire. Then there was a pleasant, middle-aged woman whose name was Mae Matthew. Willard and I never saw her at any other sort of occasion, but she came to every party, quietly wrote her sonnet, and joined in with us all, mostly with her cheerful smile. I remember the Tates bringing their great friend Robert Penn Warren, who was at Oxford and who came to Paris for his Christmas vacation. We called him "Red" because of his beautiful bright hair and we all loved him.

Ford would prepare in advance many copies of the last word in every line of a sonnet—he used those of different poets; Shakespeare and Christina Rossetti come to my mind now. The copies would be passed to the guests and everyone would write a sonnet based on the same rhyme words. I never would write one until the very last sonnet party that we had—I don't remember what prompted me to do it that time, but, to the complete surprise of everyone, Polly Boyden and I tied for first prize. I have a copy of it still and also one that Ford wrote and dedicated to me. But until that time there were three of us—Alice Bandy, Lee Hirsch, and I—who didn't, couldn't write the sonnets, and we were the judges. We were the only ones who were not professionally literary and were there at all only by virtue of our having literary spouses. . . . I can see the whole scene now—sitting where one could for light and comfort and often sacrificing both in the crowded room out of politeness—the movement of the firelight shadows, and each one solitary in the involutions and evolutions of creation. Ford always wrote his on the typewriter in the little adjoining study. After everyone had read his sonnet aloud, we judges would take the sheaf of them and go into the next room. We knew that our choice must be very conscientiously made—the authors waiting for our announcement were knowing and sensitive. My husband got the first prize often and really merited it, but one night Ford put his head in the door of the study and said, "Ah, I see what happens in here. You two sit and hold hands and Mary gives the prize to Willard." When all the exclamations over the prize-giving and the discussions of it were over, Ford would give us delicious petits fours and glasses of mousseux and we sat and talked on for ever so long in that passionate way of a group with a common interest.

Ford and the Tates and Willard and I had dinner together nearly every night, and often we were joined by Polly and by Léonie Adams. We had a few favorite restaurants—Michaud, where Allen always ordered the same thing, tournedos and a compôte de fruit, and the Cochon au Lait, next door to our hotel, where the suckling pigs were roasted on spits and where Ford introduced me to eau-de-vie de framboise and we sat sipping and sniffing it in the huge glasses, and Lipp's with the famous sauerkraut, though I never ate it without thinking that it couldn't compare with the sauerkraut my Czechoslovakian grandmother made on her farm in western Nebraska.

In late February Willard and I went to London, and Ford came over on some business of his and also to talk with us about a plan he had in mind. He took us to the Café Royal, the first time I had ever been there, and while we drank sherry Ford unfolded his plan, which was that when we went back to Paris we would come and live with him in a larger apartment that he was taking in the same house. Willard would act as Ford's secretary. And that is how it happened that when we returned to Paris our home, too, was 32 rue de Vaugirard. Ford used to call it, jokingly, our "ménage à trois."

This apartment was also on the fourth floor, but in the front of the building. Our bedroom was in the back of the apartment, Ford's in the front, and there was a living room, a small dining room, and a small kitchen.

Ford got up very early every morning, started writing at five o'clock, and worked through until noon. This was his day's work and he never did otherwise no matter how late he had stayed up the night before. In the afternoon and the evening until all hours he led a very full social life. We used to wonder how he could possibly keep up such an arduous schedule.

We had a *bonne,* whose name was Madame Yvonne, who used to come in every day to do the cleaning and to prepare the large dinner that we had at noon. We never saw Ford until dinner-time. When we were seated at the table Ford would say, "And what is today's great thought?" And that would start our conversation. I wonder what were Madame Yvonne's own "great thoughts" about us as she served us her delicious dishes—the elderly, patriarchal Englishman and the two young Americans somehow islanded on the top floor of an apartment house in Paris that was "home" to all of them?

A wise man once said to me, "It is difficult to live with anyone." And with Ford's complex artist's nature it was very difficult living with him. Willard seemed to take it better than I did. Perhaps it was just that much harder for me, with my Nebraska prairie background, to find a common ground with Ford and his association with the Paris and London literary worlds. I must have seemed very gauche to him. He was constantly teaching me manners: "You must say, 'Pardon,' when you pass anyone on the stairs" (no matter how ample and broad the stairway). "You, the woman, must be the one to suggest leaving" (this when he and Willard and I had been at some party together). On and on went my lessons and though I think now that they were necessary lessons, at that time they were irksome and embarrassing. Also, his indirectness, and what to me with my blunt ways seemed like evasiveness, disturbed me. I remember Willard quoted a line of Pope's to me one day, one that had delighted him, "Obliquely waddling to the mark in view," and I exclaimed instantly, "That's Ford!"

. . . It was spring! We used to walk every afternoon in the beautiful Jardin du Luxembourg, just across the street from our apartment. We walked very slowly because of Ford's difficulty in breathing. But this pace gave us more time to delight in every spring wonder. It was like slowly, slowly sipping an eau-de-vie—we had time to see each flower, each budding bush and tree, time to hear the children at their singsong games, to watch the little girls who already displayed in their small gloved hands and short, short skirts the famous French chic. If I could I would go back to Paris every spring, where the days are lighted twice over by the bright candelabra of the chestnut trees. Spring in the country is wonderful, but I believe spring in a beautiful city—a tree-lined, flower-filled city—is even better. There the glory of nature is compounded by human joy—the joy of the many people who become participants in a great procession.

Sometimes in our walks we would get as far as the Closerie des Lilas, that charming old café on the opposite side of the gardens. There we would sit under the trees and have an apéritif before getting back for our supper.

We often had our suppers at home. Ford and I would take turns doing the cooking and there was where we really ran into trouble. Ford was very proud of his cooking and I'm sure with good right, but he used to make me nervous and irritated coming into the kitchen when it was my turn, standing over me instructing me (I should have been grateful for his instruction; I wish now that I had had the good sense to profit by it—but then it only exasperated me). I remember one night losing my temper and being very rude to him —and all over a dish of baked bananas! I often said to Willard, "Ford is like an old woman in the kitchen."

When Ford had a dinner party of any pretensions, he never sat down at the table himself but devoted all of his attention to the cooking and serving. After one such party, and I forget who came to that one, Ford said that the menu would be syndicated in hundreds of papers throughout America.

Ford's daughter, Julie—then just ten years old—was living with her mother, but she came regularly to spend an afternoon with Ford and to go to Mass with him now and then on Sunday mornings. They seemed to be content in this arrangement, and very content and happy with their relationship. Ford, who loved her devotedly and was very proud of her, often quoted her droll or precocious sayings (she spoke only French, as I recall). I can see them still walking down the street, Ford looking very impressive and beside him his little female replica.

. . . I now come to the place in my memories where I want to tell you about what was possibly the most important night in Ford's life.

Willard's friend, Eileen Lake, from America, had come for a visit to Paris, bringing with her her best friend, Janice. Willard had invited the two girls to one of Ford's Thursdays, and soon after we asked them for supper and, of course, invited Ford to join us. We had a lively supper, the liveliest our little salle à manger had ever contained. There were many questions to ask about America and much to tell about our new life. Ford was at his best, appreciative in listening and joining in enthusiastically. In the living room after supper he sat between the girls on the sofa and I sat facing them in my big chair. Ford did most of the talking then—leading it, anyway—and I felt that they all had quickly become friends; they laughed and talked easily, delighted with each other. Then it was that I had one of the strangest experiences of my life: I saw, literally *saw,* the transformation of Ford, as though he were a monarch moth shedding his cocoon. We had always thought of him as an old man (he was then fifty-eight). But here he was, become a young man. Ford, of course, always liked women and I knew that he was especially fond of one of the women in our group that year; but never had I seen him like this. He was ardent, he was charming, he was a man in love!

Later that evening Ford took Eileen and Janice out to see some boîtes and to do some dancing, and the girls told us later that he danced with them all night long. I heard him come in after dawn; nevertheless, he met Willard and me for our noon dinner. Our conversation that day was entirely about the night before and the two girls from New York. Eileen was really the showpiece of the pair. She was a poet, tall, blonde, and fascinating, born and raised in Antigua, which fact always seemed to increase her interest for everyone, and we thought that naturally she would be the one that Ford would be taken with. So we started talking about her—wasn't Eileen charming, wasn't she attractive, and so on? Ford listened and agreed with all we said, and then paused and said very quietly, "And the little dark-haired one is nice." And, just from the way he said it, I knew instantly that he was in love with Janice, that it was for her that he had been transfigured the night before.

We were all quite horrified when we learned they were really planning to be married—it seemed to upset all our socially prescribed and approved codes. She was twenty-eight and he was fifty-eight—impossible! And I remember saying, "But it isn't sexually aesthetic." But they were married, and codes, aesthetics, or any other disapprovals had to undergo a reevaluation, because they had one of the best marriages I have ever known, and I believe that Ford felt about Janice the way that T. S. Eliot did about his wife, that he also had "never imagined that he would have such felicity." And Janice said to me one day, "I have looked all my life for a man with a mind as old as my own and what difference does it make if, when I find the man, he has a pot belly?"

Ford and Janice's marriage didn't happen until several weeks after they met. In the meantime it became June and the birth of our child drew nearer and nearer. On 6 June I went out to the American Hospital for a checkup and the doctor told me that the baby would come in about a week. But at six o'clock in the morning on 7 June I awakened with signs that the baby would come that very day. We called the doctor at once, and after he examined me he said just to lie quietly all morning and that he would come back to see me in the afternoon. Ford evidently believed in the doctor's judgment because he sent Willard on an errand over to the Right Bank. Willard was angry about having to leave me then, but there seemed no choice except to comply. He was gone a long time and my pains were getting worse and worse. That was the only morning that Ford didn't work. I could hear him moving restlessly around in the dining room next to my bedroom. Every now and then he would put his head in the door and ask, "How are you now?" He knew then that things weren't going as the doctor expected. As soon as Willard came back I said that I was sure that we shouldn't wait for the doctor but should go to the hospital immediately. Ford walked down those four long flights of stairs to get a taxi for us and have it waiting at the door when we had made our slower descent. He stood on the curb waving good luck and au revoir as we drove away. Then, as I learned later, he walked all the way down to the Church of Saint Sulpice to light a candle for me. . . . Our baby was born at six o'clock that evening and at a dinner party that night Ford proposed her first Parisian toast in champagne.

The birth of our baby marked the end of our living with Ford—there was no room for a baby in our small ménage, and also Ford would marry soon. But Ford and Janice and Willard and I stayed fast friends for the remaining three years of our stay in Paris.

The last time that I saw Ford was in New York—by that time I had read many of his books, I knew him far better, and I had grown up. He and Janice were living in an apartment on lower Fifth Avenue, and I stopped in one afternoon for a visit with them. We talked about the old Paris days and I said, "Oh, Ford, it was so good of you to offer to give Polly and me that course in French literature. You always had so much to do—how could you have been so generous?" And he said in his slow, thoughtful way, "Well, you see —I was very fond of you." And I know that I was, and am, very fond of him.

The following two sonnets, written at Ford's sonnet parties, were saved by Willard Trask. (Ford used to call me either "Joan" or "Mary": Joan was my confirmation name, which I used when I was a dancer in New York.)

For Joan (Mary)

Were there no love but only lives to save
Were there no kisses only coins at hand
Were there no sanctuary in all the land
For our short lives on this side of the grave
And if in heaven that the planets pave
We must join in with that unmarried band
That chant *eleisons* or that waiting stand
Beside the margin of the crystal wave

And if of kindness there remained no hope
Where the far planets frozen sway and shine
We must go seeking and in blindness grope
For the lost pattern of the august will
But since we love what matters the design.

FMF

Gently the summer closed with first leaves' fall
And the world turns a sacrificial flame,
The fields and forests cry a boisterous shame,
And twenty asters brown against the wall,
Only tanned rushes hear the herons' call.
Please answer now, my love, or the white frame
Of winter comes and misconstrues our aim
Or puts a smothering silence over all.

It must come, this hour of our magic flight,
To that warm land where all things lovely seem
And mountains touch the sea in lines that swerve
And fruit is warm; the sun there takes his right,
It is all true; this is no idle dream,
Then wait not, love, but come with me and serve.

Mary McIntosh

JEAN RHYS

I am writing my autobiography and have tried to say all I know about Ford Madox Ford in that. Of course his great generosity to young writers was very well known both in London and in Paris. He was willing to take a lot of trouble for those he thought of promise.

I learnt a good deal from him and can't think of anyone who has quite taken his place.

Letter to the editor, 28 July 1978.

WALLY TWORKOV

I met Janice and Ford in 1934, on their first visit to New York after I had gotten to know Janice's brother, whom I was to marry the following year.

I was eighteen, a college dropout in my sophomore year, without an idea in my head except the sad state of the world—very much the lost adolescent. Ford thought he could use my help, I was available, and I just drifted into what is known as a secretarial position, although I myself never thought of it that way. Time spent with Ford was too pleasant and relaxed for that. He was no perfectionist taskmaster or I wouldn't have lasted an hour. My frequent errors were taken for granted and tolerated.

Mostly I typed letters: to friends, to family, to publishers. Ford's way of dictating varied. Sometimes I would take down what he dictated in longhand (I did not take shorthand), sometimes directly on the typewriter. Or I would type from his longhand or retype what he had already typed and corrected in pencil. I think that I took direct dictation only for letters and not for the books. If I did any typing for the books, I am almost sure it was always from Ford's longhand, usually written on yellow unruled paper. Ford would sit beside me, smoking Gaulois as he talked, and I was forever in awe at the ease with which he could turn out one graceful phrase after another.

I am aware that some people found Ford difficult to understand. He had a way of dropping his voice long before the end of a sentence. I was, fortunately, not one of them. For some reason I could never understand, I was able to take his dictation in French with sufficient accuracy, despite my very limited knowledge of that language.

I remember two of their New York apartments, both on lower Fifth Avenue, but the one I remember more clearly was No. 10 Fifth Avenue (the other, I think, was No. 85), a small beehive of activity with Janice painting in the bedroom, Ford typing on a table in the living room, both taking turns cooking. Ford liked to cook, was very good at it, and both of them gave me my first lessons in French cooking. And always, no matter what was going on, the tenderness of the Fords toward each other.

If, when I arrived, I found Ford playing solitaire, it meant that he was not feeling well, maybe just out of sorts, or that he was thinking something through. Sometimes he would already be at the typewriter, patiently typing away with his two-finger method. The books in progress were *Provence, Great Trade Route, Portraits from Life,* and later, *The March of Literature.*

The "job" was part-time. I must have gone there some mornings, because I remember occasionally staying on for lunch. But I must have also worked some afternoons, especially Thursday, because that was the day set aside for open house, and I remember helping them get ready. It was their way of seeing as many of their American friends as possible during their stay here. Anyone who wanted to see them could and did come, and the apartment would fill up with all sorts of friends and acquaintances. A frequent visitor was Edward Dahlberg, towards whom Ford went out of the way to be kind and supportive. Dahlberg could be ornery and acerb.

Ford said of himself: "I am an old man mad about writing," and one aspect of this "madness" was that he was never too busy or too tired to read any of the numerous manuscripts that were sent to him—and never once a crushing reply to an author. There was also occasional excitement over a manuscript, like Eudora Welty's, sent to Ford, I think, before she was published.

I remember William Carlos Williams, unaffected and genial, dropping in one morning to thank Ford for having formed the Friends of William Carlos Williams. And I was, of course, thrilled to be included in a dinner with the Fords and the Dreisers at a little Italian restaurant on West 13th Street. I don't remember the conversation, but I do recall that in my innocence I was surprised at how "established" the Dreisers looked in their evening clothes, considering Dreiser's subjects and sympathies.

Between 1934 and 1937, the Fords made several trips to the States, and if I were free during their stay, my typing days would resume.

In the spring of 1937, I accompanied Ford and Janice on their visit to the Tates in Clarksville, Tennessee, not far from Vanderbilt University, where so many of the figures in the Agrarian and Fugitive movements were teaching, many of whom we met in the Tates's living room, usually on Sunday afternoons over mint juleps. Robert Lowell, aged nineteen, I think, arrived unannounced and set up a tent on the Tates's property for the purpose of studying at the feet of Tate and Ford; he was for the most part unsmiling and so shy that his requests at lunch and dinner to "please pass the bread" could hardly be heard. And I was to discover, after a week of lunches, when visitors were most frequent, that the animated talk around the table was not about the Spanish Civil War which was then taking place and which was preoccupying most of my friends in New York, but about the Civil War between the States. But Ford and I went about our business for part of the day and Janice painted.

To satisfy Ford's desire to see as much of the country as possible, we traveled to Tennessee by Greyhound bus. Our first stop was in Washington, D.C., where Ford had a friend who took us to a dark little Mexican restaurant for an "exemplary Mexican dinner." Janice and I did nothing but complain afterwards: about the poor judgment of the friend, about the food, about our indigestion—but not Ford. And so it was with all the other discomforts, small and large, that went with this trip, including the greasy spoons known as Greyhound diners. It was as if Ford had made up his mind not to fret.

The Fords made their numerous trips back and forth from France with little fuss. Duffle bags were filled, and off they were, looking forward to the sea voyage, especially if it was going to be on the *Ile de France.*

When they left for what was to be Ford's last trip back to France, I was pregnant with my first child. Ford's final illness coincided with the imminent birth of my daughter. During this period, Janice wrote of Ford's concern for me, which is why she asked us, after his death, to add his name to the one we had already chosen. And so we did, and Hermine Ford Tworkov was born 13 July 1939, three weeks after Ford died.[1]

I was of course touched by Ford's concern but should not have been surprised. It was the same affectionate interest he had shown in so many of the letters I had typed for him to his friends.

Whenever I now speak or think of Ford, I become acutely aware that being *that* young and unformed made it impossible for me really to know him and I am overcome by a sense of frustration and great loss.

[1] *Editor's note:* The Tworkovs' daughter—"another working Ford"—is the painter Hermine Ford.

An Interview with Janice Biala (1979)

INTERVIEWER: Readers tend to think of Ford's life as a sad one. Would you say his temperament was sad as well?

BIALA: I don't think Ford had a sad life. I think of his great vitality (think of all the books he wrote, how *much* he lived), his gaiety, his confidence, his optimism, his wild sense of humor. Ford did what he pleased all his life. He lived exactly the life he wanted to live. And he looked at unhappiness as part of life. But he enjoyed life. Those last days in Deauville, I had in a local doctor. He was a little mean-looking man, and after the first visit, Ford having been not a very good patient, he said: "It is obvious that Monsieur has always done whatever he wanted in his life." He said it spitefully and I could see *he'd* never done anything he wanted to do in his life. But how right he was.

INTERVIEWER: But the temperament that produced the books seems complicated and subtle and far from being understood. How did you see it?

BIALA: I didn't find him complicated. He was very intuitive. That made him a sympathetic observer of life—as well as an ironical one: he had a considerable sense of humor, not always understood.

INTERVIEWER: H. G. Wells claimed that nobody knew who Ford was, including Ford: "What he is really or if he is really, nobody knows now and he least of all; he has become a great system of assumed *personas* and dramatized selves." Can you tell me about the Ford you knew? And can you see what Wells might have meant, or how Ford might have impressed people in the way Wells saw him?

BIALA: I have no idea what Wells meant or any of the people who've followed him. Ford romanticized—but in an extremely candid way, so

Editor's note: The following pages had their origin in a series of meetings in Paris in the summer of 1979. I had invited Biala to contribute a new memoir to *The Presence of Ford Madox Ford.* "I am a painter, not a writer," she said. But she agreed to answer my questions, and later to send me written answers to further questions. The conversations in Paris and the later written interview are put together here.

no one was fooled. He said once that some relative of his was called Hill, and since Shakespeare too had a direct something or other called Hill, he felt he was probably descended from Shakespeare. Then he added, *"Someone* has to be."

He looked like the portrait I did of him, of which you have the photograph—large and blond, very gentle, very blue eyes. And the quality of his conversation . . . Olive Garnett, who had taken Elsie's side, said: "His conversation was like caviar."

I think the answer to the "real Ford" could be found in what Ford wrote about the czar reading *A Sportsman's Sketches* by Turgenev. The czar was Yermolai, found out in some fault; he was a poor servant girl, twisting her apron in her hands, weeping; he was all the unhappy serfs on his mother's property being sold or flogged. Ford too was nearly all his characters. He was Tietjens and Leonora, Sylvia and The Young Lovell, but probably not Florence, who was a cheat. How else could he understand them if he didn't put himself in their place?

He could find material in the most trivial acts. I remember once we were in Boston. The whole of Beacon Hill was agog over a broken marriage. We heard all kinds of gossip about the young wife and the husband. The young woman was very frank about it. She loved her husband and wanted to keep him. She told us that she had had a heart embroidered on her nightgown in the hope that it would bring back her husband. I thought this a silly way of trying to keep a husband, but Ford thought it pathetic and touching.

INTERVIEWER: How can you explain the impression of arrogance he left on some observers?

BIALA: Not all observers are necessarily good observers. Ford was proud, but not arrogant. He gave others the impression of being so sure of himself because he believed so firmly what he believed, and they thought he was condescending or arrogant or pretentious to make such statements. But Ford treated a *femme de ménage* and an Important Person in exactly the same way. He didn't treat one human being with more respect than another because both were human beings and deserved the same respect. But of course some people like to be treated as superiors, not equals. Ford often made sweeping statements that were contrary to current beliefs—and enraged some people, but his statements were most often true; and he used exaggerations to heighten a truth, as one does in any art.

INTERVIEWER: Why did Ford never defend himself against the charges against him? His reputation was very much damaged in his lifetime and even now. The same charges are restated—the question of the veracity of his facts, his involvement with a number of women—and these "issues" have often dominated any consideration of his merit as a writer.

BIALA: Ford was a very private person and a very proud one. He never replied to any charge. Nothing has been heard from Ford's side because he thought it beneath his dignity to answer. But you might say his silence was used against him, and he was judged as in the trial in *Alice in Wonderland.* His critics were the judges, the jury, and the executioners.

INTERVIEWER: Since Ford never defended himself, is there anything you feel ought to be said in his defense?

BIALA: Ford didn't want to be defended. He often quoted "Though thou be cold as ice and chaste as snow thou shalt not escape calumny." I don't know anything about Elsie Hueffer except that she brought an action for divorce in which her lawyer, like every divorce lawyer, covered Ford with mud and withdrew the action before Ford's lawyer could reply. So her public view of him has prevailed. Her *private* view of him seems to have been different. I have a letter from Katharine Lamb [Ford's second daughter by Elsie] in which she tells me that her mother asks me to put a particular quotation (I don't recall the words) on Ford's tombstone because, Katharine said in another letter, her mother "feels as you do that he is one of the people one has to thank God for having existed . . ." and Elsie "wished, to the extent that a tombstone can be a tribute, to be associated in that tribute." This letter and the previous one on the same subject were written in 1947. I presume that is why she always refused to divorce him, even as late as 1930.

INTERVIEWER: Is there any special understanding of Ford's attitude toward the women he lived with that you may have gotten from having lived with him for nine years?

BIALA: I don't think I'm qualified to talk about Ford's relationships with other women. But Ford used to say, when you come down to breakfast and you have nothing to say, the marriage is pretty well over. I mean "the marriage of true minds." And that's probably what Ford meant. In any case, most marriages break up because of incompatibility. One more thing: Ford was ahead of his time. Today nobody would give a damn. Nearly everyone I know has been married or not married three or four times and God knows how many women or men in between. But Ford committed the unforgivable sin: he introduced and considered as his wife each woman who shared his life. That wasn't done in England at that time. If all that happened today, no one would pay the slightest attention.

INTERVIEWER: But a good many critics and reviewers, writing then, rather than now, when attitudes toward marriage are different, have left the impression of a disordered life.

BIALA: A man who never missed a day's work in his life can't be said to have a disordered life.

INTERVIEWER: There's been an extraordinary amount of denigration—a general habit, almost automatic with some reviewers in the past, of rehearsing the "facts" of Ford's life as a prelude to, or a substitute for, any sort of critical statement about the book itself; and there's been a sort of tradition of condescension to Ford.

BIALA: I don't understand this sort of Peeping Tom interest in his life. But if he were just anybody, would they still be interested? I think the critics who feel obliged to repeat the whole thing do so (1) because they want to show that they are in the know and (2) because if they couldn't gossip about his life, they would have to write about his work, and that is much harder. For forty years since Ford's death, I have been enraged and baffled, trying to find an explanation why a man so honorable, so generous, and so gifted should be so denigrated. But perhaps that is exactly why he was denigrated—*because* he was generous and honorable and gifted. Take the case of *A Moveable Feast* by Hemingway. I was startled and unbelieving that a civilized man could write with such obscene hatred of any other man. Surely it throws a great deal of light on Hemingway and none on Ford—but I have never heard of Hemingway's being reviled for these lapses from decency, and all this because he couldn't forgive Ford for the fact that some people said Ford had helped him, discovered him, and published him.

INTERVIEWER: Ford used to speak of Les Jeunes, the young writers he was interested in and whom he tried to help and often did. They have written about Ford, but always about Ford the literary personality, rarely about his books, about the books he was writing during the years they knew him. Why was this so?

BIALA: Probably because they only saw Ford as a source of admiration and help for themselves. Later some, like Robie Macauley, did write about his books. There was also Edward Crankshaw and one or two others. Ford's enthusiasms always carried him away. He convinced these young writers that they were more important than he was, and they believed him. When I asked him about it, he said, "Did you ever hear of the pride that apes humility?"

Ford read, and tried very hard in the months before his death, to get published a manuscript by Wanda Tower Pickard. He didn't succeed. He said it was the best first novel he'd ever read. She lived in Evanston, Illinois. I saw her after Ford's death but then I lost her address and she was too sensitive to remind me of her existence, I suppose. I wonder if the book was ever published.

INTERVIEWER: Can you describe Ford's encounter with the American Midwest? What was life like at Olivet? Most readers assume it was bleak. How did Ford feel about being there?

BIALA: Life at Olivet was really very gay. It had been some kind of Baptist or Presbyterian College, but when Joseph Brewer became president, it changed radically. He introduced the tutorial system and artists-in-residence, and he brought in many new people. The old left-overs didn't like us newcomers (Ford didn't teach; he was writer-in-residence). The dean, of the *ancien régime,* gave a lecture entitled "Do Gentlemen Drink Wine?" knowing perfectly well that Brewer had a very good wine cellar, and anyone could see the empty bottles outside our back door. There used to be terrific wine sales because few people bought or drank wine in Michigan, and we used to get the best wines for fifty cents a bottle. Brewer also introduced the writer's conference, and the biggest names in the literary world passed through Olivet. He had a collection of modern art, the first seen in those *parages,* and he was a terrific tap dancer. Ford and I did a lot of good to that place in another way. Socially the sexes were rigorously separated. There were constantly parties either for men only or for women only. We put a stop to that. The first time Ford was invited to one of those men-only parties he replied politely, "Sorry, I don't go to parties where there are no women." And the first time I was invited to one of those only-women parties, I replied, "Sorry, I don't go to parties where there are no men." So then the younger crowd decided to follow suit and pretty soon all the parties were mixed.

We liked being there and Ford was surrounded by young aspirants to literature, and people from all over Michigan sent in manuscripts to be read. Wanda Pickard was one of these.

INTERVIEWER: How equal did he make you feel in private life?

BIALA: Ford was a confirmed feminist long before the movement as we know it today. . . . The years I spent with him were a long passionate dialogue. Starting from opposite points of view, opposite backgrounds, each convinced the other, converted the other.

INTERVIEWER: Could you elaborate?

BIALA: We had such a hell of a lot to say to one another. There wasn't enough time for everything we had to say. . . . He was extraordinarily considerate both to me and in respect to my work.

INTERVIEWER: Ford was always an admirer of strong-minded and independent women—as early as in the fairy tales, as Alison Lurie has pointed out.

BIALA: I don't know about strong-minded women—but unlike most men, Ford truly liked women—aside from being in love with them, etc. Ford liked to quote his friend, Arthur Marwood, whom he claimed to use as a model for Christopher Tietjens. Ford would say, "Marwood told me once that I would always pick women of low vitality." He generally told me that when I was raising hell about something. I didn't get it until years later.

INTERVIEWER: How did you meet Ford—under what circumstances?

BIALA: I was taken to one of his Thursdays. I went because I'd heard Ezra Pound would be there and I was a great admirer of Pound.

INTERVIEWER: Stella Bowen, in her book *Drawn from Life,* spoke of Ford as needing propping up—a great user-up of other people's energy.

BIALA: Perhaps after the war he needed propping up. He had been shot to pieces. But he didn't need any propping up in my time. It is true that Ford was terribly demanding, but of no one more than of himself. And he lived at the top of his bent. He was very demanding, both of himself and of me. This took the form of our doing things together—housework, cooking, gardening, typing. There was no one else to do these things. And besides, he wanted us always to be together, side by side in everything, before the world.

INTERVIEWER: Did his demands interfere with your work? Did he help you with your work—by taking it seriously, by giving you serious criticism? Was he able, given the size of the tasks he imposed on himself, to be genuinely interested in your work?

BIALA: Ford was very much interested in my work. He claimed to be more interested in mine than his. He gave me every kind of encouragement. The few dust jackets I did for his books—*Provence, Great Trade Route, The Rash Act*—I did because Ford insisted, though I am really not very good at making jackets.

INTERVIEWER: As a painter, can you help the literary critics try to understand what Ford meant by impressionism? Was there any connection between Cézanne's aesthetic (you painted Ford in a deck chair reading a book with the title *Cézanne*) and Ford's?

BIALA: As a painter, I can't speak for a writer. But what does come to my mind are the waterlilies of Monet. The waterlilies are floating on the water. They are blue and violet and pink. But when you look close, there are no waterlilies, no water, no trees—just blobs of paint. You step back, and once more the waterlilies are floating on the water shadowed by the drooping willow trees. In short you need a certain distance in front of any work of art. The artist is not concerned with scientific truth or facts. Both Raphael and Ingres used considerable distortion in their portraits —for the purposes of a greater reality—not realism. So when Ford said that Conrad threw the teacups into the fire, it was not the literal truth —it was a creation of the ambiance, the climate of Conrad's passionate rejection of a criticism of Marie Antoinette. This explains some of those famous "lies" of Ford, I think.

INTERVIEWER: How many portraits of Ford did you paint? The image of Ford reading in that deck chair turns up in the dust jacket you designed for *Provence.*

BIALA: I painted three portraits of Ford. None of them does either of us justice. Incidentally, the fact that I painted him reading a book on

Cézanne is not significant in any way, although he was an ardent admirer of Cézanne. The features in this portrait are not accurate, but the painting nevertheless gives a pretty good idea of him—the amount of space he took up.

INTERVIEWER: Who indexed his books—those that are indexed? For example, It Was the Nightingale has a fascinating index, with such listings as Animals, thoughtfulness to; Earnestness; Memory, loss of; Omens; Secretaries; Shallots; Swine fever; White blackbirds; Writer's cramp.

BIALA: I can't remember, but in this particular book it could have been himself—though I'm not sure.

INTERVIEWER: Did Ford write a cookbook—under a pseudonym perhaps? It seems to me he mentioned somewhere that he'd written one.

BIALA: No.

INTERVIEWER: I wish he had—though I'm still working up to the recipe in Provence for chicken cooked with two pounds of garlic, to be eaten like haricots blancs. But he did write so persuasively about food—about cooking it and raising it.

BIALA: We had a few chickens which we were raising so Julie [Ford's daughter by Stella Bowen] could have chickens to eat when she came. Ford insisted on letting them wander all over the garden, though it was hell to get them into the chicken coop at night—because, he said, if you raise animals for the table, you should give them the best life possible while they are alive. Julie, incidentally, refused to eat a chicken she had known personally. We tried one, but couldn't swallow it for the same reason.

INTERVIEWER: You spoke of a little film on Ford, made in 1930 in the Luxembourg Gardens. Who made it, and where is it now?

BIALA: It was made by George Keating, and I have it in Peapack, New Jersey.

INTERVIEWER: It surprises me that The Good Soldier has never been filmed, say, for television.

BIALA: Granada made arrangements with me but still hasn't done it.

INTERVIEWER: Ford was perfectly tri-lingual—his French and German were excellent. What did his French sound like?

BIALA: Like French with an English accent.

INTERVIEWER: By the way, how did Ford pronounce Hueffer? There are at least three different indications by contemporaries, who rhymed it with buffer or with opera buffa or else pronounced it as Heffer.

BIALA: Hueffer was pronounced like opera buffa.

INTERVIEWER: Sooner or later the question of Ford's attitude toward money comes up in reminiscences about him. And his generosity. It's as if he had an idea of money that was really at odds with received notions about its value.

BIALA: One day one of those innumerable Georgian princes turned up. He introduced himself as a friend of some American girl that Ford knew and liked. He came to ask Ford for money because he couldn't pay his hotel bill, etc., etc. Ford asked me to make out a check for a small sum. I looked protestingly at him—but Ford paid no attention. The prince was outraged and insulted by the smallness of the sum. We didn't tell him that it was exactly one-half of the Ford account, and he left, another enemy. Ford used to boast that every member of his family died poorer than he'd been when he was born. He was very proud of that.

INTERVIEWER: Do you remember Ford's saying anything about Conrad, anything about the collaboration between them?

BIALA: Ford spoke of Conrad with the greatest admiration and affection, but he'd written so much about him and their collaboration that he didn't need to talk about it.

INTERVIEWER: Did Ford speak of his experience in World War I?

BIALA: Ford didn't speak much about his past life. He was interested only in his current one. But it is true that when he was dying and he was delirious, he was back in the trenches; and once he said, "They can't do this to us. We are British officers." I suppose being in the trenches was an expression of how sick he was feeling.

INTERVIEWER: His Catholicism has never been a clear matter. He was nominally a Roman Catholic. So far as you knew, what were his feelings as a Catholic? About religion generally?

BIALA: I don't remember any talk about religion. It didn't play any role in our life. I am an unreconstructed Jew. Ford was certainly no practicing Catholic. He brought his children up as Catholics because he thought all children should be brought up in some religion, and he preferred Catholicism because he said if you wanted to break away from it you could make a clean break. Apparently Catholics have to believe the whole works—or nothing. He did say he admired the organization of the church. . . . When we entered a church Ford would make a half-hearted bow in the direction of the Virgin—but perhaps more because she was a woman than because she was the Virgin. And I imagine he believed in Catholicism philosophically.

INTERVIEWER: What was Ford's daily reading like? Did he read history, poetry, novels? What periodicals did he habitually read?

BIALA: He didn't have the time for that kind of reading. He was always reading books that other writers had sent him or manuscripts. When he was writing *The March of Literature* he reread everything he wrote about.

INTERVIEWER: Recently I noticed how different the two editions of that book are, as if the American publisher, which published it first, had one set of assumptions about readers of the book, and the English publisher had quite another. The English edition has a detailed table of contents; the American has none. And the contents are again given at the beginning of each section in the English edition.

BIALA: Those differences are due to the fact that the Dial Press threw out most of Ford's quotations at the last minute, because they were simultaneously publishing an anthology of world literature, and Ford had to rewrite the massacred passages so that they would make sense. The changes in the page headings were made by the American publisher. Ford did not approve of them. The book needs to be republished on the basis of the original manuscript typescript as Ford wrote it before the Dial got to work on it. I wish the book could be republished. It was Ford's last book and he put so much hope into it. The English edition (Allen and Unwin) was based on the American edition rather than on the original manuscript.

INTERVIEWER: Do you know anything about the projected collected edition of Ford that Allen Tate spoke of?

BIALA: The collected edition by McGraw-Hill was never more than an idea by one of the editors there. It never came to anything. Nothing happened with Allen and Unwin either.

INTERVIEWER: Harvey spoke of a locked trunk in 1962—"a locked trunk containing manuscripts of published and unpublished material [which] has not, during the compilation of this bibliography, been accessible to anyone."

BIALA: That "locked trunk" has been following me around for years. It sounds mysterious, like the dark lady of the sonnets. . . . It was just a trunk in which I kept the manuscripts and some letters. All of this is now in Cornell and absolutely without mystery.

INTERVIEWER: How did the Violet Hunt papers make their way to Cornell?

BIALA: The Violet Hunt papers were sent over to Stella Bowen by Violet's executors. They told Stella they didn't know who Ford's executors were, and Stella wrote me about it saying we would go through the papers together when I came to London. She asked me to come when she knew she was dying of cancer. (She said there was no one she could talk to about her "real life" but me. We became very good friends after Ford's death when we really got to know each other. She wrote me the most moving letters.)

INTERVIEWER: Which of his unpublished manuscripts did Ford particularly want published?

BIALA: *A History of Our Own Times.* Ford started out in life as a historian, he said, and so it was inevitable that sooner or later he would write our history. It was to be in three volumes.

INTERVIEWER: He had sustained a memory loss because of World War I, and afterward he recovered, though it's not clear whether he recovered everything. His memory, like Tietjens's, had been considered remarkable.

BIALA: His memory was still remarkable when I knew him.

INTERVIEWER: Can you talk about his habits of writing in the thirties?

BIALA: The only thing I know is that Ford played patience for several hours before he began to write. When he had thought out every word he began to write. There are very few corrections in Ford's manuscripts. Ford said he had to know where every door, window, object was in a room before he could write a scene. Once he knew where everything was, he didn't need to mention it.

INTERVIEWER: Ford is generally thought of as the writer of *The Good Soldier* and *Parade's End.* The other books he wrote are generally waved aside as having little importance or interest; and the charge that many of them are just potboilers has often been made. How did Ford himself regard the mass of his writing? Did the distinction between potboiler and serious work exist for him?

BIALA: I don't think Ford *ever* wrote a potboiler. He was always interested in whatever subject he attacked. People just haven't read his work. He wrote some very beautiful books before *The Good Soldier* and after. If one reads all his books one sees that he always wrote the history of our times.

INTERVIEWER: Did Ford read reviews?

BIALA: Yes, sometimes he read his reviews. He used to say—when they were good—he could have done them better himself, and he was irritated when they were bad, and I think he could have done *them* better himself.

INTERVIEWER: The novels of the thirties—*When the Wicked Man, The Rash Act, Henry for Hugh, Vive Le Roy*—these are virtually unread today.

BIALA: With reference to all those unread books, the publishers all went bankrupt shortly after they were published. These were written and published in the thirties. And attention was focused on books of social consciousness at that time.

INTERVIEWER: During the thirties, Ford admired writers with very different political sentiments—Dreiser, Pound, the Fugitives. How much did politics matter to him? Did he think politically?

BIALA: I don't think Ford was political at all. He had the greatest contempt for all politicians. He would say either that he was a Tory or that he was a Communist—to make a point.

INTERVIEWER: You spoke of the detective novel and Ford's respect for its construction. Which detective novels was he reading in the thirties?

BIALA: He read most of those that were available to us. He had a special admiration for early Simenon, whom he tried very hard to get published in New York. But no dice. He thought the detective stories of the period better constructed and written than most novels. His own novels seemed like detective stories to me in that respect, but intensely alive detective stories. By the way, Ford had the greatest admiration for certain criminals. He said that they had genius, and if only it were put to acceptable ends. . . .

INTERVIEWER: His own value as a writer—did he question this?

BIALA: All artists have days in which they doubt the value of what they are, of their work. Other days they think they're terrific. Ford was like that too. He used to joke about Thackeray, who, after finishing *Vanity Fair,* struck his forehead and exclaimed, "This is genius." But Ford was firmly convinced that—and used to say—"The world needs us." He wanted his books read after his own death. He had certain beliefs; he was absolutely certain about the value of the artist to society.

FRANK MACSHANE
Two Such Silver Currents

... I must absolutely have
encouragement as the crops rain.
GERARD MANLEY HOPKINS

In quantity, American literature is flourishing. There are more literary magazines than there have ever been before, more poetry readings, more writers
teaching in schools and colleges, more grants and fellowships. The National
Endowment for the Arts, the New York State Council on the Arts—and all
the other state arts councils—not to mention the Guggenheim Foundation,
the Rockefeller Foundation, the MacDowell Colony, Yaddo and other artists' retreats all spend millions of dollars every year to encourage and support
writers. Some have complained that this largesse is ill-conceived and that
mediocre writers are the main beneficiaries. But public agencies have given
a chance to women writers and to poets and novelists from racial and ethnic
minorities who otherwise might have remained silent. This alone should
insure that the egalitarian basis for support will not be changed.

Apart from financial assistance, public support has also lessened the
feelings of helplessness and despair that overcome all sensitive writers, especially at the beginnings of their careers. Many young writers are forced to
work all day in offices and write only at night when they are tired and
drained; others take jobs as taxi drivers, construction workers, or janitors in
the hope they will either make money quickly or be able to write a few hours
while on the job. Even publication does not solve the economic problem for
most writers, since few can live on the small earnings of a first novel or the
meagre fees paid for short stories in magazines. For poets, there is practically
no income at all, except from readings. Beyond the economic conditions are
the psychological. "How much it takes to become a writer," says Tillie Olsen
in *Silences*. "Bent (far more common than we assume), circumstances, time,
development of craft—but beyond that: how much conviction as to the
importance of what one has to say, one's right to say it. And the will, the

229

measureless store of belief in oneself to be able to come to, cleave to, find the form for one's own life comprehensions."

A grant or fellowship will restore confidence, for it represents a voice from the public the writer is addressing: it is a response to the writing itself. But the impersonality of state and foundation aid robs it of the warmth that comes with individual interest. Thoreau said, "If you give money, spend yourself with it, and do not merely abandon it to them." But few foundations or government officials become involved with grant recipients. They do not, and probably cannot, do much to lessen the feelings of isolation and loneliness that afflict most writers. Only an individual, and preferably a fellow-artist, can supply the understanding and sympathy that is required. This psychological help will not buy groceries, but it will replenish the emotional bank that creative activity quickly exhausts. Moreover, many artists and writers are, in Tillie Olsen's phrase, "mediocre caretakers of their talent." They are frequently inept at completing application forms for foundation or state grants, and many hesitate to beg references from those who have already spoken well of their work. It is easier to withdraw than to suffer the humiliation that comes with almost certain failure. Women in particular, knowing the weight of custom and opinion against them, are often the first to give up; they settle for something less and perpetuate their condition.

Psychologically, state and foundation aid has not mattered much, and it may even have reduced the sense of caring that in former times came from an individual patron or friend. How important this caring is can be seen by considering Ford Madox Ford, who from the beginning of his career devoted much of his time to helping others. Brought up among Pre-Raphaelite painters and poets, he learned early about the need for loyalty among artists. However much the Rossettis and Holman Hunt and his own grandfather Ford Madox Brown abused one another in private, toward outsiders they always presented a solid front of mutual support and esteem. They were literally a "brotherhood" in this sense. Ford Madox Brown also gave Ford what he himself later called a "Rule of Life": "Fordie," said his grandfather, "never refuse to help a lame dog over a stile. Never lend money: always give it. When you give money to a man that is down, tell him that it is to help him get up; tell him that when he is up he should pass on the money you have given him to any other poor devil that is down. Beggar yourself rather than refuse assistance to any one whose genius you think shows promise of being greater than your own."

As a young man without much money, Ford had few opportunities to be of financial assistance to writers whose work he admired. Instead, he wrote letters of encouragement to his contemporaries—to H. G. Wells, John Galsworthy, and Joseph Conrad. He did not merely flatter and praise them; he paid them the compliment of taking their work seriously enough to criticize it. "I find I have attacked you somewhat viciously," he apologized rather unnecessarily at the end of a letter to Galsworthy; then he explained that his comments were mainly "theoretic disquisitions upon art, as I see it in my limited field of view." In fact, Ford's letters are full of generous praise and understanding, although he was always serious and frank. He believed that "imaginative literature is the only thing of any permanent worth in the world," and therefore he had a passionate commitment to those whose work he admired. Ford also urged a greater understanding of art itself. He suggested to Edward Garnett, a publisher's reader, that he bring out a series of books on the art of writing "as distinct from the general line of tub-thumping about moral purposes" that occupied most critics in Edwardian England. In weekly and monthly magazines, he also wrote about older writers he admired, such as Henry James, Stephen Crane, and W. H. Hudson, because he hoped that by increasing an understanding of good writing, he might indirectly help his talented contemporaries. In 1908, he founded the *English Review* with the express purpose of publishing the most gifted young writers he could find. Moreover, he wanted to run his magazine on a profit-sharing basis so that it would benefit the writers who made it possible. "I am an idealist," he said, "and my ideal is to run the 'English Review' as far as possible as a socialistic undertaking. The kicks I shall get will be the price I will pay for indulging my idealism and these I trust to bear with equanimity." Ford's financial arrangements did not work, but his literary intentions remained unchanged. He published the best established writers in England—James, Conrad, Hudson, Wells, and Bennett among them—as well as such unknown writers as D. H. Lawrence, Wyndham Lewis, Norman Douglas, and Ezra Pound. Being in favor of one group of writers put him automatically against others, and the critics and litterateurs he would not print soon turned against him and his magazine. Ford's altruism was not vaguely humanitarian like the foundation director's; it was a fierce commitment to literary excellence. Inevitably, his sense of duty in supporting young and promising writers earned him the enmity of the old guard who had no talent but occupied positions of power and influence.

Beneath these literary motives, there were other reasons for Ford's generosity. One of his early novels, *The Benefactor*—originally called *The Altruist*—is the story of a man who devotes his whole life to helping others. Although (or perhaps because) he has no ambitions of his own, he is ruined in the end and hated by all whom he has helped. The same theme appears in *Parade's End* when Christopher Tietjens offers himself to others and allows himself to be ruined by his wife, his colleagues, and his social acquaintances. Ford's portrayal of Tietjens and the benefactor shows that he is aware of the psychological and religious implications of altruism. Both characters know they will be rejected and that they will suffer for their generosity, yet they persist in it. The pleasure they receive from this painful condition is knowing that like the saints and martyrs they are imitating Christ, and this "imitatio" gives them a gratifying sense of their spiritual superiority to others. In *A Man Could Stand Up*—, the third part of *Parade's End,* Ford has Tietjens reject his Christ-like altruism and accept his own dependence and humanity. Nevertheless, as a Roman Catholic with latent aristocratic leanings, Ford retained his own sense of altruistic duty, as imparted to him by his grandfather, although lacking the lordly trappings and the unconscious masochism he attributes to Tietjens. By the 1920s, Ford's generosity was a fixed habit. He told Gertrude Stein that he had become "a sort of half-way house between nonpublishable youth and real money" and described himself as "a sort of green baize swing door that everyone kicks both on entering and leaving."

But Ford was not neurotic. He did not brood about the hurts he received, nor did he imagine he was saintly. When attacked or criticized, he could give as well as receive. Like Tietjens, he had learned to stand up. Moreover, he was too involved in life, and not merely literary life, to worry about failures. As a farmer in Sussex and later in Provence, he was involved with pigs and vegetables, nurturing their world as he did his own. In the early Mediterranean dawn, he would go out to his Provençal garden to arrange the irrigation of his plants. "The semi-tropical plants and trees—the oranges, lemons, peppers, vines and the rest can do without water for a long time. Musk- and water-melons must have a little water and the Northern plants that for his sins the pink Nordic has imported here—the peas, beans, string beans, cabbages, carrots and such gross, over-green matter, must have a great deal or incontinently die. It was a whole campaign of irrigation channels that I had mentally to arrange for a day given up entirely to writing and the affairs of the parched earth." In the same way, he looked after writers. If there was a secondary literary motive for his generosity to young writers, it was his desire to be part of a movement, to join with others in the fight for what was vital and true in literature. As a young man, he sought out his contemporaries and those slightly older than himself such as Hardy, Conrad, and James. Then, after World War I, in Paris, he befriended a new generation of writers including Ernest Hemingway, Herbert Read, Jean Rhys, and Katherine Anne Porter. He would read their stories and poems, offer suggestions for improvement, and send what he admired to magazines and publishing houses with accompanying letters urging that they be accepted. For a year in the early 1920s he had his own magazine, the *Transatlantic Review,* where he published what he could of their writings. By the end of his life, he was spending his days with students and with such writers as Robert Lowell and Jean Stafford, who were forty years younger than he. Almost always he had with him stacks of manuscripts young writers had sent him for guidance and suggestions.

Sooner or later, most of those he helped drifted away from him and some returned his kindness with personal attacks and invective. Ford appears as the blimplike Braddocks in Hemingway's *The Sun Also Rises* and is treated openly and viciously in *The Moveable Feast;* Jean Rhys pilloried him as a lecherous old man in her novel called *Postures.* This reaction is not so unexpected. As early as 1932, Katherine Anne Porter noted that Ford seemed to have "a special genius for nourishing vipers in his bosom, and I have never seen an essay or article about him signed by any of these discoveries of his. I can make nothing of this, except that I have learned that most human beings —and I suppose that artists are that, after all—suffer some blow to their self-esteem in being helped, and develop the cancer of ingratitude. As if, somehow, they can, by denying their debt, or ignoring it, wipe it out altogether."

To some extent, it was natural that, as they became more independent, those Ford helped gradually moved away from him. Ford had the personal enthusiasm and partisanship of a father for the young writers he helped, and so he had to be outgrown. This is part of the price the benefactor must pay for his generosity. Also, with some of the young women writers he helped, Ford mixed a romantic element with his literary instruction and assistance. Growing older and lacking the public success he deserved, he was gratified by the attention he received from them just as they benefited from him. It is always easier to help a pretty girl than a plain one, and all his life Ford was in love with someone, and often more than one at the same time. These personal involvements tended to make Ford move on from one generation to another, surrounding himself always with younger and younger writers.

It may have produced an unsettled life, but it was never dull. If Ford never had the cozy experience of sitting round the fire with childhood friends reminiscing about the days when they were young together, he had what was far more invigorating, the companionship of the young at the outset of their careers. When an English contemporary of his started a magazine of his own, Ford urged him not to "forget les jeunes—the quite young and extravagant; it is only in them that you can put your trust." Ford's trust kept him always young; he never adopted the cynicism of old age, nor the dullness, so that the benefit he received from his continuing generosity was the vitality of youth that fed his own.

By the time he was sixty, Ford's unwavering support of fellow artists had become such a habit that when a New York publisher finally agreed to bring out Ezra Pound's *XXX Cantos,* Ford automatically wrote to a number of friends and acquaintances, including Ernest Hemingway, T. S. Eliot, Hugh Walpole, James Joyce, Allen Tate, and William Carlos Williams, asking them to contribute to a pamphlet of tributes to Pound that could be circulated by the publisher in order to give the book a good send-off. Although he was penniless himself, he even offered to pay the printing costs for the pamphlet. This campaign he organized by mail; generally he became socially involved with those he helped. Soon after inviting the English writer A. E. Coppard to contribute to the *Transatlantic Review* in 1923, he urged Coppard to visit him in Paris, and on receiving his acceptance, he wrote, "How delightful! But of course you will stop for more than a day—if you can put up with the moderately primitive housing and a very warm welcome. For Paris cannot be seen in a day. Neither can the Fords." To be so treated by an older writer was obviously pleasing, but Ford easily combined personal charm and literary seriousness of purpose. "I profess to a certain inherited flair for—a certain sense that it is the duty to forward—the recognition of young men with, to change the idiom, individualities, practicing one or other of the arts."

Ford's continuing enthusiasm for *les jeunes* led Ezra Pound to question the quality of his discoveries: "you by persistent settin on goose/eggs have occasionally hatched a swan," he wrote, "but more often a one-legged duck." Inevitably Ford's net caught small fish as well as big, but it is astonishing how high the quality of his discovering was. Counting only American writers whom he encouraged in the last ten years of his life, we find the names of John Crowe Ransom, Allen Tate, Caroline Gordon, Eudora Welty, Jean Stafford, Robert Lowell, Edward Dahlberg, and William Carlos Williams. The year before he died he even established a special society called the "Friends of William Carlos Williams," whose purpose was to call attention to the work of unjustly neglected writers, of whom Williams was one at the time. For all the effort he made to help others, Ford never received any material reward. Writing to his daughter in 1935, he commented, "You inherited certain duties from people who for generations have ended their lives in indigent circumstances. So that, not only should you not be so abhorrent of indigence—which nowadays is a thing rather to be proud of; but to carry out those duties you should eschew all easy triumphs."

Although he was scorned or neglected by many he helped, some acknowledged their debt and were grateful to him. Edward Dahlberg wrote: "I know of no literary man in America who has your goodness, who is what I from young manhood believed an artist to be. My gratitude to you: it is good to have a human being to whom I can offer my little flower." And W. H. Auden wrote: "I was very touched by your wishes at the end of your letter, because few people nowadays have any feeling for a writer's difficulties. It is disheartening to be praised by people who one knows have never read a line of one's work with understanding, but think that one can be useful to their cause."

At the end of his life, Ford wore patched clothes, lived in a simple room, and ate frugally. Most of his books were out of print and he had trouble placing new work. Yet he could look back on his life with some satisfaction, knowing that he had not wasted his time. In 1976, Katherine Anne Porter wrote, "I have enjoyed my work, it has been my only happiness." Ford would not have been so extreme, for he had other pleasures. And he probably would have agreed with Sherwood Anderson's tribute to him after his death: "Ford was a rich man. He was rich in a way we would all secretly like to be rich. He was rich in good work done, in self-respect."

It is not enough to sit on a panel for the National Endowment for the Arts or to write a letter of recommendation to the Guggenheim Foundation, or even send to a check to the Authors League fund for impoverished writers. Ford set an example which is not so much a duty as a way of life, and at least some of those who knew him have followed in his footsteps. Allen Tate and Stanley Kunitz, for example, have been noted for their concern for beginning writers. To have a feeling of responsibility for young novelists and poets is a source of pleasure. It is easy to write a letter of recommendation or send a check in the mail, but as Emerson said, "Your goodness must have some edge to it—else it is none." Personal involvement usually produces emotional reactions that may include anger and despair. But that is a side of living that those who are willing to commit themselves are glad to assume. It is also likely to encourage the kind of literary excellence that cannot be nourished by impersonal aid. Help that is mingled with discussion of the work, with talk about the writer's own development as an artist, has a greater chance to affect literary quality than checks in an otherwise empty envelope. The very success of the National Endowment and of the state arts councils therefore makes the need for private involvement greater than ever, since institutional assistance is by nature impersonal. When there is private involvement, the giver and receiver are united through the project, the work that engages them both. In this exchange, the true benefactor is the artist who shares his work with the one who wants to help him. Then "two such silver currents when they join / Do glorify the banks that bound them in." In the face of almost universal narcissism, it is worth remembering these lines from Shakespeare, as Conrad did when he described his collaboration with Ford Madox Ford.

EDWARD CRANKSHAW
Afterword

It is too easy to make fun of Ford's often absurd pretensions, his vanity, his compulsive romancing—or lying. Certainly he asked for it—the natural and incorrigible Bohemian who dreamt of himself as an English country gentleman; the most impractical of men who presented himself as the casual master of all trades; the dedicated novelist who would have gone to the stake for those he considered to be his masters (Conrad; James) and yet boasted in the silliest way about his own superiority . . . .

It is one thing to make fun of this sort of nonsense, quite another to use these follies and frailties as an excuse to exclude Ford from the novelists' roll of honor.

One of his sympathetic critics, Granville Hicks, wrote somewhere that it is "difficult to take seriously a man who exposes himself so recklessly to the charge of asininity." As I remember, Hicks was exasperated by Ford's intrusion of his own pretensions into his discussion of other writers. If a friend could feel like this, how violent must have been the reaction of his enemies. And Ford, for one reason and another, made a great many enemies. Almost invariably hostile feelings were exacerbated by the air of lofty superiority which he carried about with him like a stammer—and then made worse still by the uneasy feeling that he had in fact a great deal to be superior about.

Thus there was a time when pretty well the whole of the British literary establishment (including many individuals who owed much to his help and encouragement as editor and mentor) felt justified in refusing to take him seriously. But I think this tells us more about Ford's contemporaries than about Ford himself. Admittedly he was tiresome, and sometimes worse. But it is a poor commentary on his contemporaries that they allowed themselves to be blinded not only to his genius, but also to the good and generous human qualities which underlay the nonsense. Hicks would have done better to ask how it was possible for a man of such marvelous gifts to behave like such an ass—why a man so gifted should find it necessary to pretend to far less important attributes and talents which he knew he did not possess. But there was an element behind the foolishness, and the romancing which has not been adequately recognized: I mean Ford's immense courage.

In some ways he was childish indeed. He was forever looking at the greener grass on the other side of the fence. In Stella Bowen's memorable phrase, when he wanted something "he filled the sky with an immense ache that had the awful simplicity of a child's grief." And yet with this infantilism there went a highly adult, an austere dedication to his vocation, to writing, to *all* good writing and writers, which was absolute, and for which he was prepared to suffer great hardship and pain.

Some of his contemporaries knew this very well. Conrad knew it (but not Mrs. Conrad). Wells knew it: on one occasion he warned a friend (was it Stephen Crane?) who was about to meet Ford (then Hueffer) for the first time: "Hueffer will patronise you, but never mind. One day Hueffer will patronise the good God Himself; but God won't mind, because Hueffer is all right."

And so he was.

He was more than all right.

No doubt it was easier for me than for his own generation to discount the nonsense in Ford and open myself not only to his brilliancies but also to the profound generosity and humility of spirit which lay beneath the surface arrogance. I was twenty-four when we first met and he was sixty. This meant that I did not in the least mind being patronized by a man I saw as a master. It did not mean that I was uncritical of his work or unconscious of its irregularity, much as I admired it, or that I was unaware of his more obvious failings (they seemed to me too obvious to matter). It meant, simply, that he was far above me in talent and experience—and I knew it; whereas a great many writers of his own generation, who should have known better, thought of themselves, erroneously as a rule, as being in competition with him and bitterly resented his superior attitude, still more his too frequent defensive offensiveness. But they resented still more, I believe, his gifts, his disinterestedness, his courage.

There was no need for him to get himself commissioned as an infantry officer in 1915. He was forty-two and his chest was bad. He was not remotely fit to stand up to the mud and murder of the Somme. But he tried. And even if his enlistment was in part a flight from the muddle of his private life and his disappointments as a writer, it was still more an acknowledgment of the obligations which followed from his own high-flown image of himself: he was prepared to pay for that image with his life, and he very nearly did so.

The same rather desperate but ever-responsive courage showed itself, less obviously, in the way in which against a background of chronic muddle, emotional and material, he kept a brave face to the world over the years, almost regardless of the cost. He fought for his independence and he paid for it by living in a manner Spartan even in his day, but almost inconceivable in this age when the main function of literature sometimes seems to be to forward the careers of corn-fed academics on their way to satisfying pensions.

This heavy, rather lumpy figure in shapeless, battered tweeds, panting, often gasping like a fish, would sit upright, legs apart, on a hard chair in a bare attic room like a king on his throne—and talk like an angel about everything under the sun—without the faintest suggestion that he had no idea where next week's rent was coming from—showering on his listeners pure gold. His personal possessions when he died were minimal. One of his favorite remarks was that he enjoyed luxury but despised comfort; but the discomfort of some of his perches was excessive—and unrelieved by the least touch of luxury. My first meeting with him was on one of his transit visits to London on the way from Paris to New York. He had established himself with Biala and her pictures in one of the Bohemian quarters of his youth, in Fitzroy Square—a couple of attic rooms in a very run-down house. The living room, to the best of my recollection, was furnished with a packing case or two (covered with some sort of cloths) to serve as tables, and two or three hard chairs. I never saw his New York roosting place; but the Paris apartment in the rue de Seine (I speak, of course, of those last few years) was larger, had some simple furniture, attic rooms again, but spacious—a perfect setting for *La Bohème,* splendid for the very young, not so splendid for a grand old man of English letters. As for the Villa Paul at Cap Brun just outside Toulon —it had a fine view of the blue sea and a good terrace with a stone table round which life revolved in fine weather; but the interior was Spartan to a degree. Stella Bowen recorded that when she allowed herself to be per- suaded to take it for the winter of 1931-32 she had never felt "so sharp a pang of desolation" as when she looked round and took stock of the "domes- tic difficulties" in store. Five years later the kitchen arrangements were still primitive beyond belief.

But Ford might have been living in a palace. He would complain that he was not treated like a prince or respected as a grand literary figure, but he never complained that he was as poor as a churchmouse. Riches or poverty —he was above them both. It was fantasy, of course, but it was fantasy in a noble cause. He could not raise a finger to help himself; and to try to help him (as, for example, bringing him together with a publisher) was like trying to drag a horse out of a burning stable. But even in these very difficult years when he received so little encouragement himself, he never for a moment ceased from urging the claims of others. All his life he leapt to meet and welcome talent. The spirit which made so memorable his editorship of the *English Review* before the first world war was revived with the appearance of the *Transatlantic Review* in Paris when the war was over. And in the very last years of his life he was planning to start a new *Transatlantic,* to gather in yet another generation of young writers, as he had gathered in Lawrence and Hemingway in years gone by. Many of his cygnets turned out to be geese, and many of the swans he nurtured gave him no thanks. But nothing would deflect him; and when he should have been collecting all his energies to exploit the slight turn in his own fortunes in the middle 1930s—he found a sympathetic and imaginative publisher in Sir Stanley Unwin—he still, and to the very last moment of his life, spent himself on helping and promoting others. With all his faults, which he wore blazoned on his sleeve, he was a hero of letters.

Chronological List of Ford's Books

(Including Collaborations and Ford's Own Translations)

Date given is actual year of publication, not necessarily year on title-page.

1891. *The Brown Owl.* Children's fairy tale.
1892. *The Feather.* Children's fairy tale.
1892. *The Shifting of the Fire.* Novel.
1893. *The Questions at the Well* [pseud. "Fenil Haig"]. Poems.
1894. *The Queen Who Flew.* Children's fairy tale.
1896. *Ford Madox Brown.* Biography.
1900. *Poems for Pictures.* Poems.
1900. *The Cinque Ports.* "A Historical and Descriptive Record" (half-title) of Kent and Sussex port towns.
1901. *The Inheritors.* Novel, written in collaboration with Joseph Conrad.
1902. *Rossetti.* Art criticism and biography.
1903. *Romance.* Novel (historical adventure story), written in collaboration with Joseph Conrad.
1904. *The Face of the Night.* Poems.
1905. *The Soul of London.* Sociological impressionism.
1905. *The Benefactor.* Novel.
1905. *Hans Holbein.* Art criticism.
1906. *The Fifth Queen.* Novel (historical romance; first of the "Katharine Howard" trilogy).
1906. *The Heart of the Country.* Sociological impressionism.
1906. *Christina's Fairy Book.* Children's fairy tales.
1907. *Privy Seal.* Novel (historical romance; second of the "Katharine Howard" trilogy).
1907. *England and the English.* Sociological impressionism; published only in America; composed of the previously published *The Soul of London* and *The Heart of the Country* plus *The Spirit of the People.*

From David Dow Harvey, *Ford Madox Ford 1873–1939: A Bibliography of Works and Criticism.* (Princeton: Princeton University Press, 1962).

1907. *From Inland.* Poems.
1907. *An English Girl.* Novel.
1907. *The Pre-Raphaelite Brotherhood.* Art criticism.
1907. *The Spirit of the People.* Sociological impressionism; previously published, only in America, in *England and the English.*
1908. *The Fifth Queen Crowned.* Novel (historical romance; third of the "Katharine Howard" trilogy).
1908. *Mr. Apollo.* Novel.
1909. *The "Half Moon."* Novel (historical romance).
1910. *A Call.* Novel.
1910. *Songs from London.* Poems.
1910. *The Portrait.* Novel (historical romance).
1911. *The Simple Life Limited* [pseud. "Daniel Chaucer"]. Novel (satire).
1911. *Ancient Lights.* Reminiscences; published in America in 1911 as *Memories and Impressions.*
1911. *Ladies Whose Bright Eyes.* Novel (historical fantasy).
1911. *The Critical Attitude.* Essays in literary criticism.
1912. *High Germany.* Poems.
1912. *The Panel.* Novel (farce).
1912. *The New Humpty-Dumpty* [pseud. "Daniel Chaucer"]. Novel (satire).
[1913] *This Monstrous Regiment of Women.* Suffragette pamphlet.
1913. *Mr. Fleight.* Novel (satire).
1913. *The Desirable Alien.* Impressions of Germany, written in collaboration with Violet Hunt.
1913. *The Young Lovell.* Novel (historical romance).
1913. *Ring for Nancy.* Novel (farce; adaptation of *The Panel;* published only in America).
1913. *Collected Poems.*
1914. *Henry James.* Critical essay.
1915. *Antwerp.* Long poem (pamphlet).
1915. *The Good Soldier.* Novel.
1915. *When Blood Is Their Argument.* War propaganda (anti-Prussian essays).
1915. *Between St. Dennis and St. George.* War propaganda (pro-French and anti-Prussian essays).
1915. *Zeppelin Nights.* Historical sketches (told Decameron-fashion against the background of the war), written in collaboration with Violet Hunt.
1917. *The Trail of the Barbarians.* Translation of the war pamphlet, *L'Outrage des Barbares* by Pierre Loti.
1918. *On Heaven.* Poems.
1921. *A House.* Long poem (pamphlet).
1921. *Thus to Revisit.* Literary criticism and reminiscence.
1923. *The Marsden Case.* Novel.
1923. *Women & Men.* Essays.
1923. *Mister Bosphorus and the Muses.* Long narrative and dramatic poem.
1924. *Some Do Not. . . .* Novel (first of the "Tietjens" tetralogy).

1924. *The Nature of a Crime.* Novella, written in collaboration with Joseph Conrad; previously published in 1909 in *English Review.*

1924. *Joseph Conrad: A Personal Remembrance.* Biography, reminiscence, and criticism.

1925. *No More Parades.* Novel (second of the "Tietjens" tetralogy).

1926. *A Mirror to France.* Sociological impressionism.

1926. *A Man Could Stand Up—.* Novel (third of the "Tietjens" tetralogy).

1927. *New Poems.*

1927. *New York Is Not America.* Essays in sociological atmospheres.

1927. *New York Essays.*

1928. *The Last Post.* Novel (last novel of the "Tietjens" tetralogy; titled *Last Post* in England).

1928. *A Little Less than Gods.* Novel (historical romance).

1929. *The English Novel.* Essay in literary criticism and history.

1929. *No Enemy.* Disguised autobiography (concerning the war years; written shortly after the war).

1931. *Return to Yesterday.* Reminiscences (up to 1914).

1931. *When the Wicked Man.* Novel.

1933. *The Rash Act.* Novel.

1933. *It Was the Nightingale.* Autobiography and reminiscences (from 1918).

1934. *Henry for Hugh.* Novel.

1935. *Provence.* Impressions of France and England.

1936. *Vive le Roy.* "Mystery" novel.

1936. *Collected Poems.*

1937. *Great Trade Route.* Impressions of France, the United States, and England.

1937. *Portraits from Life.* Essays in personal reminiscence and literary criticism about ten *prosateurs* and one poet; published in England in 1938 as *Mightier than the Sword.*

1938. *The March of Literature.* Survey of literature "From Confucius' Day to Our Own."

1965. *Letters of Ford Madox Ford,* ed. Richard Ludwig. Princeton: Princeton University Press, 1965.

Books in Print

Between St. Dennis and St. George (Haskell)
The Brown Owl (Braziller)
The Critical Attitude (Arno)
Critical Writings of Ford Madox Ford, ed. Frank MacShane. Regents Critics Series
    (University of Nebraska Press)
The English Novel (Folcroft; Arden; Somerset)
The Fifth Queen (Vanguard)
Ford Madox Brown: A Record of His Life and Work (AMS)
The Good Soldier (Random House)
Henry James (Octagon)
Hans Holbein the Younger (Longwood)
It Was the Nightingale (Octagon)
Joseph Conrad (Octagon)
Ladies Whose Bright Eyes (Folcroft)
A Mirror to France (Folcroft)
New York Is Not America (Folcroft)
Parade's End, consisting of *Some Do Not . . . , No More Parades, A Man Could Stand
    Up—* and *The Last Post* (Random House)
Portraits from Life (Greenwood; Houghton Miflin)
Provence (Ecco)
The Queen Who Flew (Braziller)
Return to Yesterday (Liveright)
Rossetti: A Critical Essay on His Art (Folcroft)
The Soul of London (Haskell; Folcroft)
Thus to Revisit (Octogon)

Contributors

JANICE BIALA, the painter, lives in Paris.

JENNY SERRUYS BRADLEY is the widow of William Aspenwall Bradley, Ford's literary agent and friend.

EDWARD CRANKSHAW is a critic and historian of Central Europe, especially Habsburg Austria and Russia. His most recent book is a study of Bismarck. He was the translator of René Béhaine, the little-known French novelist Ford greatly admired.

DENIS DONOGHUE holds the Henry James Chair of Letters at New York University and is the author of *Connoisseurs of Chaos, The Ordinary Universe,* and *The Sovereign Ghost.*

L. L. FARRAR, JR., teaches European history at Trinity College, Hartford, Connecticut. He is the author of *The Short-War Illusion: German Policy, Strategy and Domestic Affairs, August–December, 1914* (1973) and *Divide and Conquer: German Efforts to Conclude a Separate Peace 1914–1918* (1978). He has written numerous articles and reviews and edited *War: A Historical, Political, and Social Study* (1978).

WILLIAM GASS, novelist and critic, is a professor of philosophy at Washington University. He is the author of *Omensetter's Luck* and *In the Heart of the Heart of the Country.*

CAROLINE GORDON is the author of the following novels: *Penhally, Aleck Maury, The Women on the Porch, The Strange Children, None Shall Look Back, Malefactors, Garden of Adonis,* and *The Glory of Hero.* She has also written two volumes of short stories, *The Forest of the South* and *Old Red and Other Stories,* as well as three books of criticism.

GRAHAM GREENE is the editor of *The Bodley Head Ford Madox Ford.*

DAVID DOW HARVEY is the author of *Ford Madox Ford 1873–1939, A Bibliography of Works and Criticism* (1962).

RICHARD HOWARD is the author of seven volumes of poetry and two of criticism; he has translated over 150 works from the French and teaches literature at several universities.

EDWARD KRICKEL teaches English at the University of Georgia. He was an editor of the *Georgia Review* from 1971 to 1974.

JULIA M. LOEWE is the youngest daughter of Ford Madox Ford. Her mother was Stella Bowen.

ROBERT LOWELL, major American poet, died in 1977.

ALISON LURIE has written six novels, of which the most recent is *Only Children.* She is the author of many articles on children's literature as well as two collections of folktales retold for children. She is a professor of English at Cornell University.

ANDREW NELSON LYTLE was a member of the Agrarian movement. He is a former editor of the *Sewanee Review* and describes himself as a writer and reader of fiction. Among his books are *A Novel, a Novella and Four Stories, The Hero with the Private Parts,* and *A Wake for the Living.*

FRANK MACSHANE is the author of a biography of Ford and editor of two collections, *The Critical Writings of Ford Madox Ford* and *The Critical Heritage.*

MARY MCINTOSH was married to Willard R. Trask, translator and author. As Joan McIntosh she was a dancer in the Fokine Ballet in New York.

EDWARD NAUMBURG, JR., bibliophile and patron of music, began collecting Joseph Conrad and Ford Madox Ford about 1926. A brief checklist by him of Ford's works appeared in the 1942 New Directions *Homage to Ford Madox Ford—A Symposium.*

HOWARD NEMEROV is the Edward Mallinckrodt Distinguished University Professor of English at Washington University. His most recent books are *The Collected Poems of Howard Nemerov, Figures of Thought* (essays), and *Sentences,* a collection of new verses.

WILLIAM H. PRITCHARD teaches English at Amherst College and is on the editorial board of *Hudson Review.* His most recent books are *Seeing through Everything: English Writers 1918–1940* (1977) and *Lives of the Modern Poets* (1980).

JEAN RHYS, author of *Left Bank and Other Stories, Postures,* and *After Leaving Mr. Mackenzie,* as well as *Voyage in the Dark, Good Morning, Midnight, Wide Sargasso Sea,* and *Tigers Are Better Looking,* died in 1979.

ROGER SALE teaches English at the University of Washington and is the author of *Modern Heroism.*

C. H. SISSON, English poet and translator, has recently published *Exactions* (poems), *The Divine Comedy of Dante* (translation), and *The Avoidance of Literature* (collected essays). He is a co-editor of *PN Review.*

SONDRA J. STANG teaches English at Washington University in Saint Louis. She has written a book on Ford and is editing *A Ford Madox Ford Reader.*

ALLEN TATE, major figure in American letters—poet, critic, editor, novelist—died in 1979.

WILLIAM TREVOR, novelist and short-story writer, is the author of *The Children of Dynmouth, Lovers of Their Time,* and the forthcoming *Other People's Worlds.*

WALLY TWORKOV, married to Jack Tworkov, the painter and brother of Janice Biala, did some typing for Ford between 1934 and 1937.